I0130802

AUDIENCE GENRE EXPECTATIONS IN THE AGE OF DIGITAL MEDIA

This volume bridges the divide between film and media studies scholarship by exploring audience expectations of film and TV genre in the age of digital streaming, using qualitative thematic and quantitative data-driven analyses.

Through four ground-breaking surveys of audience members and content creators, the authors have empirically determined what audiences expect of various genres, the extent to which these definitions match those of scholars and critics, and the overall variation and complexity of audience expectations in the age of media abundance. They also examine audience habits and preferences, drawing from both theory and original empirical analyses, with a view toward the implications for the moving image in a rapidly changing media environment. The book draws from the data to develop a number of new concepts, including genre repertoire, genre hybridity, audience interest maximization, and variety seeking, and a new stage of genre development, genre bending.

It is an ideal resource for students and scholars interested in the symbiotic relationship between audiences and the moving image products they consume, as well as the way the current digital media environment has impacted our understanding of film and TV genres.

Leo W. Jeffres is a Professor Emeritus of Communication at Cleveland State University. His research interests include audience analysis, communication technologies, media effects, and urban communication. He has authored four books, including *Mass Media Processes*, *Mass Media Effects*, and *Urban Communication Systems: Neighborhoods and the Search for Community*. He has authored dozens of refereed journal articles, book chapters, and papers over the past 45 years. He was a Fulbright scholar and Peace Corps Volunteer.

David J. Atkin is a Professor of Communication at the University of Connecticut. His research interests include the diffusion of emerging media and program formats, political communication, and media policy. He has coauthored several books, including *The Televiewing Audience* (both editions), *Communication Technology and Society*, and *Communication Technology & Society*. The author of more than 175 articles, Atkin is Associate Editor at JMCQ and does grant-supported work on adoption and uses of digital media.

Kimberly A. Neuendorf is a Professor Emeritus of Communication at Cleveland State University. The second edition of her methods textbook, *The Content Analysis Guidebook*, was published in 2017. Her research has examined both the content and the effects of media, with emphases on marginalized populations and new technologies. She is an author of over 100 articles and chapters. Neuendorf has been engaged as an expert witness on the methods of content analysis in multiple litigation actions.

AUDIENCE GENRE EXPECTATIONS IN THE AGE OF DIGITAL MEDIA

Leo W. Jeffres, David J. Atkin, and Kimberly A. Neuendorf

Routledge
Taylor & Francis Group

NEW YORK AND LONDON

Cover image: izusek/Getty Images

First published 2023
by Routledge
605 Third Avenue, New York, NY 10158

and by Routledge
4 Park Square, Milton Park, Abingdon, Oxon, OX14 4RN

Routledge is an imprint of the Taylor & Francis Group, an informa business

© 2023 Leo W. Jeffres, David J. Atkin, and Kimberly A. Neuendorf

The right of Leo W. Jeffres, David J. Atkin, and Kimberly A. Neuendorf to be identified as authors of this work has been asserted in accordance with sections 77 and 78 of the Copyright, Designs and Patents Act 1988.

All rights reserved. No part of this book may be reprinted or reproduced or utilised in any form or by any electronic, mechanical, or other means, now known or hereafter invented, including photocopying and recording, or in any information storage or retrieval system, without permission in writing from the publishers.

Trademark notice: Product or corporate names may be trademarks or registered trademarks, and are used only for identification and explanation without intent to infringe.

Library of Congress Cataloging-in-Publication Data
A catalog record for this title has been requested

ISBN: 978-1-032-20709-4 (hbk)
ISBN: 978-1-032-20131-3 (pbk)
ISBN: 978-1-003-26482-8 (ebk)

DOI: 10.4324/9781003264828

Typeset in Bembo
by KnowledgeWorks Global Ltd.

This book is dedicated to the late Dennis L. Giles, Ph.D., whose passion for both the practical and the scholarly in film studies informed and inspired our work.

CONTENTS

FIGURES

TABLES

ACKNOWLEDGMENTS

This book is literally more than 30 years in the making. And a lot of people have supported us along the way; we would like to acknowledge the scholarly contributions of: Paul D. Skalski, Ph.D., Carolyn Lin, Ph.D., Jim Denny, Frank Biocca, Ph.D., Annabelle Atkin, Ph.D., John Christensen, Ph.D., and Steve Stifano, Ph.D.

Like the audiences we study here, our work has not occurred in a vacuum but occurred across two academic institutions and several communities, as well as with the support of our families.

To Charlie, Alesha, and Violet, who have enriched my life beyond measure when we became family, I thank you for allowing me to make so many memories with Violet. To Angie, who has supported me and provided "in house" medical advice, I thank you for all the years we have shared together. To Bryanna and Joe, whose creativity and artistry I admire, I thank you for bringing so much joy to my life, and joining me in apple picking and other adventures. Love you all.......Leo W. Jeffres.

To family and friends who helped formulate ideas for this book: Quinn Neuendorf, Justin Centa, Dorian Neuendorf, Evan Chrisman, Blake McKean, Bob Neuendorf......Kim Neuendorf.

To Carolyn Lin, Arthur Atkin, Annabelle Atkin, and Robert Vazquez, who have all helped provide the inspiration that helps carry me through life.......Dave Atkin.

1

INTRODUCTION

When the 2011 film *Cowboys and Aliens* appeared, reviewer Roger Ebert noted that it was neither a satire, nor a comedy, and he wished it had been a western: "You know, the old-fashioned kind, without spaceships" (Ebert, 2011, para 6). Lamenting the decline of the western genre, he still liked the science-fiction-western hybrid and predicted that the film would be popular. The release proceeded to bring in more than $175 million worldwide.

Ebert (2011) described the film's "cockamamie" ingredients: "Here is a movie set in 1873 with cowboys, aliens, Apaches, horses, spaceships, a murdering stagecoach robber, a preacher, bug-eyed monsters, a bartender named Doc, a tyrannical rancher who lives outside a town named Absolution, his worthless son, two sexy women (one not from around here), bandits, a magic bracelet, an ancient Indian cure for amnesia, a symbolic hummingbird, a brave kid with a spyglass, and a plucky dog who follows the good guys for miles and miles through the barren waste and must be plumb tuckered out" (para 1). Ebert's characterization makes the point that this was not a typical "genre film."

So how do audiences define film genres and television formats? And do those expectations match the criteria cited by film scholars and critics? To date, no empirical research has tackled these particular questions. Within film studies, the limited empirical work has tended to either focus entirely on details within the texts/films (e.g., Fischer et al., 1995; Ma et al., 2021) or, if examining audiences, take a physiological (e.g., Shimamura, 2013) or economic (e.g., Shon et al., 2014) approach. Further, given the preponderance of classic film genre literature that appeared in the 1970s and 1980s, the current volume attempts to (a) provide an update of notions related to film/television genres and audience expectations, and (b) add quantitative and qualitative empirical evidence to an arena that has not featured such types of inquiry.

DOI: 10.4324/9781003264828-1

The concept of genre has its roots in Greek philosophy; Aristotle argued in *Poetics* (335 BC) that the different functions of comedy, tragedy, the epic, and the ballad were characterized by different stylistics, including poetic meters or rhythms (Altman, 2004; Creeber, 2015; Grant, 2007). Kaminsky with Mahan (1985) note that the word "genre" means order, and that we understand such ordering due to "shared cultural understanding" (p. 21). Indeed, as Grant (2007) notes, "popular cinema is organized almost entirely according to genre categories—science fiction, horror, thriller, pornography, romantic comedy, and so forth" (p. 1).

With growing opportunities for creating and viewing the moving image, older and more limited lists of film genres have been expanded as creative producers seek new forms and structures to attract audiences. In addition, the same situation has occurred for television genres, where differentiation and creation have led to not only new genres but also to entire channels devoted to them. The TV news magazine genre, for instance, has extended beyond its roots in the 1960s (e.g., *60 Minutes*, 1968-) to encompass characteristic unscripted discussions of current events in domains ranging from entertainment (e.g., *Entertainment Tonight*, 1981-) to automotive repair (e.g., PBS's *MotorWeek*, 1981-). This emerging "long-tail" of the multichannel environment is forcing a reconsideration of the concept of genre.

Genre: A Background

The use of the term "genre" has grown in popularity, and has been applied to almost any type of content structure. For art history scholars, the term has referred to paintings with unidealized scenes of daily life. Such "popular" subjects were not deemed worthy of critical attention until the late 20th century (e.g., Newcomb, 2007), and the concept has a similar history in film. Genre films were seen as those appealing to the masses, in contrast to the cinema produced by artists who experimented with structures, often intentionally violating audience expectations. From film, the concept migrated to television, capturing the same notion of form and structure in that medium. Defining film genre, and television genre, has been a matter of some debate. As Jeffres et al.'s (1990, p. 3) summary of the early literature on film genre definitions suggests:

> Definitions of genre abound, including: contemporary myths (Grant, 1977); type of writing, story-telling, presentation (McConnell, 1977); hidden archetypes (McConnell, 1977); inner form and outer form (Buscombe, 1977); subject matter, theme, techniques (Geduld & Gottesman, 1973); common themes, certain typical actions, certain characteristic mannerisms (Tudor, 1977); plot, character, visual effects–the "shibboleths of conventional criticism" (McConnell, 1977);

formalized characteristics of an artistic convention (McConnell, 1977); preordained forms, known plots, recognizable characters and obvious iconographies-visual codes-photographed elements that audiences need not ponder to understand (Sobchack, 1977).

One team of scholars—defining genre as a category, or form of film distinguished by subject matter, theme, or techniques—lists 75 genres of film, including fiction and non-fiction (Geduld & Gottesman, 1973, p. 73). As Creeber (2015) notes, "put crudely, genre simply allows us to organize a good deal of material into smaller categories." Extending these typologies to TV genres/formats, Mittell (2004, 2015) argues that scholarly definitions should conceptualize genre as an assemblage of discourses—one that resides within these texts—to include "interlocutors" such as industry, audience, and academia. Thus, while scholars and critics often have a set model or typology of the defining characteristics of genres across narrative forms—e.g., Pye (2012) lists (1) plot, (2) other structural features, (3) character, (4) time and space, (5) iconography, and (6) themes—the current research is interested in discovering whether any such typology emerges from the responses of spectators.

Four Stages of Genre Evolution

How are genres "born" and how do they develop? Scholars, including Schatz (1981), Altman (2004), and Creeber (2015), have acknowledged and elucidated stages in genre evolution. All schemas of the "life span" of a genre seem to flow from Henri Focillon's four ages of a cultural art form (*The Life of Forms in Art*, 1942, as cited in Schatz, 1981). As summarized by Schatz, a cultural form (e.g., genre) begins with an *experimental* age, during which its conventions are isolated and established, a *classic* age, during which conventions reach an "equilibrium" and are understood mutually by the source and the receiver, an age of *refinement*, in which form/style details provide embellishment, and ultimately a *baroque* age, when the form becomes self-reflexive to the point of the details or embellishments becoming the substance of the work.

A popular adaptation of this schema to film genres by Giannetti (2011) makes the assumption that over time, genres become more complex—this is true of both form and thematic range—suggesting that genres ultimately "veer into an ironic mode, mocking many of the genre's original values and conventions" (p. 359). The four cycles in the life span of a film genre, according to Giannetti, are *primitive*, a naïve but powerful phase during which conventions of the genre are established; *classical*, an intermediate stage that provides balance and richness and during which the genre's values are shared by the audience; *revisionist*, a stylistically complex phase that also finds the genre more symbolic and ambiguous, and during which the genre's now-established conventions are "exploited as ironic foils to question or undermine popular beliefs"; and *parodic*, a phase of comic presentation of the genre's conventions that constitute an outright mockery (p. 359).

For example, the venerable film genre, the western (Cawelti, 1974; Hoberman, 1994; Kaminsky, 1985; Maynard, 1974; Nachbar, 1974; Schatz, 1988b), began with primitive exemplars such as *The Great Train Robbery* (1903), developed in its classical form during the golden age of the Hollywood Studio System in the 1930s and 1940s (with such films as *Stagecoach* (1939)), was used to express contemporary concerns and themes such as racism (e.g., *Sergeant Rutledge*, 1960) and political criticism (e.g., *Little Big Man*, 1970), and was ultimately parodied with laser precision by Mel Brooks (i.e., *Blazing Saddles*, 1974).

Abelman and Atkin (2011) extended this typology to the evolution of television genres, noting that these expressive cycles define the process whereby "the form finds new audiences and producers attempt to maintain the form's integrity while at the same time bolstering its popularity" (p. 39). Within the western genre, for instance, examples range from primitive (e.g., *The Lone Ranger*, 1949-57) to classical (e.g., *Gunsmoke*, 1955-75), revisionist (e.g., *The Wild Wild West*, 1965-69), and parodic (e.g., *F Troop*, 1965-67). The authors linked the ongoing evolution of these forms to larger cultural changes that are continually driven by commercial imperatives, outlined in the section to follow.

Industrial Process and the (Re)packaging of Television Genres

While film critics used to ignore "genre films" as fodder for the masses (Braudy, 1976), film studios rely on such forms. Indeed, the film industry, notably in the US—spearheaded by the classic Hollywood Studio System (Grant, 2007)—has actively participated in the development of recognizable commercial genres. This was aided over time by the activities of entertainment news media. Neale (2012) points out the importance of "industrial and journalistic discourses," the discussion about films that helps define their genres and develop audience "expectation and anticipation" (p. 182).

Parallel work in television studies (e.g., Grant, 1994; Litman, 1978, 1979; Litman et al., 1994; Wakshlag & Adams, 1985) has offered genre categories numbering as high as several dozen program archetypes. Trend analyses suggest that only a fraction of these genres are employed in any given season; content diversity increases during times of heightened network competition, although most programs fall into a handful of categories (i.e., movies, situation comedies, and action adventure). Later work (e.g., Picard, 2000; Potter, 2016) documents the rise of reality TV genres in the current millennium, although the range of program genres remains rather limited, despite the rise of multichannel competitors like cable and streaming services. Ocasio (2012), for instance, documents that the number of reality shows grew from 4 in

2000 to 320 in 2010. Potter (2016) further broke this category down to the following subgenres: *documentary-style, reality-legal, reality competition/game show, self-improvement/makeover, social experiment, hidden camera, supernatural/paranormal,* and *hoax.* That said, his larger typology identifies only a handful of traditional genres: action/adventure, tragedy, mystery, horror, comedy, romance, and reality television.

Economists have long attributed the relative lack of TV genre diversity to the industry's oligopoly structure, documenting that the networks have historically displayed interdependent content in the realm of program duplication, prompting some to question whether network ownership is in the public interest (e.g., Litman, 1978). Wakshlag and Adams (1985) classified all prime-time programming into 37 categories, finding no decline in the variety of network programming between 1950 and 1982. They found that two to four categories dominated each season, with each accounting for 12–25% of available screen time. For instance, Signorielli (1986) found that the percentages for action-adventure programming were 40% in 1970, 12% in 1975, 27% in 1980, and 27% in 1985. Despite the relative constancy of most genres/formats, some have ebbed and flowed in popularity over the years. Westerns were the most popular TV format in the 1950s and 1960s—accounting for hundreds of programs—before virtually disappearing after 1980. Abelman and Atkin (2011) document these trends through the start of the new millennium, concluding that while there have been moments of true genre innovation, "most television history reflects a lack of diversity and a limit in format choices" (p. 168).

Jeffres (1994) notes that although the number and diversity of genres/formats is limited by human creativity, audience filters can further narrow the range of available options:

> Most of us do not seek constant stimulation, particularly the kind that requires attention to structure in order to understand the context or to enjoy the process. Were that the case, all film would be experimental and TV content would represent public acceptance of the artist's desire to be "expressive." A format or genre reduces the need to pay close attention for understanding. It also allows the audience to plan one's behaviors…In low involvement situations like TV viewing, the public has certain expectations about the redundancy of content.
>
> *(p. 332)*

Sociologists note that such genre/format conventions facilitate the (re)packaging of content in order to attract a loyal audience. As Gitlin (2000) observes, "nothing succeeds like success" (p. 1). Under this genre structure, programs become standard—as hegemonic processes might dictate—eventually giving rise to new variations on established themes; these, in turn, challenge conventional standards, and the new idea/ideology then becomes incorporated into the system. More broadly, this parallels a larger dynamic in capitalist ideology encompassing the notion that, as new products become available, they displace the old and feed into a loop of increasing consumption and, inevitably, production.

Similarly, Jeffres (1994) contends that genres embody a successful compromise between creative ideas and public expectations. In particular, "new formats generally represent combinations of older formats or subtle changes in the elements generally associated with an existing one. 'New' also often means a return to the 'old,' as formats from the past appear new when recast with today's popular culture...Although TV is a relatively new medium, its history is long enough to suggest that formats or genres may go through cycles of popularity and acceptance" (p. 332). He concludes that blending of genres (e.g., from pure comedy and dramatic adventure to comedy adventure programs) became more common in the latter 20th century.

Critical scholars (e.g., Hall, 1980) maintain that such genres/formats (alongside message formulas) can be essential to content producers as well as audiences, however, with the latter using them as "guides." The film critic is also complicit in this relationship (Jameson, 1994). Hall (1980) incorporates the language of "encoding" and "decoding" to illustrate these processes, noting that producers (un)consciously imbue their programs with encoded meanings. Audiences, in turn, decode these broad conventions—e.g., the familiar suburban setting for a sitcom—and subtly use them to glean a preferred reading. This confluence of supply-push and demand-pull factors thus reinforces the old adage that "imitation is the truest form of Hollywood." As Abelman and Atkin (2011) note, such risk aversion prompts the industry to move cautiously when providing variations on any themes underpinning a given genre.

One of the aims of this book is to make headway in transcending the boundaries of "camps" that have grown up over time concerning genres—TV vs. film perspectives, critical studies vs. social science approaches, and academic vs. industry perspectives. Feuer (1992), for example, argues that the study of TV genres should take place on a number of different criteria levels, including the Aesthetic Approach, where genres are defined in terms of a set of conventions of artistic expression involving individual authorship, the Ritual Approach, where genres are viewed as an exchange of audience and industry, and the Ideological Approach, where genres are an instrument of control, providing advertisers an audience supporting the larger capitalist system.

Identifying and Defining the Concept of Genre

Commercial cinema can be identified by recurring formal and narrative elements (Schatz, 1981). For example, these might include a story of a certain length, particular standards of production, an editing style, and/or use of a musical score. Grant (2007) has put it simply: "[G]enre movies are those commercial feature films which, through repetition and variation, tell familiar stories with familiar characters in familiar situations" (p. 1). These traditions may be a continuation of characteristics set in earlier art forms, such as western narrative fiction's informing of the western film genre (Pye, 2012), black comedy films' reliance on literary precursors (e.g., the works of Jonathan Swift; Gehring, 1988a), and horror films as derived from older forms, including mythology and classical tragedy (Kawin, 2012).

Screenwriter Eric Williams (2018) has devised a system of genres, supergenres, and microgenres, in a practical effort to provide writers in film and television a guide for "collaborative storytelling." In his taxonomy, Williams notes about 60 discrete genres defined by the three essentials of Story, Character, and Atmosphere. However, "those sixty genres can stand beneath eleven genre umbrellas. I call these 'supergenres' because they actually define the Story, Character and Atmosphere that all other genres subsequently use" (p. 21). Nested below supergenres are macrogenres and then microgenres, which further delineate the expected features of various types of moving image content.

In stark contrast to Williams' top-down hierarchical structuring of genres at different levels is Allocca's (2018) description of YouTube's bottom-up, inductive process of "genre" development for videos on the website. He notes that as of 2017, YouTube's "discovery algorithms" were being updated automatically with more than 80 billion signals (likes, views, etc.) daily. "This helps make YouTube different from any other entertainment medium we've ever had, an extension of our individual tastes and collective psyche" (Allocca, 2018, p. 10).

As creative producers experiment, variations and iterations complicate the task facing audiences who come to the screen with different expectations. At the same time, the increasing hybridity of genres (Altman, 2004; Creeber, 2015; Neale, 2012; Staiger, 2012; Williams, 2018) affords both content producers and spectators greater opportunities for matching needs and interests.

The Audience Role in Defining Genres

The essential role of the audience in the establishment and evolution of film and television genres has also been widely discussed by scholars and critics. As Creeber (2015) notes, genre is not simply a method of classifying modes of communication and art but it also attempts to explain how the different genres may create differential meanings for an audience. Film critic Richard Jameson's (1994) highly practical approach rests on the assumption that when given the name of any classic film genre, "even the most casual movie-goer will come up with a mental image of it, partly visual, partly conceptual" (p. ix). Altman (2004, p. 15) makes the claim that "genres are defined by the film industry and recognized by the mass audience." That said, audience dimensions undergirding (social) scientific conceptions of genre structures—which are generally assumed—remain subordinate to conceptions of the medium as an art form (e.g., Potter, 2016).

While developing a theoretic position regarding the role of the audience in defining genres, Neale (2012) has perhaps been the most explicit in declaring that spectator expectations are critical. "Genres do not consist only of films: they consist also, and equally, of specific systems of expectation and hypothesis that spectators bring with them to the cinema and that interact with films themselves during the course of the viewing process" (p. 179). He notes that both memories of the films themselves and the set of generic images produced by advertising, posters, etc., serve as bases of genre expectations.

Neale further argues genres are best understood as *processes*, through which each new genre film, featuring a selection from the repertoire of genre elements of the past, constitutes an addition to an existing genre corpus and necessitates some measure of development and change. This is a reason, says Neale (2012), "why it is so difficult to list exhaustively the characteristic components of individual genres, or to define them in anything other than the most banal or tautological terms" (p. 189).

Beyond the theoretic stylings of Neale (2012), additional prior scholarship on audience expectations for film and television genres has appeared, either taking a qualitative approach (e.g., Höijer, 2000) or examining one specific genre (e.g., Palmgreen & Rayburn, 1982). Work by Jeffres et al. (1990) was unique in its quantitative exploration of expectations for multiple film genres, which we explore in the context of multichannel environments below.

The Media of Abundance

The entertainment environment facing consumers has been shaped by a constant expansion of possibilities in recent decades, and the digital shift has magnified that dramatically. Each mass medium offering audiences "moving images" in one form or another has contributed to that growth (Jeffres et al., 2004, 2011; Neuendorf et al., 2000). First, multiplexes provided not only many more options for filmgoers but they also made it more convenient and enticing to exercise those choices, providing single destinations and more comfortable surroundings for viewing. Hollywood was quick to provide the films occupying those screens, as the sheer volume means that producers from around the world have found niches for viewers with expansive tastes.

Then cable television, and later, satellites, provided the same growth in home viewing, expanding the TV menu from the early three networks and then a dozen or so cable options to an almost limitless supply of films and television programs. The addition of computer and mobile devices with streaming capabilities has merely made the limitless supply of content—films, and TV programs but also the newest "medium," videos—omnipresent possibilities.

How have audiences kept up and reacted to this growth in supply? Noted communication scholar Frank Dance is reported to have said that "message" is the one concept unique to communication as a discipline. In the present context, that "message" is the moving image represented in films, television programs, and videos accessed through various platforms. It is easy for communication scholars, other social scientists, and certainly commentators to get lost focusing on the technologies and market shifts and lose sight of what's happening with the most important concept—the message, which bean counters refer to most often as "content."

Content theory, thus, is communication theory, representing a negotiation between creative producers and audiences (e.g., Abelman & Atkin, 2011). With people becoming active contributors as well as members of audiences, the characterization of "content" is not cut and dry. Consequently, media content forms have become more variegated and sophisticated, making it harder to function as a viewer (e.g., Johnson, 2005).

From the early days of film, audiences came to recognize various genres, or forms that films assumed, from westerns to comedies to musicals. While film certainly drew inspiration from other sources, such as books and storytelling, it is fair to say that early film producers were "inventing" genres. The concept of genre was borrowed from art history terminology, referring to paintings with real, contemporary subjects and scenes of everyday life. Such commonplace subject matter was not seen as worthy of critical attention. In film, the concept came to refer to popular film forms and structures that appealed to the masses, contrasting with cinema produced by experimental artists. Audiences reacted to the moving images offered to them by seeking out those they enjoyed most, creating the most popular film genres. Similar dynamics unfolded in television, as producers experimented with what forms to offer audiences at home. Here too, they borrowed from film, and radio, but also experimented with forms and formats (Jeffres et al., 2011).

Importing a concept from sociology, we note that the expansion of a social system prompts structural and functional differentiation—the creation of more specialized institutions to serve social uses (Parsons, 1951). Similarly, as the volume of films, programs, and videos expands, that differentiation occurs through the proliferation of different forms to serve diverse gratifications that attract audiences to cinema. This is the overall descriptive, but not the underlying communication theory we need to develop and examine.

According to the Theory of the Long Tail, as products become increasingly available to audiences, consumers desire more obscure items that are more closely aligned with their own needs and interests (Anderson, 2004). As a result, the marketplace will shift from a relatively small number of universally appealing options (i.e., "hits"), to include more individually appealing options (i.e., "niche" fare) as well. Like many changes in the larger marketplace, this theory can be explained by economic shifts in the digital environment. As Anderson (2004, para 7) notes:

> Many of our assumptions about popular taste are actually artifacts of poor supply-and-demand matching—a market response to inefficient distribution... Hit-driven economics is a creation of an age without enough room to carry everything for everybody. Not enough shelf space for all the CDs, DVDs, and games produced. Not enough screens to show all the available movies. Not enough channels to broadcast all the TV programs, not enough radio waves to play all the music created, and not enough hours in the day to squeeze everything out through either of those sets of slots. This is the world of scarcity. Now, with online distribution and retail, we are entering a world of abundance. And the differences are profound.

The long tail envisaged in Anderson's (2004) original conception—arrayed across several online modalities—is portrayed in Figure 1.1. He applies the concept to television as well as film content structures, including documentaries. What does this long tail mean for genre development? Anderson notes three rules that help govern the proliferation of emerging genres: (1) *Make everything available*, (2) *Cut the price in half. Now lower it*, and (3) *Help me find it*. What does this age of abundance mean for audiences?

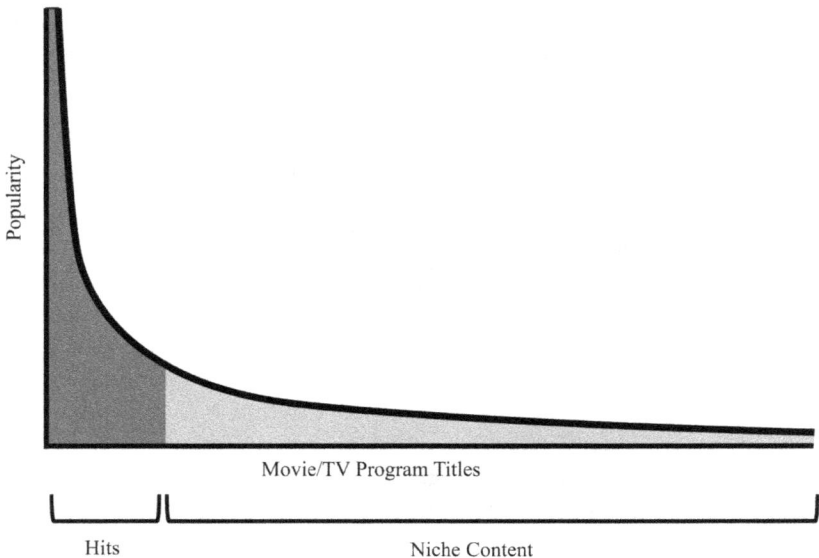

FIGURE 1.1 The Long Tail of Digital Media Content

Note: Image adapted from picture by Hay Kranen/PD and concepts by Milosz Krasinski (n.d.).

Johnson (2005) argues that popular culture—notably television and film—has been steadily growing more challenging over the past 30 years (via proliferating genres/formats, characters, intersecting plot lines, etc.). He discusses three aspects of his own, to help conceptualize how audiences must "grow smarter" as they grapple with these more cognitively demanding contents: (1) "multiple threading," (2) "flashing arrow," and (3) "social networks" (Johnson, 2005, pp. 194–199).

Multiple threading refers to the melding of complex narrative structures to complex subjects, involving multiple plots/subplots. Johnson cites the example of programs like *ER* (1994-2009)*, The Sopranos* (1999-2007), and *24* (2001–14), which each offered as many as 10 threads/episode. Audiences can then make sense of these challenging contents through the use of *flashing arrows*, or narrative signposts that are deliberately planted to aid viewer comprehension; he notes these arrows have appeared less frequently over time, although they're still used to signify obscure references and intricate plotlines. Viewer tracking of these multiple relationships triggers social intelligence, defined as "our ability to monitor and recall many distinct vectors of interaction in the population around us" (p. 199). This, in turn, enhances viewer understanding of *social networks* embedded within those televisual or filmic texts.

This interaction of creative producers and audiences who process those messages is the basis for the generation of forms over time. Thus, it makes sense to examine the perceptions audiences have of those messages and what uses and gratifications are derived from exposure to them. Tudor (1977) noted that to call a film an example of a particular genre means that it draws on a tradition and a set of conventions. This is based on the assumption that people do not go to films or watch programs or videos that fail to provide some minimum of uses and gratifications. Over time, the labels we give to genres come to represent shorthand efforts to describe expectations.

How do audiences face this decision-making, or choice for viewing? With a couple of theaters in town, or a couple of channels to watch on televisions, the process was quite easy. But as the menu expanded, audiences had to narrow their options. The concept of "channel repertoire" (Neuendorf et al., 2001) represents the constraint people place on their own decision-making in television. We defined repertoires as the set of channels used regularly and frequently by audience segments. In this book, we introduce and develop the concept of "genre repertoire" to capture people's regular and specialized viewing of film and television genres. While there is likely to be some "sampling" process as people face more choices, some people will have larger repertoires than others. Differences can also be found in repertoires and sampling patterns by social groups. Spurred on by economic incentives, producers will of course attempt to influence that sampling process with advertising and commercials, added to by other communication influences. This will be the focus of Chapter 4.

Four Studies Examining Audiences for the Moving Image

In this book, we draw on data from four online surveys that capture viewers' perceptions of film and television genres and their mass communication behaviors as audiences cope with the "media of abundance" (Neuendorf et al., 2000). After laying out the survey design and concepts measured—developed over several decades of media audience research tapping media habits, audience perceptions and expectations, demographics/social categories, psychographics, etc.—subsequent chapters will examine relationships among those variables and attempt to develop content theory for audiences' selection and processing of the moving image. Although an international sample would be desirable, we need to limit the number of television genres that can be incorporated into a survey instrument, so the US context was chosen for all four studies. One of the four studies captures how the COVID-19 pandemic affected people's viewing patterns and expectations moving forward, which will be the focus of Chapter 8. Two of the studies focus on "creators" of moving image content for the Internet. All four surveys were approved by the relevant university IRB(s).

Study 1 (2015 Users Survey)

An online survey netted 543 respondents from across the United States, who were invited to participate after a screening process that limited participation to those aged 18 or older and living in the United States. The survey was conducted via SurveyMonkey with recruitment through Amazon MTurk (Sheehan & Pittman, 2016). Respondents were asked about their general media habits (e.g., television viewing, theater attendance, streaming, and smartphone watching). In addition, respondents were asked how often they watched specific film genres and television genres from a battery of 31 film and 11 television genres. Open-ended items tapped respondents' perceptions of what they would "expect" when watching each of these genres. These textual responses were subjected to qualitative thematic analyses (Neuendorf, 2019). Semantic as well as linguistic elements of the definitions and typologies were incorporated in the thematic analyses; those elements include: Time frame, material culture/symbols, people/roles, types of activities, reactions/feelings, special effects/techniques, plot/story line, evaluations/assessments, descriptive/abstract references, specific films or programs cited, miscellaneous, and don't know/don't watch.

From the results of the thematic analyses, comparison models were developed with expert definitions and typologies (extracted from both scholarly and industry sources, e.g., Altman, 1984, 2004; Cabral, 2021; Dirks, 2020; Ebert, 2020; Fischer et al., 1995; Gehring, 1986, 1988b, 1999, 2002, 2016, 2019; Grant, 1977, 1984, 1986, 2003, 2007, 2012a; IMDb, 2020; Kaminsky,

1985; Kaminsky & Mahan, 1985; Rotten Tomatoes, 2020; Sanders, 2009; Schatz, 1981; Tudor, 1977). This modeling will be presented in Chapter 2.

Respondents were also asked how much they agreed or disagreed on a 1–7 scale with items tapping perceptions that film and television reflect reality, reflect culture, are realistic, or represent high quality. In addition, three scales were constructed from items tapping media delivery system preferences, including whether someone was a mobility/social media enthusiast (e.g., I often search for videos on YouTube to watch; I often share videos on Instagram), a technology enthusiast (e.g., I love the options at my fingertips today, watching videos on my phone, texting, streaming films), or a communication traditionalist (e.g., I'm more a traditionalist, preferring to read physical copies of books, magazines, and newspapers rather than digital versions).

Respondents were asked about their viewing context preferences for the various film and TV genres—in a theater, at home, or on a mobile device. This was asked to see whether the nature of a genre would affect whether people wanted to watch on a large screen, at home, or in a mobile context. Another set of items sought reasons as to why audience members decide to go see films in a theater—uses and gratifications sought—as well as specific selection criteria—the film genre, the director of the film, stars in the film, whether it's a recent release, the country of origin, and the language of the film. Additional items looked at patterns of audience viewing, including repeat viewing dimensions such as "fandom viewing" and viewing with companions. In the current era of active audiences, viewers also are often creators of messages, so a set of items sought to describe video making and sharing behaviors, as well as online searching and mobile viewing activities. The survey instrument was rounded out with measures of the typical social categories (gender, age, ethnicity, education, and income).

While the dataset is not a random sample of viewing audiences, it does provide diversity on the social categories important for identifying viewers. The sample is slightly biased toward females, who account for 60% of respondents. The ages range from a minimum of 18 to 65, with a mean of about 35 and a median of 32 years. The sample is relatively educated, with 15% having advanced degrees, 46% college graduates, 28% some college, and 11% high school or less. Median household income is in the $40,001–$50,000 range. The sample also overrepresents White/Caucasians, who account for 77% of respondents, with 7% Black/African American, 5% Hispanic, 6% Asian, and 5% other ethnicities (or mixed background).

Study 2 (2021 Users Survey)

A national (US) online survey was executed in 2021 to tap contemporary attitudes and behaviors concerning film/television genres and viewership, notably during the COVID-19 pandemic. The instrument was hosted on

SurveyMonkey, with recruitment via MTurk. Respondents provided information about their changing habits and expectations as related to newer viewing options (e.g., streaming via TVOD and SVOD, user-generated content (UGC), online videos (with their own growing menu of genres)), as well as habits and attitudes forged by pandemic-related structural changes (e.g., the resurgence of drive-in theaters, the rent-a-theater phenomenon).

Repeating key measures from the 2015 Users Survey, the 2021 Users Survey asked about a variety of media behaviors, including viewership frequency of the battery of 31 film and 11 television genres. Three scales were constructed from items tapping media delivery system preferences, including whether someone was a mobility/social media enthusiast, a technology enthusiast, or a communication traditionalist.

A number of new measures were included to tap self-reported adjustments made by viewers during the COVID-19 pandemic. Respondents were asked about whether their media habits had changed during the pandemic (including a roster of items measured on a 6-point response scale, from "Have not done this at all during pandemic" and "Have done this much less during pandemic" to "Have done this much more often during pandemic than before"). They were also asked in open-ended questions whether there are certain film and TV genres they have avoided, and sought out, during the pandemic. Respondents were asked whether they have engaged in adaptive viewing behaviors during the pandemic, including renting out a movie theater to see a first-run film with family and/or friends, going to a drive-in movie, watching outdoors with family and/or friends, and simultaneously streaming content with others at another location.

Also new in the 2021 Users Survey were measures tapping cable and satellite TV subscription, and access to streaming services for the delivery of film and TV (from a roster of 33 options). Respondents were asked whether they watch videos on seven different social media platforms (e.g., YouTube, TikTok). TikTok videos may differ from other social media videos and in open-ended questions, respondents were asked about their expectations for videos on social media, how TikTok videos may differ from other social media videos, what types of social media videos seem aimed at building an audience, and how they think social media videos have changed over time. Measures were included that tapped reasons for viewing social media videos and reasons for posting videos (a set of 10 Uses and Gratifications items), as well as whether they post videos of various types on social media themselves, and reasons for posting videos (a set of eight Uses and Gratifications items).

Other new measures were focused on additional contemporary issues regarding viewing behaviors. Respondents were asked to what extent they binge watch film and TV, and whether they feel that current film/TV offerings provide adequate representation of ethnic/racial diversity, and LGBTQ+ diversity. Further, they were asked in an open-ended question whether they could identify any film/TV content that has "bent" a genre: "Can you name one movie or TV program you've seen that really 'bent' the genre by introducing aspects of other genres? Please explain."

The 2021 Users Survey included several psychometric scales. The Short Big 5 Scale (Rammstedt & John, 2007) taps extraversion, agreeableness, conscientiousness, neuroticism, and openness. Also included was the four-item Narcissism Scale by Jonason and Webster (2010) and a Novelty-Seeking Scale adapted from Lee and Crompton (1992). These were joined by measures of the typical social categories (gender, age, ethnicity, education, and income), with the addition of political philosophy and political party identification.

A total of 207 respondents completed the 2021 Users Survey. The sample represents a gender split near that of the population, with 48.2% female and 51.8% male. Respondent age ranges from 19 to 67, with a mean of 38 and a median of 36. The sample reports a fairly high level of education, with 27% having advanced degrees, 65% having a college degree, and 9% some college or less. Median household income is in the $50,001–$75,000 range. The sample again overrepresents toward White/Caucasians, with 79% of respondents indicating that identity, and 11% Black/African American, 4% Latinx/Hispanic, 4% Asian, and 4% Native American/American Indian (multiple racial/ethnic identities were allowed). Regarding political philosophy, 46% indicate a strong conservative or leaning toward conservative orientation and 38% indicate a strong liberal or leaning toward liberal orientation. When asked which political parties they identify with (multiple endorsements were allowed), the most common parties are the Democratic Party at 57%, the Republican Party at 30%, and "Independent" at 11%.

Study 3 (2021 Creators Survey)

For Study 3, the focus shifted to those who *create* videos for posting on social media. The purpose was to track how film and TV genre conventions might provide frameworks for the production of videos by a contemporary generation of moving image "creators." Once again, a US national survey was conducted online in 2021, hosted on SurveyMonkey and recruited via MTurk, with specific instructions to recruits that they must be social media video creators.

Repeating key measures from the 2015 Users Survey and the 2021 Users Survey, the survey asked about a variety of media behaviors, including viewership frequency of the battery of 31 film and 11 television genres. Again, three scales were constructed from items tapping media delivery system preferences, including whether someone was a mobility/social media enthusiast, a technology enthusiast, or a communication traditionalist. Maintaining measures used in the 2021 Users Survey, this study included measures tapping cable and satellite TV subscription, and access to streaming services for the delivery of film and TV (from a roster of 33 options).

Respondents were also asked whether they watch videos on seven different social media platforms (e.g., YouTube, TikTok), and in open-ended questions, they were asked about their expectations for videos on social media, how TikTok videos may differ from other social media videos, what types of social media videos seem aimed at building an audience, and how they think social media videos have changed over time. Measures were included that tapped reasons for viewing social media videos (a set of 10 Uses and Gratifications items), as well as reasons for posting videos (a set of eight Uses and Gratifications items).

Additional measures pertinent to the creation of videos for social media were added for the 2021 Creators Survey: Open-ended queries asked where they post, what types of videos they post, how long they have been posting, whether they have a particular style or theme for their videos, whether they include particular subject matter, and what their future plans are. A list of nine types of content was presented, and respondents were asked which types they feature in their videos (e.g., political ideas, "how to" videos, their own lifestyle).

Other measures from the 2021 Users Survey were included in the 2021 Creators Survey: Measures of binge watching, whether they feel that current film/TV offerings provide adequate representation of ethnic/racial diversity and LGBTQ+ diversity, and the open-ended question regarding the identification of any film/TV content that has "bent" a genre.

The 2021 Creators Survey included a number of psychometric scales: The Short Big 5 Scale (Rammstedt & John, 2007), tapping extraversion, agreeableness, conscientiousness, neuroticism, and openness; the four-item Narcissism Scale (Jonason & Webster, 2010); a five-item Novelty-Seeking Scale adapted from Lee and Crompton (1992). Also, this survey included an eight-item composite Very Short Authoritarianism (VSA) Scale (Bizumic & Duckitt, 2018; Duckitt et al., 2010) and the four-item Brief Social Desirability Scale (Haghighat, 2007).

The 2021 Creators Survey included the same measures of social categories as the 2021 Users Survey: Gender, age, ethnicity, education, income, political philosophy, and political party identification. A total of 327 respondents completed the 2021 Creators Survey. The sample skews toward male, with 54% male and 46% female respondents. Age ranges from 21 to 73, with a mean of 39 and a median of 35. The sample reports a fairly high level of education, with 23% having advanced degrees, 62% having a college degree, and 16% some college or less. Median household income is in the $50,001–$75,000 range. The sample overrepresents White/Caucasians, with 85% of respondents indicating that identity, and 7% Black/African American, 5% Latinx/Hispanic, 5% Asian, and 1% Native American/American Indian (multiple racial/ethnic identities were allowed). Regarding political philosophy, 39% indicate a strong conservative or leaning toward conservative orientation and

43% indicate a strong liberal or leaning toward liberal orientation. When asked which political parties they identify with (multiple endorsements were allowed), the most common parties are the Democratic Party at 60%, the Republican Party at 23%, and "Independent" at 16%.

Study 4 (2021–22 Young Creators Survey)

A companion study to the 2021 Creators Survey is the 2021–22 Young Creators Survey, which was conducted with undergraduate college students at a large Northeastern public university. Basically, the same instrument was used as for the 2021 Creators Survey MTurk sample. A total of 557 students completed the 2021–22 Young Creators Survey. The sample shows a balance of gender, with 46% male and 54% female respondents. Age ranges from 18 to 36, with a mean and median age of 19. Median household income is in the $100,001–$125,000 range. The sample is less biased toward White/Caucasians than the other three studies, with 66% of respondents indicating that identity, and 8% Black/African American, 11% Latinx/Hispanic, 18% Asian, 2% Middle Eastern/North African, and 0.4% Native American/American Indian (multiple racial/ethnic identities were allowed). Regarding political philosophy, 19% indicate a strong conservative or leaning toward conservative orientation and 51% indicate a strong liberal or leaning toward liberal orientation. When asked which political parties they identify with (multiple endorsements were allowed), the most common parties are the Democratic Party at 33%, the Republican Party at 13%, the Communist Party at 4%, the Green Party at 3%, the Libertarian Party at 2%, and "Independent" at 27%.

A Concluding Note

The present chapter provides an introduction to the concept of genre, outlining its origins in early film and developmental stages. Escaping the constraints of the traditional definitions of genre, the concept as it now is applied includes both film and television, with acknowledgement to literary forms (e.g., Altman, 2004). Print and online sources explicate a variety of compilations of film and television genres, illustrating the growth and differentiation of genres (e.g., Jeffres et al., 2011). Adding in examples from television, we outline the role of economic as well as aesthetic influences shaping the evolution of genres since the mid-20th century.

We discuss the influence of emerging media forms in light of industrial processes and fragmenting platforms, which can support narrowing taste publics. By focusing on these macro-level perspectives derived from humanities and economics, the literature on film has generally bypassed individual-level perspectives stressing the audience's role in defining genres. The current framework nominates empirical approaches stressing individual differences—as derived from such disciplines as Communication, Sociology, and Psychology—to fill that void. The limited empirical work in film studies has largely focused on psychological or economic approaches (e.g., Shimamura, 2013; Shon et al., 2014), and our current efforts expand that into the communication discipline. Theories stressing audience interest maximization as well as uses and gratifications can help inform our understanding of how audiences process genres.

In an attempt to bridge the gap between those audiences and media creators, we discuss four surveys, each with unique information to help inform our understanding of film and television genres. Study 1 involves a 2015 survey of audience expectations for key genres. Study 2 focuses on changes in viewing accompanying the COVID-19 pandemic. Study 3 involves a survey of content creators, and Study 4 surveys college students, or "young creators." Results from these studies are further detailed in the chapters to follow, beginning with empirical evidence regarding audience support for these dimensions in Chapter 2.

2

AUDIENCE EXPECTATIONS FOR FILM AND TELEVISION GENRES

What do we know of audience expectations for film and television genres from critical observers and the scant empirical data available up to now? The concept of film "genre" has a considerable history, generally coming to mean the recurring formal and narrative elements associated with a type of film. With an almost unlimited opportunity for experimenting and developing variations or forms of the moving image, producers have expanded from the earlier limited set of film genres to lengthy lists compiled by observers. Here we examine the literature outlining what critics, scholars, and online fan communities have identified as referential aspects of 31 film genres and 11 television genres that are examined in our data. There is a practical reason for the existence of stable forms of genres since people seek some but not constant stimulation and often look for the comfortable content that fulfills their uses and gratifications (for a conceptual review, see Chapter 3).

Gitlin (1979) discusses genre as one of the key formal conventions supporting a larger hegemonic structure defining a "prime time" ideology, one that can indicate the interrelated ways in which television messages are integrated into the dominant system of discourse and the prevailing structures of politics, labor, and consumption through these formal features of prime time network programs:

> (1) format and formula (including the rigidity of program length and the narrative curve of action); (2) genre; (3) setting and character type; (4) topical slant; and (5) the solution imposed on the fictional problem. Within certain definite limits—related both to the core of dominant values and to market tolerances—these formal structures are flexible; for example, some of Norman Lear's comedies have disrupted stereotypical conventions of static character and imposed solution. The hegemonic

DOI: 10.4324/9781003264828-2

commercial cultural system routinely incorporates some aspects of alternative ideology and rejects the unassimilable.

(p. 251)

Given these various influences and effects of visual media, it's useful to explore the larger socio-cultural factors governing genre development.

Macro Factors Stimulating Genre Development

Video consumption was transformed this century by dramatic changes in the media environment, including the growth of digital media as well as the convergence of countless wired and wireless distribution platforms (e.g., Grant & Meadows, 2020). As we'll explore in this chapter, the concept of genre has continued to evolve as legacy media like the broadcast networks—who commanded over 90% of prime time audiences through the 1980s—face withering competition from emerging platforms ranging in scope from streaming services to social media. As industry analyst Ed Papazian (1998) recounts "… the medium's power structure is being shaped by a convergence of interactive forces. Thanks to the impetus of advancing technology, coupled with short-sighted intransigence of the major network establishment, alternate forms of television have multiplied and prospered" (p. i).

Broadcast economists have utilized several typologies of TV forms—numbering as high as several dozen—to gauge the impact of network competition on program diversity. Litman (1978, Litman et al., 1994) found that program duplication represents an area where the networks have historically displayed interdependent conduct (alongside cooperation in advertising pricing, program input costs, affiliate compensation payments, and the number of minutes aired per hour). His own analysis suggests that network ownership has encouraged great similarity in programming, prompting the conclusion that network ownership is not in the public interest. Subsequent empirical work (e.g., Abelman & Atkin, 2011; Dominick & Pearce, 1976; Ocasio, 2012; Wakshlag & Adams, 1985) found support for this dynamic, as new genres/formats continued to proliferate into the new millennium.

This work was inspired by Schumpeter's (1971) perspective on competition, which foretold a gale of "creative destruction" summoned by competitive innovation, one that would blow asunder existing monopolies. Atkin and Litman (1986) referenced the predictive value of this framework when documenting the erosion of network audiences during the 1980s; that is, the exogenous shock of technological innovation—coming in the form of competition from home video, cable, and emerging networks—would claim most of their audiences in the decades to follow. Abelman and Atkin (2011) later recounted that "as long as each of the broadcast television networks have only one channel choice to offer its audience—an audience with an increasing array of channel and programming options at its immediate disposal—their domination of the airwaves becomes increasingly fragile and fleeting" (p. 167).

Seel (2012) argues that five technological attributes have affected the production, storage, and transmission of media: (1) scalability, or the ability to create smaller file sizes, (2) extensibility, or the ability to create new and improved software without making earlier versions obsolete, (3) replicability, or the ability to make copies of digital files, (4) interoperability, or the ability for hardware and software to function together, and (5) metadata, or data about data, such as the date and time a picture was taken. Together, these have transformed the ways that media are acquired, processed, and distributed.

The diversity of genres/formats thus continued to expand over time, as spasms of intra-network competition were joined by the greater existential threat posed by emerging digital channels. Lin and Atkin (2002) document how these trends were exacerbated by deregulatory measures (e.g., the Telecommunications Act of 1996)—including cross-ownership bans for broadcasting, cable and telephone companies—which were designed to eradicate the modality-based silos that had accreted through the 20th century. As Jeffres et al. (2010) conclude, the networks' "quiet life of oligopolistic competition"—where ABC, NBC and CBS collectively accounted for 92% of the viewing audience in 1979—has been dramatically shaken by a 60+% decline in (recent) decades (p. 5).

Anderson (2008) referenced this dynamic when positing his Theory of the Long Tail (see Chapter 1), which sees the economy increasingly shifting from a focus on a relatively small number of "hits" to a huge (and growing) number of niches. In particular:

> Every year network TV loses more of its audience to hundreds of niche cable channels. Males age eighteen to thirty-four, the most desirable audience for advertisers, are starting to turn off the TV altogether, shifting more and more of their screen time to the Internet and video games. The ratings of top TV shows have been falling for decades, and the number one show today wouldn't have made the top ten in 1970. In short, although we still obsess over hits, they are not quite the economic force they once were. Where are those fickle consumers going instead? No single place. They are scattered to the winds as markets fragment into countless niches.
>
> *(p. 2)*

Despite the onslaught of digital media competition, audience research (e.g., Kunst, 2022) confirms that TV dramas account for the bulk of prime time viewership and ad spending in the US. On the larger global scene, Waisbord (2004) documents the relative constancy of a rather fixed set of formats through the early 20th century, arguing "that television is simultaneously global and national, shaped by the globalization of media economics and the pull of local and national cultures" (p. 359). As Potter (2016) concludes, this model includes a wider diversity of offerings in domestic as well as international contexts, including several sub-categories in such genres as reality TV.

Defining Film and Television Genres

As noted earlier, regardless of its origins, commercial cinema can be identified by recurring formal and narrative elements (Schatz, 1981). Beyond these general film devices, the "genre film" contains a predetermined structure where the setting, characters, plot, and techniques have prior significance to the audience. Tudor (1977) notes that calling a film as an example of a particular genre means it draws on a tradition and set of conventions. While film critics once ignored genre films as fodder for the masses (Braudy, 1976), film studios rely on such forms. Television genres also can be defined in a similar manner. Barker (1991) looks at the emergence of what he calls "repertoires of representation," referring to the aural and visual codes of television genres—sound effects, music, camera and performer blocking, editing patterns, lighting, and set design.

As noted earlier, older, more limited lists of genres have been expanded as creative producers seek new forms and structures to attract audiences facing an almost unlimited supply of moving images. The same situation has occurred in television, where differentiation and creation have led to not only new genres, but entire channels devoted to them. In books and online, numerous compilations of film and television genres can be found, illustrating the growth and differentiation of genres.

CHANGING TERMS...

A note about the use of terms. For many years, the term "format" was used to refer to different types of television programs, but it has largely been replaced by "genre" in usage. This may be due in part to the use of format to also refer to several concepts of the moving image: (a) length and frequency forms—half hour, hourly, or miniseries forms; (b) technical aspects of the moving image on screens—which are "formatted" to fit images for different sizes of screens; (c) video file format, e.g., MP4, Apple's mov, for viewing. In addition, format is used also to refer to copyrighted television shows that are licensed by networks and other producers to be remade in multiple markets with local contestants, allowing them to adapt the format to perceived tastes of local audiences. Examples include game shows (*Wheel of Fortune*, 1975-) and reality shows (*Big Brother* (2000-), *Survivor* (1997-)). In the complex world of the moving image, terms such as genres, formats, technology platforms, and online platforms are important but here we focus on the use of genre to refer to the general shape and features of films and television programs, many with long histories in popular usage.

Filmsite.org lists action, adventure, comedy, crime & gangster, drama, epics/ historical, horror, music/dance, science fiction, war, and westerns as the main film genre types, with descriptions capturing the elements most essential to each (Dirks, 2020, https://www.filmsite.org/genres.html). Added to this list are sub-genres representing more specific forms of the larger categories, each with its style, formulas, iconography, and subject matter: Biopics, "chick flicks," court-room dramas, detective/mystery films, disaster films, fantasy films, film noir, "guy" films, melodramas (or "weepers"), road films, romances, superhero films, sports films, supernatural films, thrillers/suspense, and zombie-horror films.

Moreover, as creative producers experiment, we have hybrids and iterations that complicate the task facing audiences who come to the screen with different expectations. The searchable IMDb website lists 24 film genres (Action, Adventure, Animation, Biography, Comedy, Crime, Documentary, Drama, Family, Fantasy, Film Noir, History, Horror, Music, Musical, Mystery, Romance, Sci-fi, Short Film, Sport, Superhero, Thriller, War, Western) as well as 26 television genres (Action, Adventure, Animation, Biography, Comedy, Crime, Documentary, Drama, Family, Fantasy, Game Show, History, Horror, Music, Musical, Mystery, News, Reality-TV, Romance, Sci-fi, Sport, Superhero, Talk Show, Thriller, War, Western) (IMDb, 2020).

All media content structures evolve, so there is no stable, definitive list to select from. Jeffres (1994) shows how even the format of radio stations, defined by news and music or types of music, has evolved, with "new" formats appearing (new age, modern vs. traditional jazz, film soundtracks, and comedy talk shows on satellite radio) as older archetypes decline (e.g., ethnic language radio). The new formats are created to fit market segments or rejuvenate old ones. Jeffres (1994) notes "The number and diversity of formats is limited only by human creativity…" (p. 332).

Most viewers seek some variety but also are more comfortable with the familiar; otherwise, more film and television programming would be experimental. A genre reduces the need for audiences to pay close attention for understanding. The concept allows us to plan our behaviors, to watch a situation comedy in order to laugh, or enjoy predictable characters in roles that make us feel good about our own lives. The task here is to see what audiences "expect" and the extent to which they match the definitions of film critics, observers, and scholars. To some extent, the selection of which film and television genres to examine is problematic. Netflix, for example, has 27,002 individual genres into which films are sorted (e.g., Cabral, 2021).

Profiles for 31 Film Genres

In our 2015 and 2021 surveys, we chose 31 film genres designed to reach a variety of audience tastes and preferences. Following are the film genres and descriptions of their structure according to film scholars, critics, and observers.

Musical

Schatz (1981) notes that musicals may be either backstage (in which all musical numbers are realistically set on a Broadway stage or other entertainment venue) or integrated (in which musical numbers may take place anywhere within the film's diegesis). Grant (2012b) provides a definition of the film musical as one that involves the performance of song and/or dance by the main characters and also relies on song and/or dance as an important element overall. These musical numbers are typically presented in an imaginary space. Feuer (1993) points out how dancers often use props such as room furnishings to help create an imaginary world.

The musical usually, but not always, focuses on romantic couples. Sobchack (1977) says musicals end with a wedding or a promise of one as the boy and girl come together after overcoming all obstacles (see also Scheurer, 2008). Altman (1984) notes that all aspects and sections of the musical recapitulate and reinforce the basic male-female duality (e.g., use of color, costume, setting), with dance serving as a sexual metaphor (Grant, 2007). Scheurer (1977) says music and dance help tell a story; feelings, emotions and instincts are given expression through music and dance; a libretto is essential—fusing music, dance, and book. Collins (1988) reports that the musical is the most audience-accessible genre because of its transparent plots, familiar music, and a visual style that is not confusing or elliptical.

Western

According to Schatz (1988b), the western is an "American foundational myth" (p. 25) that focuses on community conflict, which is resolved via a climactic gunfight. Tudor (2012, p. 5) says the western "has certain crucial established conventions—ritualistic gun-fights, black and white clothing corresponding to good and bad distinctions, revenge themes, certain patterns of clothing, typed villains, and many, many more." Maynard (1974) observes that most westerns take place during a very narrow time period: 1870–1890. This time period seemingly was "crammed with the romantic deeds of the nerves-of-iron gunfighter, the Robin Hood outlaw, the scrupulous lawman, the dashing cavalry officer, and the noble cowboy" (p. 1). The range of locations for the western is also narrow—the US Southwest or Mexico, places of rugged beauty shown with spectacular panoramic images (Tudor, 1977; Williams, 2018).

Nachbar (1974) contends that due to their immense popularity during the mid-20th century, "Westerns came to define for all classes of white Americans their traditional ethics, values and sources of national pride" (p. 2), a myth of national identity. There is a centrality of the Whites' confrontation with the immense frontier of North America, and as Cawelti (1974) notes, there is a thematic conflict between civilization and savagery, with "Indians" as a representation of the "inhospitable and uncontrollable elements of the surrounding landscape" (p. 59).

Horror

Hardy (1995) says that horror deals with fantasies and ideologies rather than social realities; it serves as a direct conduit to the unconscious and therefore reflects the time period that produced it (p. ix). Kawin (2012) acknowledges the importance in early horror films of a perverse love triangle (boy, girl, monster) that must ultimately be resolved. White (1977) notes that fear and pity are aroused by spectacular means, often supernatural, violent death, bizarre love, manipulation of fear, fear of the unknown, fear of rejection or isolation, abnormal mental processes, and suspension of normal frames of reference. Wood (1988) discusses the popularity of the genre in terms of how it maintains a "delicate balance between the goodness it show[s] as powerful and eventually victorious and the fascinating evil it makes visible but then return[s] to the closet" (p. 212). Williams (2018) reiterates the common theme of the horror film as a morality tale.

Often, special effects are used to generate monsters, ghosts, and other supernatural or extraordinary entities (Grant, 1984). The mechanisms generating fear are wide-ranging, from spiders and snakes to homicidal maniacs and zombies (Neuendorf & Sparks, 1988); aliens and atomic-generated monsters are part of the mix since the 1950s (Prawer, 1980). Vampires, bats, wolves, and crumbling castles are likely to be shown under the light of a full moon (Douglas, 1989).

Science Fiction

Hardy (1984) states that essentially all science fiction films call into question the world in which we live and also represent attempts to think speculatively about the future. Sobchack (1977) says there is no survival outside the group and science will save us if anything, not the individual, while V. Sobchack (1988) indicates that sci-fi is less concerned with individual psychology and personal crises than in societal crises and public situations. Tarratt (2012) notes that science fiction genre films exhibit a deep involvement with concepts of Freudian psychoanalysis and anxieties about repressed sexual desire.

Berg (2012) notes the centrality of the extra-terrestrial alien throughout much of the genre. Screenwriter Eric Williams (2018) characterizes the science fiction film in this way: "Regardless of who or what antagonizes the hero, we expect tentpole scenes in which our protagonist faces the unknown head-on and learns an important truth about humanity before the final confrontation in which she will risk 'everything'" (p. 35). Film critic Tim Dirks (2020, box 6) summarizes: "Sci-fi films are often quasi-scientific, visionary and imaginative—complete with heroes, aliens, distant planets, impossible quests, improbable settings, fantastic places, great dark and shadowy villains, futuristic technology, unknown and unknowable forces, and extraordinary monsters ('things or creatures from space'), either created by mad scientists or by nuclear havoc." In a practical sense, science fiction is the most dependent of any genre on special effects and studio art departments (Jameson, 1994).

Detective

Sobchack (1977) notes that crime or detective genre films have anti-social, violent acts but somewhere there is a moral order of community and group benefit, with the police, detective, or someone vindicating the ideal as the community is restored. The "detective" may be a private citizen, a private eye, or a police officer who is "hard-boiled," "worldly, cynical, and decidedly unsentimental" (Berger, 1992, p. 109).

Schatz (1981) indicates that the detective film in fact overlaps with film noir, although as Borde and Chaumeton (1996) note, detective films are more documentary-like in style and examine crime from the perspective of law enforcement rather than that of the criminal. Williams (2018) situates detective films within the "supergenre" of crime films.

Comedy

Scholars have noted the overly broad label of "comedy" in film and elsewhere (Neuendorf, 2020). As Leach (1977, p. 75) notes, "A genre which encompasses the visions of Jerry Lewis *and* Ernst Lubitsch is already in trouble." Nevertheless, Dirks (2020, box 6) has provided a broad definition: "Comedies are light-hearted plots consistently and deliberately designed to amuse and provoke laughter (with one-liners, jokes, etc.) by exaggerating the situation, the language, action, relationships and characters."

Comedy encompasses at least four disparate types of humor and numerous separate sets of conventions that are typically identified by such labels as slapstick, screwball, romantic comedy, dark comedy, parody, and mockumentary. Entire volumes of scholarship have been devoted to each of these so-called "subgenres" (e.g., Gehring, 1983, 1986, 2002, 2016, 2019; Grindon, 2011; Jenkins, 1992; Kendall, 1990), as well as auteur-as-genre treatments of comic giants such as Charlie Chaplin, Buster Keaton, the Marx Brothers, and Ernst Lubitsch (e.g., Kerr, 1975; Mast, 1979). Horton and Rapf (2012) explore the variety of ways in which comedy has been manifested on the big screen, including, in addition to the traditional genres such as slapstick and romantic comedies, such niche genres as utopian comedies and American Indian film comedies. Absent a single established scholarly/critical definition of the larger set "comedy," the current research is interested in how spectators might conceive of the generic term.

Film Noir

Schrader (2012, p. 266) identifies film noir as "those Hollywood films of the forties and early fifties that portrayed the world of dark, slick city streets, crime and corruption." Nachbar (1988) describes film noir (or "black film"; the French label was given to the films by French critics (Grant, 2007)) as dark in both storyline and physical texture. The lighting is often chiaroscuro and the environment is decadent and cynical; its iconography includes puddles, rainwater, mirrors, windows, and blinking neon lights (Grant, 2007, p. 24). "The world of film noir is the city, primarily at night, indifferent to suffering, with the possibility of violence or death around every corner" (Nachbar, 1988, p. 65). As Borde and Chaumeton (1996) point out, film noir presents a world from the point of view of the criminals. Characters include a bitter male pro-tagonist, and a jaded woman to whom he is sexually and fatally attracted, who ultimately betrays the protagonist in some mutual act of criminality (Nachbar, 1988). Further, "[T]he notion of haunting, obsessive memory is an essential feature of film noir. Some flashbacks directly involve a quest for the answer to an enigma or a series of enigmas posed in the beginning of a narrative" (Menegaldo, 2004, para. 2). More precisely, most films noir begin with a death and then use flashbacks to tell the story of how the death was arrived at; as Jameson (1994) says, "stories had a way of beginning at a dead end and wind-ing back to show how they had arrived there" (p. 1).

Documentary

In perhaps the definitive treatment of the development of the documentary, Barnouw (1993) describes the documentary simply as moving images that document some real phenomenon or action. Other definitions by early film-makers themselves include John Grierson's "creative treatment of actuality" and Dziga Vertov's "life caught unawares" (Barnouw, 1993). Nichols (1992) has said that documentaries are about reality, about real people, and tell stories about what really happened, but, that said, "documentary film practice is the site of contestation and change" (p. 12). Indeed, Barnouw presents more than a dozen schools of thought on what constitutes a documentary film.

Action

The action film focuses on the male, constructing an active masculinity (Gallagher, 2006). Grant (2007) indicates that action (and adventure) films "offer fast-paced narratives emphasizing physical action such as chases, fights, stunts, crashes and explosions, often dominating over dialogue and character development" (p. 83). Williams (2018), who identifies the action film as a "supergenre," also notes fight scenes, chase scenes, heart-racing stunts, and vivid special effects as essential: "Action films are visceral, not intellectual" (p. 21). The action film offers a display of male power and prowess dating back to the swashbuckling films of the silent era. Action stars tend to be heavily muscular with a hyperbolic masculinity; they "offer their impressive bodies for visual display and as the site of ordeals they must undergo in order to defeat the villains" (Grant, 2007, p. 83).

The heroes of action films, according to Williams (2018), are struggling against all odds to solve internal and/or external problems. The villains in action films are usually single-minded with grandiose plans, highly intelligent with extreme character flaws. According to Dirks (2020, box 6), "Action films usually include high energy, big-budget physical stunts and chases, possibly with rescues, battles, fights, escapes, destructive crises (floods, explosions, natural disasters, fires, etc.), non-stop motion, spectacular rhythm and pacing, and adventurous, often two-dimensional 'good-guy' heroes (or recently, heroines) battling 'bad guys'–all designed for pure audience escapism." Action films often show a contradiction between mundane and exotic locales (Williams, 2018).

Animated

Dirks (2020, filmsite.org/animatedfilms) notes that animated films are "not a strictly-defined genre category, but rather a film technique," in which "individual drawings, paintings, or illustrations are photographed frame by frame (stop-frame cinematography)"; he also notes that "animated films are often directed to, or appeal most to children, but easily can be enjoyed by all."

Mystery

Spiegel (2017) indicates that the mystery genre may be defined by an ambiguity in its world construction, and the audience's inability to ascertain "what logic governs the fictional realm" (p. 37). Berger (1992) offers that the genre typically involves a fictional character, an eccentric protagonist, solving a mystery by using logic and deductive reasoning. The protagonist is an outsider who works in unorthodox ways. The story is often set in a grand manor where there are servants of questionable morality.

Many scholarly sources include "mystery" as an alternative to or a subset of either detective films or film noir. Williams (2018) also combines mystery and detective films in a single "macrogenre," in which the film explores "the clues and motives that reveal a crime (the mystery) and/or the person uncovering the clues (the detective)" (p. 77).

Dark Comedy

Screenwriting professional Eric Williams (2018) offers a succinct definition of dark comedy: "Humor that makes light of subject matter typically considered taboo" (p. 17). Gehring (1988a) says that fundamentally, dark humor "is a genre of comic irreverence which flippantly attacks what are normally society's most sacredly serious subjects—especially that of death" (p. 167). Further, Gehring (2016) asserts that dark comedy films, notably those of the 1970s, are often a crossover (hybrid) with other genres such as war (e.g., *Dr. Strangelove* (1964),

M*A*S*H (1970)), western (e.g., *Little Big Man* (1970)), or musical (e.g., *Cabaret* (1972), *All That Jazz* (1979)). Dark comedy is a sophisticated form of humor that deals with topics that make the spectator uneasy and uncomfortable (Siegel & Siegel, 1994). Gehring contends that dark comedy is the "bravest" of all genres, kicking away "all the institutionalized crutches which prop up most people" (2016, p. 7), such as religion and government. It often tackles topics such as death and suicide through the lens of a sympathetic central character in an absurd environment, while undercutting any assumption of man's nobility or goodness.

Biography

Biography is a broad film genre, ranging from "everyman" stories of ordinary people dealing with monumental challenges to rags-to-riches tales (Williams, 2018). A biographical film is one that is based on the life of a real person, either living or dead. Anderson (1988) calls the biographical film, or the "biopic," an "amalgam of literature, history, psychology, and sociology" like its literary precursor (p. 331). Most biopics would fall in the fictionalized or interpretive biography categories of literature, according to Anderson. The biographical process follows norms of both history and journalism as well as fiction. The point of view or "voice" of the biography can range from autobiographical to the third-person omniscient narrator.

Parodies

"Film parody is a comic, yet generally affectionate, distorted imitation of a given genre, auteur, or specific work" (Gehring, 1988b, p. 145; see also Gehring, 1999). Williams (2018) observes that a parody film entails "humor based on imitation. All parodies are based on a preexisting work that is widely recognized. The work is summarily exaggerated to the point of mockery and trivialization" (p. 17). Parody may be seen as "creative criticism," a mechanism for learning more about the genre being parodied. It is not limited by time or space, often includes additional intertextual references beyond the content being parodied, and self-consciously draws attention to the fact that it is a film, sometimes breaking the fourth wall. Parody is different from satire in that parody focuses on literary/cinematic norms (at the level of the cultural product) while satire is aimed at social/political norms (at the level of the culture or society).

Slasher

A subgenre of the horror genre, the slasher film rose to prominence in the 1970s and 1980s. It is a post-*Psycho* (1960) form characterized by multiple killings by a psychopathic monster, with intentionally outrageous excess of gore. The slasher film highlights violence with sharp objects, by which skin is "slashed," as opposed to violence via blunt instruments or guns (Williams, 2018). Clover (1987) says the slasher film is "drenched in taboo and encroaching vigorously on the pornographic" (p. 187). She further notes that, compulsively repetitive and crude, "slasher films present us in startlingly direct terms with a world in which male and female are at desperate odds but in which, at the same time, masculinity and femininity are more states of mind than body" (p. 188). Clover identifies the trope of the "Final Girl," the one who does not die, and the character with whom male spectators are intended to identify. Most slasher films are violently misogynist and homophobic—punishing female sexuality, equating femininity with victimhood, and portraying the killer/monster as a queer figure or of non-normative masculinity (Rieser, 2001). There is emphasis on the male gaze, and occasional use of the "I-camera" showing the killer's point of view.

Mockumentary

The mockumentary is essentially a parody film in which the content being parodied is in documentary form. Mockumentaries are "fictional media texts which…imitate the aesthetics and stylistic conventions of documentaries" (Wallace, 2018, p. 3). It is reflexive both regarding its subject matter and with regard to the documentary form.

Chick Flick

Chick flicks are commercial films aimed at middle-class female spectators in their 20s and 30s. Called "prime postfeminist media texts" (Ferriss & Young, 2008), chick flicks raise questions about women's place in the world, negotiating friendships and sex, and achieving independence. The films often include a nod to femininity, designer clothing and consumer culture, and romantic attachments. According to Dirks (2020, filmsite.org/chickflicks), chick flicks may be either romantic comedies or melodramatic tearjerkers, and star a female protagonist or heroine, and feature "female bonding situations involving families, mothers, daughters, and children."

Slapstick

The term "slapstick" is derived from the name of the paddle that was once used in knockabout farces (on the stage) to slap the actors, making a loud, comic noise (Siegel & Siegel, 1994). "Slapstick is usually considered a lowbrow form of physical humor that depends upon pain and humiliation for laughter" (p. 263), with pratfalls and other physical gags. Williams defines slapstick films as featuring "humor that uses tripping, falling and cartoon-like violence as the core element" (2018, p. 18). Leach (1977) notes that both screwball and slapstick comedy show man out of keeping with his culture or man vs. woman. Slapstick comedy depends on the collision between man and things or rules, or the little man as victim.

Drama Film

Like the comedy film, the "drama film" is a wide term that encompasses many distinct subgenres, including romantic drama, melodrama, biography, historical film, and potentially epic film, film noir, mystery/suspense film, and gangster film. A general definition is provided by Dirks (2020, box 6): "Dramas are serious, plot-driven presentations, portraying realistic characters, settings, life situations, and stories involving intense character development and interaction." Williams offers the following portrait of what he calls the "straight drama" movie: "This broad category applies to those that do not attempt a specific approach to drama but, rather, consider drama as a lack of comedic techniques" (2018, p. 15).

Fantasy

Jennings (1988), while noting that the term "fantasy film" has been broadly used throughout the history of film criticism and therefore its definition is problematic, contends that "the only indispensable element in a fantasy is a central situation that defies rational or even pseudo-scientific explanation… [unlike science fiction,] the situation cannot be explained; it must simply be accepted" (p. 249). Williams (2018) categorizes the fantasy film as a "super-genre," for which the hallmark is "a sense of wonderment, typically played out in a visually intense world inhabited by mythic creatures, magic and/or superhuman characters" (p. 26).

Most fantasy films involve a quest, literal, or metaphorical. This quest may be related to the fact that the inexplicable world of fantasy is often contrasted with a more conventional reality from which the characters come and to which they may return. There is often a joyful climax to a journey toward self-knowledge in which the protagonist must make a choice between these worlds, after their "surrender of conventional understanding" and questioning of what constitutes "home" (Jennings, 1988, p. 251). The theme of freedom is also central. Typical characters include a hero or villain with supernatural powers, a child hero, and a supernaturally wise mentor to the human hero. Dirks (2020) indicates that fantasy films often include mythical creatures, and are sometimes based on fairy tales or other folklore. Williams (2018) also notes the importance of props and costumes for fantasy films.

Adventure

T. Sobchack (1988) acknowledges that the adventure genre encompasses a broad range of films (further, he notes the existence of subgenres that are often included in this category—swashbucklers, war films, jungle films, and disaster films). Nevertheless, he characterizes adventure films as those in which "mankind is depicted as living in a world fraught with perils of all kinds, but through the exemplary effort, cooperation, and bravery of individuals and groups, the social order, without which man would perish, is maintained against all threats to its stability" (pp. 9–10). In an adventure film, the characters are situated in the past, or in a location that is quite separate from ordinary life, posing few restraints on the characters. Correspondingly, exotic locations, flamboyant character actions, unusual characters that the protagonist encounters, and the use of spectacle are common elements (Williams, 2018). Bourget (2012) notes that the subgenre of swashbuckler adventure films reveals a pattern of social unrest and revolution to solve social ills.

Foreign

The "foreign film" is not really a genre with a scholarly literature that describes it. It is of interest to discover what the range of responses to a spectator survey will be.

Romantic Drama

Using the label "Romance," Dirks (2020, box 3) describes the genre thusly: "These are love stories, or affairs of the heart that center on passion, emotion, and the romantic, affectionate involvement of the main characters (usually a leading man and lady), and the journey that their love takes through courtship or marriage. Romance films make the love story the main plot focus." It has been noted that romantic drama often ends sadly (i.e., it may be a tearjerker or "weepie") (Siegel & Siegel, 1994). Williams (2018) also identifies one of his "supergenres" as "Romance," with an expectation of outcomes that are emotional and possibly sexual.

Romantic Comedy

Simply put, romantic comedy (the "romcom") is the "'boy meets girl, boy loses girl, boy gets girl' formula played for laughs" (Siegel & Siegel, 1994, p. 240). Romantic comedy takes a look at relationships of the heart "with a light and humorous touch…One of the central attributes of this [macrogenre] is that the audience quickly recognizes that the two characters are perfect for each other, even though the characters themselves may not" (Williams, 2018,

p. 81). Gehring (2002) notes that romantic comedy, while focusing on a romantic couple, accents "love" over "funny" when compared with other comedy genres such as screwball comedy. It is largely reality-based, with no slapstick and mainly realistic characters, and highlights a traditional dating ritual, with a slowly paced conclusion that leaves the spectator agonizing over whether the couple will ultimately get together (p. 3).

Gangster

Gangster movies tend to explore characters "within a specific social construct... organized crime" (Williams, 2018, p. 69). McArthur (1977) says gangster films show recurrent patterns of imagery, the physical presence-attributes-dress of actors, the milieu and the technology, with racketeers, gangsters, cops, private eyes, complex technology of firearms, autos, and phones, speeding cars, screaming tires, and images of aggression. Mitchell (2012) identifies patterns within gangster films that are more abstract and philosophical. Schatz (1981) notes that the unique origins of the genre were the contemporary newspaper headlines, and Raeburn (1988) cites the importance of prohibition to the genre's genesis. Schatz contends that gangster films romanticized the gangster-hero and painted an unflattering picture of contemporary urban life (and no nature is shown). He also notes that the classic movie gangster "represents the perverse alter ego of the ambitious, profit-minded American male" (p. 85), a kind of parallel to the American Dream (Raeburn, 1988).

Samurai

Kaminsky (1985) notes that "In a Japanese samurai film, a samurai, or ronin, can, with ease, defeat fifteen or twenty opponents at a time with his dazzling swordplay" (p. 63). The male protagonist is equally successful against guns, flying or invisible opponents, or if he is blind or otherwise disabled or "deformed" (p. 64). While similar to the American western in some respects, the samurai film (unlike the western) extends its plot and action beyond the limits of possibility.

Epic

"Epics, by their very nature, are long, detailed stories of heroic adventures" (Williams, 2018, p. 67). Durgnat (1977) says epic films are always connected with action, and exhibit extroversion, often extravagant, expensive, historical, large size, and grandeur. Dirks (2020, box 6) notes that epic films "cover a large expanse of time set against a vast, panoramic backdrop" and "take an historical or imagined event, mythic, legendary, or heroic figure, and add an extravagant setting or period, lavish costumes, and accompany everything with grandeur and spectacle, dramatic scope, high production values, and a sweeping musical score."

Sports

Williams (2018) notes that in a sports movie, of course, "people will be playing sports, and it will basically be the story of 'Our Team' versus 'Their Team'" (p. 37), with nearly every sports movie presenting an underdog story. Sayre (1977) says themes of sports genre films include the transitory nature of success and feature sports settings such as locker rooms. Dirks (2020, box 1) defines sports films as "Films that have a sports setting (football or baseball stadium, arena, or the Olympics, etc.), event (the 'big game,' 'fight,' 'race,' or 'competition'), and/or athlete (boxer, racer, surfer, etc.) that are central and predominant in the story. Sports films may be fictional or non-fictional."

Historical

Burgoyne (2008) identifies historical films as those that share a basis in the "documentable past" (p. 2). A more specific definition comes from Davis (2002, cited in Burgoyne, 2008): "dramatic feature films in which the primary plot is based on actual historical events, or in which an imagined plot unfolds in such a way that actual historical events are central and intrinsic to the story" (p. 2). Williams (2018) says that screenwriters do not consider the fact that the story takes place in the past as the most important aspect; rather, it is important that "the audience is given new insight into their own understanding of history" (p. 70).

Burgoyne (2008) claims there is overlap of the term "historical film" with the genres of war films, epics, and the biographical film. Although centered on the past, the historical film often arouses critical and popular controversy. The films are often scrutinized for their verisimilitude or their departure from accepted historical records. Burgoyne also refers to the films' ability to establish an emotional connection to the past, impacting on viewers' sense of national identity. Burgoyne further states that "By re-enacting the past in the present, the historical film brings the past into dialogue with the present" (p. 11).

Referencing primarily British films, Galpin (2016) identifies "heritage films" as those aimed at an older, middle-class audience, valued for their quality more than their commercial prospects, and motivated by a "nostalgic desire to escape…from an unpleasant or problematic present" (p. 433; see also Vidal, 2012).

Superhero

A definition of the live-action superhero genre is provided by Brown (2017): "filmed stories about costumed and/or super powered characters, performed by actors, who battle villains and defend the greater community" (p. 5). Common conventions include colorful costumes, secret identities, and traumatic origin stories (Williams, 2018).

Brown (2017) notes that an ongoing wave of live-action superhero blockbusters dominates world film box office. The reasons for this vast success are complicated, Brown indicates, including "In the traumatized post-9/11 climate, superhero movies provide a reassuring fantasy of America's ability to withstand terrorist attacks" (p. 2). There is a comforting nostalgia for America as not just a nation but an ideal; at the same time, the genre represents "the climate of late capitalist consumerism" (p. 3) and an industry reliance on cross-platform tent-pole films. The films are obviously dependent on advanced digital effects technologies, while needing to provide the spectator with believable, if fantastic and super-powered, characters with whom they can identify. Contemporary superhero films often challenge cultural beliefs about race, gender, nationalism, morality, and capitalism, but these are often glossed over as "vague assumptions about 'truth, justice, and the American way'" (Brown, 2017, p. 3).

War

Williams (2018) classifies the war film as a "supergenre," in which the typical story portrays a small group of isolated individuals who are facing death and then—one by one—are killed by some outside force, leaving a smaller group or individual to fight the final battle. Sobchack (1977) says the most popular plot involves a group of men, individuals thrown together from disparate backgrounds, who must be welded together to become a well-oiled fighting machine. The hero's primary function is to mold the group. Kane (1988) reinforces the notion that the protagonists did not choose to be where they are, but rather are "swept up by forces of history beyond their understanding" (p. 87). Eberwein (2010) identifies the essential features of the war film in terms of characters and basic narrative elements: Familiar male characters include the older, seasoned leader, the green recruit, and the platoon clown; familiar female characters include the loyal wife/girlfriend/nurse, the prostitute or floozy, and the wise mother; basic narrative elements include bonding, successful "graduation" from basic training, activities specific to branches of the service (e.g., water landings), contact with home in the form of letters and radio, and, often, readjustment to civilian life after war service.

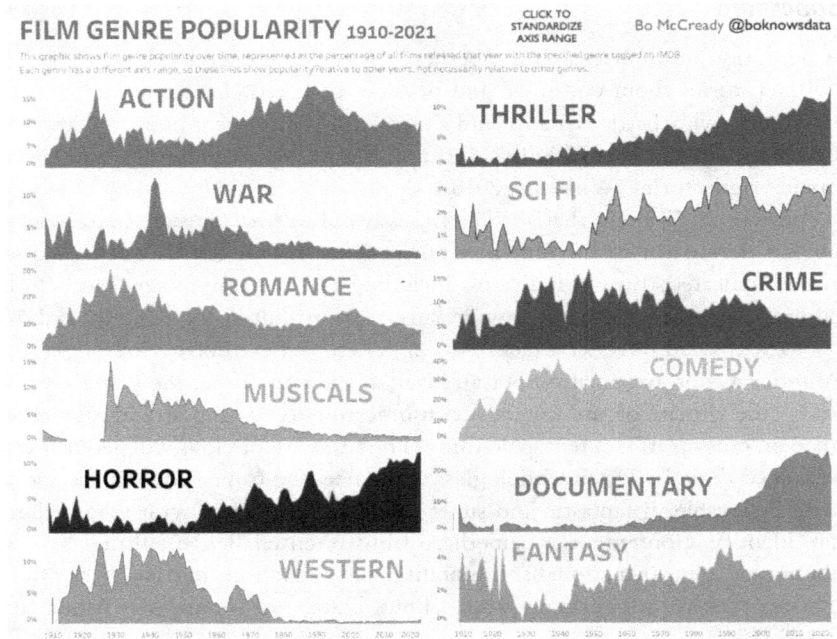

FIGURE 2.1 Film Genre Popularity 1910–2021

© *Bo McCready*

The evolution of key film genres from 1910–2021 is profiled in Figure 2.1 (reprinted with permission, Bo McCready).

Evolution of Television Genres

Brooks (2007) offers a typology of eight different eras of television programming that define commercial television's first 60 years in the US. They include:

1. *Vaudeo* (1948–1957). This era featured such programs as Milton Berle's *Texaco Star Theater* (1948-56), which was "typical of the first wave of television programming—frantic, corny, but always highly visual", with a combination of slapstick and variety that harkened back to vaudeville (p. xiv);

2. *The Adult Western Era* (1957–early 1960s). The western *Gunsmoke* (1955-75) ushered in an era that "signaled a major change in the source of prime time TV programming. All of them were on film, and most of them were produced by the major Hollywood studios…" (p. xv).

3. *The Idiot Sitcom Era* (early–late 1960s). Brooks characterized the 1960s as a "youth decade" during which "[B]izarre, comical characters turned up

on the *Addams Family* [1964-66], *The Munsters* [1964-66], *The Flying Nun* [1967-70], and *Batman* [1966-68], and slapstick silliness was alive and well on *Gilligan's Island* [1964-67], *Mr. Ed* [1961-66], *Hogan's Heroes* [1965-71] and many other shows" (p. xvi).

4. *The Relevance Era* (late 1960s–1975) reflected changes in America accompanying late-1960s era movements encompassing civil rights, women's rights, and opposition to the Vietnam War: *"All in the Family* [1971-79], about a blue-collar bigot and the folly of his ways, ranked number one among all series for five years....In its wake came spin-offs (*Maude* [1972-78], *The Jeffersons* [1975-85]) and a new wave of shows dealing with issues TV had scarcely ever touched before: interfaith marriage (*Bridget Loves Bernie* [1972-73]), anti-war sentiments (*M*A*S*H* [1972-83]), life at the bottom of the economic ladder (*Good Times* [1974-79], *Chico & The Man* [1974-78]). Maude had an abortion, and Edith Bunker was attacked by a rapist—comedy had never been like this before!" (p. vii).

5. *The ABC Fantasy Era* (1975–1980) reflected a return to escapism with programs like *Happy Days* (1974-84), which Brooks described as "the perfect inoffensive 8:00 P.M. show" (p. vii).

6. *Soap Operas and the "Real People" Era* (1980s). Brooks (2007, p. xviii) notes that "the soap opera, that serialized format so popular in daytime, became a hit in prime time as well, introducing a continuing-story element missing from most prime-time series" (e.g., *Dallas* (1978-91), *Dynasty* (1981-89), and *Knots Landing* (1979-93)). These were joined by programs like *Real People* (1979-83), which "set out to reflect the real world, especially its lighter, more entertaining aspects, without necessarily trying to change it" (p. xviii).

7. *The Era of Choice* (1990s). Brooks notes that the rise of cable and other carriers complicated the process of identifying successive eras in accordance with dominant themes. "Instead, the once tightly controlled world of national television has exploded into hundreds of channels, all with their own independent voices...no longer does programming move in lockstep" (p. xix). As cable surpassed 50% of households in 1987, a welter of networks emerged to provide continuous fare that had previously been limited as part of the commercial networks' more horizontal offerings (*MTV, CNN, The Weather Channel, Discovery, TNT, Nickelodeon*, etc.).

8. *The Reality Era* (2000s). As Brooks (2007, p. xx) notes, "The vanguard of this new wave was the quiz show *Who Wants to Be a Millionaire* in the late summer of 1999, which reminded networks of the value of audience participation (anyone could get on the show by calling in and taking some tests) and of showing us ourselves on the screen."

To this, we could add a 9th era:

9. *The User-Generated Content Era* (2007–present), ushered in as *Time* magazine named individual users as their Person of the Year for 2007 (i.e., "You control the information age. Welcome to your world" (Time, 2007)). This trend toward micro-programming was furthered by the Federal Communications Commission's conversion to a digital transmission scheme that helped open the spectrum to a growing number of channels. Online platforms like Facebook and YouTube were also available to most American households by decade's end.

Profiles for 11 Television Genres

We chose 11 television genres for our examination. This configuration is based on longstanding observations regarding the relative staying power of more frequently appearing genres/formats. For instance, after 1971, films, crime dramas, and situation comedies tended to occupy an average of 60% of all regularly scheduled prime time programs and constituted 53% of all new series. Shifts in the popularity of television genres are documented in studies by Signorielli (1986). In an analysis of 15 years of prime time television programming, situation comedies went from 45% in 1970 to 34% in 1975, 39% in 1980, and 28% in 1985. Action-adventure programming went from 40% in 1970 up to 54% in 1975, down to 34% in 1980, and to 45% in 1985. A longer timespan (1950 through 1982) was selected for a study by Wakshlag and Adams (1985). They found that each season was dominated by two to four categories, when each accounted for 12 to 25% of available time.

These rather lopsided distributions across program categories held through the 1990s (e.g., Adams, 1993) and on, although reality TV had emerged as the most frequently appearing genre/format through the early 2000s (e.g., Abelman & Atkin, 2011; Potter, 2016). Since those older studies, with an explosion of available channels, the variety of new genres has grown dramatically, as reality television, for example, has morphed into different forms and variety-talent competitions and audience game shows have captured more air time.

Elaborations of the 11 television genres we examined, from descriptions by media scholars and critics, are as follows.

TV Sitcoms

The television situation comedy (sitcom) utilizes stable characters in a given situation and is distinguished by a combination of comic performer(s) and dramatic situations and action. The comic performer(s) may be a single star comic or an ensemble (Hartley, 2015). According to Williams (2018), in a sitcom the humor is "derived from knowing a stock group of characters and exposing them to different situations to create humorous and ironic juxtaposition" (p. 18). Two main types of sitcom have been the family sitcom and the workplace sitcom, although sitcoms may alternate between home and office (Feuer, 2015). More recently, production techniques for sitcoms have shifted from recording in front of a live audience to shooting documentary style, called "comedy verité" by some (Mills, 2015).

TV Dramas

Creeber (2015) identifies television drama as having multiple subgenres that define its scope: The crime series, the detective series, the police procedural, the action series, the western, the teen drama, the hospital drama, the costume drama, the telefantasy, science fiction, and postmodern drama.

TV Soaps

The soap opera is, above all, characterized by its serial narrative, with competing and intertwining plot lines directed at a female audience (McCarthy, 2015). The narrative tends to focus on particular communities and family groups, with drama, emotion and intrigue that unfold at the same pace as the viewer's real life (p. 73). Of note also is the ironic genre name—"soap... opera"—which indicates some sense of "derision" (Derry, 1985).

TV Detective

Jenner (2015, p. 20) notes that the TV detective is a maverick outsider, working in semi-isolation and is independent or semi-independent from the official police force (unlike a police procedural). The detectives are defined by their superior intellect.

TV News Magazines

A TV news magazine is an unscripted TV format focused on detailed analysis and discussion of current events. Topics can range from news and contemporary issues (e.g., *60 Minutes* (1968-)) to entertainment news (e.g., *Entertainment Tonight* (1981-)).

TV Musical Talent

Potter (2016) characterizes this as a subgenre of the reality competition genre where performers compete for a prize, as contestants, are eliminated each episode (e.g., *America's Got Talent* (2006-)).

TV Reality

Reality television is a term that has been applied to a widening range of TV program types (Dovey, 2015). Jeffres et al. (2011) settled on a definition of a TV program that typically includes competition (usually participation in a game of attrition, for "end-game" prizes), unscripted but planned behavior, and the use of non-actors (p. 159).

TV Late-Night Talk

From its inception, the TV late-night talk show has been conducted on a set that replicates a living room, with a desk for the host and a couch for guests. The sequence of elements remains: An opening monologue by the host, a segment with studio audience involvement, interviews with guests, and performances of guests on stage. There is a sidekick for the host, and the program is recorded in front of a live audience (Shattuc, 2015).

TV Children's Programs

While children's television is not defined by its narrative structure, setting, or intended emotional impact, as are many other genres/formats, it does have a prime distinguishing feature. It is predicated on the assumption of adults imagining the intended young audience and producing cultural texts for that audience (Mittell, 2015, p. 112).

TV Animal/Nature

This unscripted format can include wildlife documentaries from such sources as the BBC and National Geographic. Programs are generally shot on location and many feature celebrity narration (e.g., PBS's *Nature* (1982-)).

TV Sci-fi

TV science fiction has often been based on a "projection into a potentially frightening future," but that future holds some promise (Kaminsky & Mahan, 1985, p. 115).

Audience Expectations for Film and Television Genres—The 2015 Users Survey

How do audiences define film and television genres? And do those expectations match the criteria cited by film scholars? First, we examined the literature to determine how film scholars, reviewers, and critics define film and television genres. Then we compared those criteria with the responses of our respondents in the 2015 survey. Our thematic coding scheme built on earlier work by Jeffres et al. (1990), which included 10 major headings subsequently broken down into 75 different categories that captured a substantial universe of audience expectations—people and roles, types of activities, plot/storyline, personal reactions and feelings, material culture/symbols, time frame, quality/ evaluations, settings, special effects and technical aspects, and analogies to other content.

In the 2015 study, we built a lengthy coding book (Neuendorf, 2019) of almost 75 pages so that we captured an even more refined set of expectations. The highest order of categories remained almost the same, but with two additional categories: (1) references or analogies to specific films, programs; (2) time frame; (3) material culture, symbols; (4) settings; (5) people and roles; (6) types of activities; (7) personal reactions and feelings; (8) special effects and technical aspects; (9) plot, storyline, format structure; (10) evaluations and assessments; (11) descriptive concepts, abstractions; and (12) miscellaneous.

The development of subcategories followed an inductive process through which individual references for each film and television genre were placed into categories added under the larger headings. This multi-year process is largely responsible for the time between the survey and presentation of results. Eventually, a separate category of descriptive concepts and abstractions, and a miscellaneous category had to be added. Following are some examples for major categories, with a fuller description available online.

References to specific TV programs, films, or analogies seem rather straightforward. The time frame category includes historical time frames, biographical frames, and references to length of running or airing. The material culture and symbols category includes everything from clothing and drugs to cell phones and sports items. Settings range from locales to the built environment. People and roles include references to specific actors, types of people, and roles. Types of activities range from routine personal activities to violence and singing and talking. Personal reactions and feelings are cited for many genres, from being cheered up to feeling scared or sad. With the popularity of superhero films, many viewers referred to special effects and technical aspects of film making. The category of plot and storyline (e.g., slice of life stories, cliff hanger, happy endings) was expanded to refer to non-fiction structures, especially television programs (e.g., contestants with judges, news magazine). Many references focused on evaluations or assessments of stories, plots—interesting plot, formulaic, or repetitive plots. The descriptive contents and abstractions category includes, for example, representational issues (poor cultural translation, stereotypes), concepts referring to social or cultural codes (life lessons, honor), describing behaviors (empathy, apathy), and describing relationships (camaraderie) or situations (despair). The miscellaneous category featured such notions as weirdness and subliminals.

Our first research question is based on an analysis of the open-ended expectations our respondents gave for each of the film and television genres.

Research Question 1: How do audiences define specific film genres?

Audiences, with their own tastes and expectations, collectively differentiate among genres when they choose what to watch. Their expectations of what a film genre is not only identifies core elements but also establishes relationships among genres.

First, how useful are the different types of referential categories for defining film and television genres? Tables 2.1 and 2.2 show how important each

TABLE 2.1 Popularity of Referential Categories by Film Genre (2015 Users Survey)

Reference Categories→ Film Genre ↓	DK	Specific Films, Programs	Time Frame	Material Culture, Symbols	Settings	People, Roles	Types of Activities
# in top 3 cited	3	0	3	9	3	11	23
Musicals	5	0	3	9	2	7	358
Westerns	10	6	3	194	38	125	138
Horror films	13	5	0	172	2	74	92
Science fiction	8	6	7	122	78	121	14
Detective films	7	5	3	63	3	116	95
Comedy films	4	9	1	7	3	58	313
Film noir films	119	7	11	20	11	37	39
Documentary films	12	6	38	14	17	14	25
Action films	5	3	2	84	5	37	308
Animated films	10	18	0	43	9	63	81
Mystery/suspense	14	3	3	9	10	36	67
Dark comedy films	38	3	0	7	2	30	234
Biography films	22	0	106	9	10	49	30
Parodies, "spoofs"	31	18	1	6	1	36	213
Slasher films	39	0	0	231	4	59	91
Mockumentaries	85	24	3	2	1	25	157
Chick flicks	20	3	2	17	1	80	184
Slapstick films	58	13	2	16	0	33	231
Drama films	10	2	7	7	2	24	117
Fantasy films	15	6	12	64	118	68	26
Adventure films	11	4	3	39	73	45	147
Foreign films	38	0	2	4	42	23	30
Romantic dramas	18	4	4	8	6	48	220
Romantic comedies	14	5	0	10	6	61	289
Gangster films	19	6	10	220	13	84	193
Samurai films	42	0	10	188	43	63	150
Epic films	54	10	63	19	39	40	62
Sports films	22	2	9	36	11	100	142
Historical films	20	4	129	45	21	33	24
Superhero films	15	30	6	60	23	149	132
War films	15	5	22	152	9	52	247

Note: Total number of respondents is 543; each respondent could give multiple responses. The most frequently reported categories are in **bold**.

TABLE 2.2 Popularity of Referential Categories by Film Genre (2015 Users Survey)

Reference Categories→ Film Genre ↓	Reactions, Feelings	Special Effects, Techniques	Plot, Storyline	Evaluations, Assessments	Descriptive, Abstract References	Miscellaneous
# in top 3 cited	15	5	15	7	0	0
Musicals	**57**	**54**	22	31	5	0
Westerns	21	14	18	22	11	0
Horror films	**118**	37	45	29	8	2
Science fiction	57	27	72	44	7	2
Detective films	70	17	**169**	29	3	2
Comedy films	**68**	9	38	51	14	1
Film noir films	47	**98**	52	34	20	7
Documentaries	**121**	77	**181**	15	26	14
Action films	**71**	51	50	27	3	1
Animated films	34	**153**	48	**105**	12	11
Mystery/suspense	**131**	60	**151**	40	14	7
Dark comedies	**64**	8	47	**49**	23	22
Biography films	**94**	32	**116**	31	26	4
Parodies, "spoofs"	**48**	14	14	**94**	25	10
Slasher films	**62**	14	41	38	8	2
Mockumentaries	46	16	37	**63**	15	7
Chick flicks	58	6	**98**	71	22	7
Slapstick films	45	13	14	**56**	14	7
Drama films	**123**	19	**136**	63	47	15
Fantasy films	54	54	59	44	11	24
Adventure films	**82**	14	**102**	26	3	8
Foreign films	**64**	**216**	43	37	9	20
Romantic dramas	**57***	8	**115**	**57***	33	9
Romantic comedies	44	6	**112**	57	22	17
Gangster films	28	14	43	23	16	9
Samurai films	32	32	22	10	23	5
Epic films	46	53	**80**	**68**	5	12
Sports films	68	3	**138**	23	14	11
Historical films	**81**	44	**109**	17	36	9
Superhero films	54	33	**95**	30	9	6
War films	45	12	**53**	18	34	4

* *Tied*

Note: Total number of respondents is 543; each respondent could give multiple responses. The most frequently reported categories are in **bold**.

category is for specific film genres. At the top of each column is the number of film genres for which the category is among the top three in audience expectations. The most important category is "types of activities" (ranging from shooting to sex to arguing), which is important for 23 of the 31 genres, followed by personal reactions (e.g., makes me laugh, feel involved, find interesting), and plot and storyline references (ranging from soap operas to slice of life and plot twists), each important for 15 genre definitions. References to people and roles comes next, being important in defining 11 genres with such references as names of specific actors and types of people—life cycle roles (children, teenagers), relationships (couples, husbands), ethnicity (Asian people, Black people), gender (old men), job or career (witnesses, jocks, doctors), or film/ television roles (underdog, sidekick, bad talent, actors, famous guests).

Less important for defining film genres are settings (from general sets, to exotic locales, landscapes, buildings, or environments), time frame (such as historical references, time spans, or certain eras), and special effects or technical aspects (references to animation, cinematography, editing, special effects, sound, or narration). References to settings are most important in defining fantasy films and foreign films, while references to time frame characterize audience perceptions of biography films, epic films, and historical films. Technical aspects of filmmaking and special effects are referenced by audiences in defining foreign films, animated films, film noir, documentaries, and musicals.

Three film genres are ill-defined by audiences. Thus, "don't know" and "don't watch" are important responses for film noir, mockumentaries, and slapstick films.

A second research question asks:

Research Question 2: How do audiences define specific television genres?

Per Research Question 2, we also examined the importance of referential categories for the 11 television genres where audiences were asked for their expectations. Tables 2.3 and 2.4 show the distribution of responses, where we note that plot or storyline is among the top three in importance for all but one television genre, animal or nature television shows. The second category that's most important is types of activities, which are important audience expectations for all genres/formats except children's shows, science fiction and animal/nature programs.

TABLE 2.3 Popularity of Referential Categories by Television Genre (2015 Users Survey)

Reference Categories→ TV Genre ↓	DK	Specific Films, Programs	Time Frame	Material Culture, Symbols	Settings	People, Roles	Types of Activities
# in top 3 cited	0	0	0	2	1	4	8
TV sitcoms	32	11	8	5	14	**61**	**160**
TV dramas	28	4	13	3	12	41	**73**
TV soap operas	37	2	8	6	6	39	**99**
TV detective shows	19	6	12	37	12	**85**	**121**
TV news magazines	58	10	21	13	1	49	**76**
TV musical talent	33	6	5	7	0	72	**146**
TV reality shows	29	6	1	7	5	51	**82**
TV late-night talk	27	7	7	11	0	**129**	**225**
TV children's shows	30	9	2	27	2	35	53
TV animal/nature shows	22	7	1	**162**	**107**	10	16
TV science fiction	29	13	7	**65**	41	**140**	31

Note: The most frequently reported categories are in **bold**.

TABLE 2.4 Popularity of Referential Categories by Television Genre (2015 Users Survey)

Reference Categories→ TV Genre ↓	Reactions, Feelings	Special Effects, Techniques	Plot, Storyline	Evaluations, Assessments	Descriptive, Abstract References	Miscellaneous
# in top 3 cited	3	1	10	3	0	0
TV sitcoms	48	60	**82**	53	15	2
TV dramas	**94**	15	**133**	67	40	12
TV soap operas	52	17	**132**	141	27	6
TV detective	66	11	**160**	55	8	7
TV news mag	**65**	11	**129**	42	16	2
TV musical talent	60	12	**128**	**77**	23	8
TV reality shows	57	11	**139**	**99**	40	10
TV late-night talk shows	53	7	**106**	41	6	6
TV children's shows	**107**	**127**	84	65	10	27
TV animal/ nature shows	**113**	58	95	30	5	7
TV science fiction	58	39	**90**	61	8	13

Note: The most frequently reported categories are in **bold.**

The Jeffres et al. 1990 study (introduced above) found that a broad range of college students varied in their agreement of what constituted popular genres. Presented with 20 different film and television genres, they were asked to match them with 38 items representing themes, character, settings, or film techniques associated with particular genres in the literature. For only eight genres did a 50% majority agree on even one component and for many others consensus emerged on only one or two components. The popular horror genre was the most precisely defined genre in that study, while musicals and epics were less clear for the young audience. Before the matching exercise, respondents were given a list of eight film genres and asked what they'd expect for each of them. In the unprompted solicitation of genre features, the respondents cited many of the features attributed to genres by critics and scholars. We'll note those in the table below alongside those of the current study with a broader range of viewers.

Austin and Gordon (1987) found a student audience agreeing on characteristics for documentary/biography/drama as well as war/crime/action/adventure genres. Glass and Waterman (1988) found that students judge new films by reference to past films with similar characteristics; in other words, they naturally use genres to classify films.

In our 2015 Users Survey, the respondents were asked to respond to open-ended items asking what they expected to find for each of the 31 film and 11 television genres. Thus, the most salient features should come to mind. Table 2.5 shows the key descriptors referenced by scholars and critics, and by the respondents in the 2015 Users Survey, along with some results from the Jeffres et al. (1990) study.

Table 2.6 shows the agreement among TV scholars/critics and audiences in expectations for television genres. Although the top item referenced by audiences for television news magazines was "don't know" or "nothing" (in particular, perhaps), the other four references do describe news and sources along with celebrity roles, so, given the quite general nature of magazine topics, audience expectations are quite realistic. Late-night television talk show expectations by audiences also demonstrate more than a passing acquaintance with this TV format—hosts, guests, and interviews along with jokes and joking that might be taken as descriptors for the monologues opening shows.

However, for both television genres, audiences reference how they expect to react—to laugh or be bored. Interestingly, structure and content items cited by scholars and critics are accompanied by the gratifications derived for audience members. The fact that audiences reference both content features and their own uses and gratifications has added significance for scholars. Biocca (1991) suggests how to link the message construction process with content structures and audiences. Media professionals use forms, conventions and structures that make media "user friendly," helping viewers to arrive at understandings that frame audience processing by guiding and limiting the types of inferences people make.

Thus, the data generated here allow us to see to what extent audience expectations for TV and film genres partner content structures and ingredients with their own expected uses and gratifications from watching the specific moving images. A look at Table 2.6 shows that most of the 11 genres include gratifications such as laughing or feeling suspense, uses such as learning, or the lack thereof—being bored. Perhaps the attention to our own reactions is a product of how much time people spend watching television and their familiarity with the various genres. But, while uses and gratifications also appear in audience expectations for film genres, they're absent in a substantial number, at least as the most popular expectations. Thus, audience expectations for westerns, action films, fantasy films, romantic dramas, gangster, samurai, sports, and superhero films seem to focus less on uses and gratifications.

A Concluding Note

In sum, this chapter sought to bridge the gulf between critical/humanistic studies of genre and empirical work on audience recognition of those structures, based on surveys with respondents evaluating 31 film genres and

TABLE 2.5 Agreement Among Film Scholars/Critics and Audiences in Genre Expectations (2015 Users Survey) with Popular Expectations by Respondents of Jeffres et al. 1990 Study Added

Film Genre	Defining Characteristic by Film Scholars/Critics	Most Popular Expectations by Respondents
Musical	(1) Performance of song and/or dance by main characters; (2) song and dance important elements overall; (3) presented in imaginary space, using props to create it; (4) usually focuses on romantic couple; (5) tells a story with feelings, emotions, instincts; (6) transparent, familiar plots	(1) Music, songs, singing; (2) dancing, parties; (3) being bored; (4) good music; (5) singing, lots of singing, great singers, lyrics In the 1990 study, some 58% cited singing and dancing.
Western	(1) Focuses on community conflict; (2) resolved via climactic gunfight; (3) conventions such as good/bad distinctions, revenge themes; (4) conventions on objects— patterns of clothing; (5) narrow 1870–1890 time period and the frontier landscape; (6) classic roles such as Robin Hood outlaw, scrupulous lawman, dashing cavalry officer, noble cowboy	(1) Cowboys, outlaws, pioneers, gunslingers; (2) shooting, gunshots; (3) horses; (4) weapons; (5) action In the 1990 study, a third cited types of people or roles, and 30% mentioned violent activities such as killing and fighting, while 23% cited types of scenes or situations one would see in westerns.
Horror	(1) Deals with fantasy, ideologies rather than social realities; (2) love triangle that needs to be resolved; (3) fear aroused by often supernatural means, with violent death, fear of unknown; (4) special effects generate monsters, ghosts, supernatural entities, such as maniacs, zombies, aliens, vampires; (5) a morality tale	(1) Blood, gore, dead bodies; (2) fear, being scared; (3) supernatural characters; (4) screaming, yelling, arguing; (5) criminal behaviors In the 1990 study, half of respondents cited material cultural symbols such as blood, gore, or weapons and a third mentioned violent activities such as murder and killing.
Sci-fi	(1) Calls into question the world we live in; (2) no survival outside the group and science will save us; (3) extra-terrestrial aliens or monsters; (4) themes of heroes, dark villains, unknown forces; (5) futuristic technology, with mad scientists, nuclear havoc; (6) special effects	(1) Supernatural characters; (2) outer space, planets; (3) spaceships, saucers; (4) sci-fi themes (tie); (4) future technology (tie) In the 1990 study, more than a fifth mentioned special effects and a quarter aliens, monsters, or the supernatural.

(Continued)

TABLE 2.5 Agreement Among Film Scholars/Critics and Audiences in Genre Expectations (2015 Users Survey) with Popular Expectations by Respondents of Jeffres et al. 1990 Study Added (*Continued*)

Film Genre	Defining Characteristic by Film Scholars/Critics	Most Popular Expectations by Respondents
Detective	(1) Antisocial, violent acts; (2) somewhere there is a moral order of community; (3) police, detective, or someone vindicating the ideal as community is restored; (4) detective may be private citizen, private eye, or a police officer; (5) detective characterized as hard-boiled, worldly, cynical, unsentimental	(1) Mystery, mysterious themes; (2) legal roles—police, courts; (3) criminal behaviors; (4) crime, perpetrator roles; (5) feeling suspense, intrigue In the 1990 study, 18% cited violent activities, and in the matching exercise a significant number cited good vs. evil subplots.
Comedy	(1) Light-hearted plots designed to amuse, provoke laughter with jokes, one-liners; (2) uses exaggerated situations, language, action, relationships, and characters to amuse; (3) four types of humor, and discrete types—slapstick, screwball, romantic comedy, dark comedy, parody, mockumentary	(1) Laughing, funny; (2) jokes, joking, humor, telling jokes; (3) types of jokes/humor (tie); (3) laughing in response to film content (tie); (4) comedian, comic actor role referenced
Film noir	(1) Portrays world of dark, slick city streets, crime, and corruption; (2) dark storyline, and physical texture; (3) chiaroscuro lighting; (4) environment is decadent, cynical; (5) world from point of view of the criminals, with bitter male protagonist, jaded women; (6) themes of sexual and fatal attraction, betrayal; (7) begins at end and provides context via flashbacks	(1) Don't know, nothing; (2) black and white picture; (3) darkness, dark colors, shots; (4) being bored; (5) criminal behaviors (tie); (5) mystery, mysterious themes (tie)
Documentary	(1) Images document real phenomena or action; (2) are about reality, real people, stories that really happened	(1) Facts, data; (2) info, knowledge, being challenged/provoked; (3) information by itself; (4) something interesting; (5) history
Action	(1) Action, fast-paced narratives with chases, fights, stunts, crashes, explosions; (2) male power and prowess with action stars and muscular, hyperbolic masculinity; (3) high energy, big-budget physical stunts, chases, battles, adventures; (4) often two-dimensional good guy/bad guy themes	(1) Actions, activities related to war; (2) chasing, chases; (3) weapons; (4) fighting; (5) action, actions

(Continued)

TABLE 2.5 Agreement Among Film Scholars/Critics and Audiences in Genre Expectations (2015 Users Survey) with Popular Expectations by Respondents of Jeffres et al. 1990 Study Added (*Continued*)

Film Genre	Defining Characteristic by Film Scholars/Critics	Most Popular Expectations by Respondents
Animated	(1) Individual drawings, paintings, or illustrations photographed frame by frame; (2) mostly appeal to children but can be enjoyed by all	(1) Cartoons; (2) colors, bright colors; (3) laughing, funny; (4) good story, plot; (5) children as target audience
Mystery	(1) A fictional character, an eccentric protagonist who's an outsider working in unorthodox ways; (2) solving a mystery by using logic, reasoning; (3) often set in a grand manor; (4) servants of questionable morality; (5) ambiguity in the logic governing the situation	(1) Mystery, mysterious theme; (2) criminal behaviors; (3) feeling suspense, intrigue; (4) plots with twists, turns; (5) being afraid, scared
Dark comedy	(1) Comic irreverence dealing with taboos or serious subjects such as death, suicide; (2) sophisticated humor that focuses on topics that make the audience uneasy, uncomfortable; (3) sympathetic central character in an absurd environment; (4) undercuts assumptions of man's nobility, goodness	(1) Types of jokes, humor; (2) laughing, funny; (3) don't know, nothing; (4) death, dying; (5) jokes, joking, telling jokes
Biography	(1) Based on life of real person; (2) are fictionalized, interpretive stories; (3) follows norms of history and journalism as well as fiction; (4) point of view or voice ranges from autobiographical to the third-person narrator	(1) Biographical, stories about people, their lives; (2) being interested; (3) facts; (4) being bored; (5) history
Parodies	(1) A comic, generally affectionate but distorted, exaggerated imitation of a given genre or work; (2) not limited by time or place; (3) self-consciously draws attention to fact it's a film, sometimes breaking the fourth wall; (4) differs from satire by dealing with literary/cinematic norms rather than aiming at social/political norms—at level of culture or society	(1) Funny, laughing; (2) humor, laughs, jokes; (3) joking, telling jokes; (4) types of jokes, humor (tie); (4) negative assessments generally (tie)
Slasher	(1) Subgenre of horror genre, characterized by multiple killings via sharp objects by psychopathic monster; (2) excesses of gore, drenched in taboos, is repetitive, crude, almost pornographic; (3) male and female are at desperate odds; (4) are misogynist, homophobic, in portraying killer/monster, equating femininity with victimhood	(1) Blood, gore, body parts; (2) weapons; (3) fear, being scared; (4) don't know; (5) criminal behaviors

(*Continued*)

TABLE 2.5 Agreement Among Film Scholars/Critics and Audiences in Genre Expectations (2015 Users Survey) with Popular Expectations by Respondents of Jeffres et al. 1990 Study Added (*Continued*)

Film Genre	Defining Characteristic by Film Scholars/Critics	Most Popular Expectations by Respondents
Mockumentary	(1) A parody film in which content is parodied in a documentary form; (2) fictional media texts; (3) imitates aesthetics and stylistic conventions of documentaries	(1) Don't know; (2) jokes, joking, telling jokes; (3) laughing, funny; (4) refers to original film source; (5) negative assessment general (tie); (5) don't, wouldn't watch (tie)
Chick flick	(1) Aimed at females in 20s, 30s; (2) question women's place in the world, negotiating friendships, sex, achieving independence; (3) nod to femininity with designer clothes, consumer culture; (4) may be either romantic comedies or melodramatic tearjerkers; (5) told from female point of view, with female bonding situations involving families, mothers, daughters, children, women's issues	(1) Romance, love; (2) crying, tears; (3) romantic themes, love stories; (4) laughing, funny; (5) youth, teenage audience (tie); (5) female gender (tie); (5) physical appearance of actors, cast positive (tie)
Slapstick	(1) Lowbrow form of physical humor; (2) depending on pain, humiliation for laughter; (3) pratfalls, physical gags that are cartoon-like; (4) depends on collision between man and things or rules, or the little man as victim	(1) Types of jokes, humor; (2) laughing, funny; (3) don't know, nothing; (4) jokes, joking, telling jokes; (5) humor, laughs, jokes with negative connotation
Drama	(1) Wide term with many subgenres—romantic drama, melodrama, biography, historical film; (2) are serious; (3) plot-driven; (4) portray realistic characters; (5) realistic settings, life situations; (6) stories involve intense character development and interaction	(1) Good story, plot; (2) crying, tears; (3) feel suspense, intrigue; (4) interested; (5) romance, love
Fantasy	(1) A central situation that defies rational or even pseudo-scientific explanation; (2) many involve a quest; (3) is a joyful climax to a journey toward self-knowledge; (4) protagonist must make choice between "worlds"; (5) typical characters include a hero, or villain with supernatural powers, often include mythical creatures; (6) often based on fairy tales, folklore	(1) Fantasy, magic; (2) supernatural characters; (3) imaginary animals, characters; (4) other, imaginary, created worlds referenced; (5) special effects

(Continued)

TABLE 2.5 Agreement Among Film Scholars/Critics and Audiences in Genre Expectations (2015 Users Survey) with Popular Expectations by Respondents of Jeffres et al. 1990 Study Added (Continued)

Film Genre	Defining Characteristic by Film Scholars/Critics	Most Popular Expectations by Respondents
Adventure	(1) Mankind lives in world fraught with all kinds of perils; (2) through effort, cooperation, bravery of individuals, groups, the social order is maintained; (3) situation is in the past or in a location quite separate from ordinary life, often exotic settings; (4) flamboyant character actions, spectacle	(1) Action, actions; (2) feeling excitement, thrilling; (3) traveling, trips; (4) quest, journey story themes (tie); (4) to have fun, be entertained (tie) In the 1990 study, more than a third cited action and a fifth types of scenes or situation one would see. And 12% noted feelings of excitement.
Foreign	(1) Not a genre but refers to non-American produced films	(1) Subtitles; (2) foreign/other languages; (3) other cultures, customs; (4) good story, plot; (5) don't, wouldn't watch (tie); (5) don't know, nothing (tie) In the 1990 study, 31% cited the use of subtitles, and 15% said foreign films were characterized by abstract ideas or were hard to follow.
Romantic drama	(1) Love stories or affairs of the heart; (2) that center on passion, emotion, affectionate involvement of main characters; (3) journey that man and lady love take through courtship or marriage; (4) drama often ends sadly	(1) Romance, love; (2) romantic themes, love stories; (3) kissing, hugging, smooches, heartbreak; (4) sex, sexual activities; (5) crying, tears In the 1990 study, some 36% cited romantic activities such as love making and sex, while a fifth mentioned types of scenes or situations one would see.
Romantic comedy	(1) Story where boy meets girl, loses girl, gets girl; (2) story is played for laughs; (3) is largely reality-based with realistic characters; (4) highlights traditional dating ritual; (5) slow-paced conclusion leaving viewer, who recognizes that the two belong together, agonizing over whether the couple will ultimately get together	(1) Romance, love; (2) laughing, funny; (3) romantic themes, love stories; (4) sex, sexual activities; (5) jokes, joking, telling jokes, humor by itself

(Continued)

TABLE 2.5 Agreement Among Film Scholars/Critics and Audiences in Genre Expectations (2015 Users Survey) with Popular Expectations by Respondents of Jeffres et al. 1990 Study Added (Continued)

Film Genre	Defining Characteristic by Film Scholars/Critics	Most Popular Expectations by Respondents
Gangster	(1) Features characters within organized crime; (2) conventional images of dress, attributes, actions associated with gangsters, racketeers, cops, private eyes; (3) complex technology of firearms, autos, phones, speeding cars, screaming tires; (4) romanticized gangster-hero in unflattering picture of contemporary urban life; (5) prohibition often involved; (6) perverse alter ego of ambitious profit-minded American male	(1) Weapons; (2) physical violence; (3) crime, perpetrator roles; (4) shooting, gunshots; (5) criminal behaviors In the 1990 study, 44% cited violent activities and more than a fifth types of roles, people, and scenes and situations typical of the genre.
Samurai	(1) Japanese samurai characters; (2) dazzling swordplay, also successful against guns, flying or invisible opponents that number even 15 or 20 at a time; (3) extends its plot and action beyond the limits of possibility	(1) Weapons; (2) fighting; (3) actions, activities related to war; (4) don't know, nothing; (5) action, actions; (6) samurai, samurai soldiers, ninjas, geishas In the 1990 study, significant percentages noted Samurai films were fast paced, filled with action, had much violence, contained minimal dialogue and showed good and evil as clearly drawn.
Epics	(1) Always connected with action and expansive, historical, large size and grandeur; (2) covers a large expanse of time set against a vast, panoramic backdrop; (3) takes an historical or imagined event, mythic, legendary or heroic figure; (4) and adds an extravagant setting or period with lavish costumes; (5) dramatic scope, high production values and sweeping music score	(1) Don't know, nothing; (2) long, too long; (3) references epics in some manner (tie); (3) actions, activities related to war (tie); (4) action, actions In the 1990 study, three items were matched by significant percentages: extravagance, action, romantic subplots and a hero at odds with the culture or community. Epics were not included in the unprompted exercise.

(Continued)

TABLE 2.5 Agreement Among Film Scholars/Critics and Audiences in Genre Expectations (2015 Users Survey) with Popular Expectations by Respondents of Jeffres et al. 1990 Study Added (*Continued*)

Film Genre	Defining Characteristic by Film Scholars/Critics	Most Popular Expectations by Respondents
Sports	(1) Themes include transitory nature of success; (2) sports settings such as locker rooms; (3) sports setting—stadium or arena; (4) sports event—big game, fight, race or competition; (5) athlete central and predominant in the story; (6) the story of "our team" vs. "their team," often with an underdog	(1) Sports roles–coach, player; (2) sports games, behaviors referenced; (3) sports objects, concepts; (4) football, soccer; (5) underdog story theme
Historical	(1) Primary plot is based on actual historical events in which; (2) an imagined plot unfolds such that actual historical events are central, intrinsic to the story; (3) re-enacting the past in the present; (4) audience is given new insight into their own understanding of history	(1) History; (2) interested; (3) historical dress/costume; (4) facts, factual (tie); (4) educational, informative, learning (tie); (4) clothing, costume referenced (tie)
Superhero	(1) Stories about costumed and/or super powered characters; (2) characters battle villains, defend the greater community; (3) colorful costumes; (4) advanced digital effects; (5) stories often challenge cultural beliefs about race, gender, nationalism, morality, capitalism but these are closed over with vague assumptions about truth, justice and the American way	(1) Superheroes; (2) action, actions; (3) dark outfits, capes, disguises, mask, robes; (4) people flying; (5) hero, villain roles
War	(1) Group of men thrown together from disparate backgrounds who must become a well-oiled fighting machine, and yet they are killed off one by one; (2) the hero's primary function is to mold the group; (3) clear roles of seasoned leader, green recruit, platoon clown, loyal wife/girlfriend/nurse, the prostitute or floozy, wise mother; (4) narrative elements of bonding, successful completion of training, activities/actions in conflicts—water landings, dogfights, interrogations—contact with home via letters, radio, readjustment to civilian life after service	(1) Actions, activities related to war; (2) weapons; (3) death, dying; (4) blood, gore, dead bodies; (5) physical violence In the 1990 study, more than half identified action as a defining characteristic and significant percentages noted a fast pace, much violence and three plots or storylines: good and evil clearly drawn, social unrest, and situations of normalcy erupting into images of death. War films were not included in the unprompted exercise.

TABLE 2.6 Agreement among TV Scholars/Critics and Audiences in Expectations for TV Genres (2015 Users Survey)

Television Genre	Defining Characteristic by Television Scholars/Critics	Most Popular Expectations by Respondents
TV news mags	(1) Unscripted TV format focused on detailed analysis and discussion of current events; (2) topics range from news and contemporary issues (e.g., *60 Minutes*) to entertainment news (e.g., *Entertainment Tonight*).	(1) Don't know, nothing; (2) gossiping, rumors; (3) news, sources referenced; (4) acting, general character, celebrity roles referenced; (5) being bored
TV late-night talk	(1) Setting replicates living room with desk for host, couch for guests; (2) opening monologue by host; (3) segment with studio audience involvement; (4) interviews with guests; (5) performances of guests on stage; (6) sidekick for the host; (7) live studio audience	(1) Jokes, joking, telling jokes; (2) laughing, funny; (3) interviews (tie); (3) program host, guest roles (tie); (5) comedy, sitcom form
TV sitcoms	(1) Stable characters in a given situation; (2) combination of comic performances, dramatic situations and action; (3) family or workplace situated; (4) recent shift from live audience to "comedy verite'"	(1) Laughing, funny; (2) laugh track, canned laughter; (3) don't know, nothing; (4) comedy, sitcom form, themes; (5) to have fun, entertainment (tie); (5) humor, laughs, jokes with negative connotation (tie); (5) jokes, joking, telling jokes (tie)
TV dramas	(1) Multiple subgenres: Crime series, detective series, police procedural, action series, western drama, teen drama, hospital drama, costume drama, telefantasy, science fiction, postmodern drama	(1) Feeling suspense, intrigue; (2) good story, plot; (3) drama general, specific; (4) don't know, nothing; (5) cliff hanger, surprise ending (tie); (5) acting with negative connotation (tie)
TV soaps	(1) Serial narrative; (2) competing, intertwining plot lines; (3) directed at a female audience; (4) focus on particular communities, family groups; (5) drama, emotion, and intrigue unfolding in "real-life"	(1) Drama; (2) acting with negative connotation; (3) being bored; (4) don't/wouldn't watch; (5) sex, sexual activities (tie); (5) romance, love (tie); (5) writing, story, with negative connotation (tie); (5) negative overall assessment (tie)
TV detective	(1) TV detective is a maverick outsider; (2) working in semi-isolation; (3) is independent or semi-independent from police; (4) detective has superior intellect	(1) Mystery, mysterious theme (tie); (1) criminal behaviors (tie); (3) legal system roles–courts, police; (4) law and order crime story themes; (5) feeling suspense, intrigue

(Continued)

TABLE 2.6 Agreement among TV Scholars/Critics and Audiences in Expectations for TV Genres (2015 Users Survey) (*Continued*)

Television Genre	Defining Characteristic by Television Scholars/Critics	Most Popular Expectations by Respondents
TV musical talent	(1) Subgenre of the reality competition genre where performers compete for a prize, as contestants are eliminated each episode (e.g., *America's Got Talent*)	(1) Singing, great singers, amazing lyrics; (2) talent competition and context theme (tie); (2) judging talent (tie); (4) specific talent, performer roles; (5) dancing, dance
TV reality	(1) Includes competition; (2) with end game prizes, in game of attrition; (3) unscripted but planned behavior; (4) use of non-actors	(1) Drama references; (2) overall negative assessment; (3) talent competition and context theme; (4) non-scripted nature of show; (5) fighting
TV children's shows	(1) Not defined by narrative structure, setting or emotional impact, but has many formats; (2) is predicated on assumption of adults imagining the intended young audience and producing cultural texts for the audience	(1) Educational, learning, informative; (2) cartoons; (3) children as target audience; (4) animation; (5) lots of colors, bright colors
TV animal/nature	(1) Can include wildlife documentaries from such sources as the BBC and National Geographic; (2) shot on location and many feature celebrity narration	(1) Animals; (2) educational, learning, informative; (3) wildlife, animal documentary scenarios; (4) nature, habitat (tie); (4) interested (tie)
TV sci-fi	(1) Projection into a potentially frightening future but one that holds some promise	(1) Supernatural characters; (2) science fictions themes; (3) don't know, nothing; (4) outer space and planets (tie); (4) spaceships and saucers (tie)

11 television genres. Inspection of study data suggests high levels of agreement among our study respondents with the genre definitions offered by film scholars and critics.

On balance, study results paint a picture of broad agreement between audiences and professional critics or creators of content. Although Uses and Gratifications Theory can help us understand how audiences process key genre types, these expectations were less explanatory for westerns, action films, fantasy films, romantic dramas, gangster, samurai, sports, and superhero films. We further explore dimensions with which audiences identify, from among these genre categories, in Chapter 3.

3
AUDIENCE VIEWING OF THE MOVING IMAGE—FILM AND TELEVISION GENRES

Today, with the advent of social media, including YouTube and other platforms, audiences not only are processors or consumers of the moving image but they're also producers. Given the omnipresence of cell phones, the quick video has become a staple of Facebook and Instagram. But even more important are videos offered through YouTube and TikTok, where an entirely new set of forms have been developing. This chapter lays out the roles that people fill in the modern media environment, then focuses on the audience as viewers, processers of the moving image in all its forms. Demographics are considered, as well as overall communication preferences and how these viewer-producer roles are related to perceptions of film and television genres.

When the Internet was in its infancy, Jeffres and Atkin (1996) argued that the emerging communication grid ultimately would allow for a wider range of communication behaviors than those originally envisaged in early Information Superhighway conceptions. They separated out the traditional media audience activities (as processors of messages—viewing, reading, and listening to the media) from sender roles (as creators of messages). Their typology distinguished the communication roles from "consumer roles" to avoid what appeared to be an undue focus on economics and technology defining the symbolic activity that constitutes communication behaviors. That imbalance seems to persist today.

The communication grid allowing people to send and receive messages via almost any mode in almost any form to almost everybody at almost any time, moreover, has most certainly arrived for the 93% of Americans who are online (Perrin & Atske, 2021). Audiences today can watch films and television programs on a host of platforms with few time constraints other than download speeds and access to streaming services. Though audiences seldom can produce or send films or television programs that mirror those examined

DOI: 10.4324/9781003264828-3

in this study of genres, increasingly people of all ages are mounting their small videos on social media, and younger audiences in particular are contributing more ambitious videos. An additional form of user-generated content (UGC)—podcasts—also fits into this discussion. Further research will need to address the genres that characterize the diverse videos on YouTube and other platforms (Grant & Meadows, 2020).

The Diverse Roles of Audiences

A 1993 study by Jeffres and Atkin (1996) used measures capturing message processor, message sender, and consumer roles that seem either quaint if not visionary given what technology has done to the communication environment over the past two and a half decades. But the distinctions and the concepts are more important than ever. It's useful to reassess those original study domains, beginning with key operationalizations underscoring each concept.

The Viewer, or *Traditional Media Audience Processor Role*: "Even if it costs more, I'd like to have a cable system that had 500 channels so there was always something that fit my personal tastes." This promise in 1993, the year the study was conducted, certainly has been fulfilled "in spades" via cable, satellite, streaming options, and such services as Netflix. Today, roughly 30 years later, we view moving images on various platforms and virtually anywhere.

Creator or *Message Sender Role*: "If there was some way I could send a message to everyone in the area using mail by telephone or some computer hookup, I'd do it regularly." Well, social media such as Facebook and Twitter certainly fulfill that role, allowing people to share or create messages with others. To this, we could add more coverage through email newsletters and online blogs or similar sender opportunities. But it's the creative role in which people use their phones and modern technology to "film" videos of varying lengths to post on social media that's most important.

Consumer Role: "I already have enough to watch on TV and don't need cable TV to pay bills, do my banking, order airline tickets or do other things that I now do in person or by mail." Even the US Postal Service could testify to the consequences of shifting consumer roles to less interpersonal contexts. The consumer role also can be expanded to include various services used through modern technology. This role is not the focus of the present volume, but it deserves mention.

People vary in the extent to which they "need" to engage in various communication activities, as senders/creators or receivers/processors of messages. The 1993 study attempted to measure the "communication need to send messages" with these items, echoing what Twitter and social media behaviors enable today:

"Sometimes I wish I were a columnist for the metro daily and could tell everybody what I thought about what's going on today."

"I often feel the need to express myself and wish I had a chance to be a writer or reporter."

That study found strong relationships between communication needs (to send messages via mass media, and need for interpersonal communication) and both the importance of the traditional audience role in receiving or processing messages and the likelihood one would be an active sender of messages using new technologies, but not the likelihood of using technologies as a consumer. There also were positive relationships between the importance of the traditional audience role in receiving messages and how often people went out to see films in a theater, as well as time spent watching television or listening to the radio.

This chapter will examine the patterns of traditional media use among our respondents (the viewing, reading, listening roles). What factors help to explain people's media use, and in particular, viewing the moving image? And how do we account for people's preferences for various film and television genres?

Traditional Media Use Behaviors—Viewing the Moving Image and Using Mass Media

First, a decision to watch a television program or go to a movie may seem like a simple decision, but it's much more complicated. Our individual decisions occur on a foundation of interests, preferences, and experiences built up over time. Clearly, we all have an initial introduction to the specific medium, particularly when it first appears on the scene. Changes in technology of course affect those preferences. For example, when color television was introduced, viewing escalated, particularly for programs made vivid, interesting, and consistent with "real life." And the introduction of mobile media and social media are within the experiences of many adults today. As children, our attention to "screens" may be limited by our parents, and even later are constrained by other factors in our lives. Let's take a look at a decision to view a specific television genre or to go see a film in a theater, modifying a "media behavior unit" introduced by Jeffres (1974) to fit our focus on the moving image.

In the natural setting, one considers initiating a viewing experience (or other media use) several times daily. When anchoring the model, we backtrack in time from the actual decision point to the existence of some function one wants fulfilled. There is some need, or desire, one wants fulfilled, whether it's simply avoiding boredom, needing to fill some time, or a more active seeking of specific information or "content." This assumes that people are aware of their needs and can identify them. In fact, our viewing and media use would persist only if they produced the desirable uses and gratifications. Though we're examining this decision process by focusing on a point in time, actual decisions to go see a film or watch a movie on TV are based on actual uses and gratifications we associate with the viewing experience built up from prior viewing. A substantial literature on uses and gratifications profiles our media habits (e.g., Knobloch-Westerwick et al., 2020).

Uses and Gratifications Theory

Uses and Gratifications (U&G) Theory focuses on what audiences do with media. The perspective posits that media fulfill a set of cognitive and affective needs for their audience (e.g., Dam et al., 2018; Katz et al., 1973). Katz et al. (1974) explicated five key assumptions of the U&G model, which Qiao and Zhu (2011, p. 233) summarize as: (1) audiences "use media with a purpose" and know their needs, so media should be designed to fit an audience's demands; (2) media use should fulfill the audience's social or psychological needs; "(3) the process of dissemination enables the audience to combine media use with demands fulfilment; (4) specific media can only satisfy some of the audience's demands, so there is competition between media; (5) audience (sic) are rational, in possession of their own needs and motives, and their needs and motivations are expressed through choice of media".

Haberlin and Atkin (2022) recount the primary U&G theoretical tenet that "level of media use is predicted by the strength of user motivations determining its use" (p. 126). This framework includes the psychological needs, motives and gratifications satisfied within a given media context (e.g., film vs. video) (Lin, 2009; Rubin, 2009). U&G Theory is also well-suited for studying the kinds of de-massified, asynchronous, and interactive capabilities characterizing emerging forms like video streaming (e.g., Haberlin & Atkin, 2022; Tefertiller & Sheehan, 2019). Key elements in this visual media use process are described in Figure 3.1.

Each of these steps, grounded in U&G Theory, can be expanded and developed to help us understand people's appreciation of the moving image and the factors that influence our expectations. Thus, individually, we have different needs related to viewing and other media experiences. As youngsters, our tolerance for boredom can be quite limited. In the current environment, many believe we've become so addicted to our cell phones, that even adults feel a "need" to be stimulated by media, specifically mobile messages, photos and videos, almost constantly. Drawing from the assumptions of U&G Theory, then, we can posit the following guiding hypothesis:

H_t: Level of visual media consumption will be positively related to strength of media use motivations.

A	B	C	D
You have some use or gratification that's stimulating the decision (e.g., to be stimulated, to fill time)	You consider the options available, first the medium, then the specific "content" (e.g., genre)	You watch the film or other medium chosen	The viewing experience fulfills one or more uses and gratifications.

FIGURE 3.1 Describing the Decision Process for Viewing the Moving Image

These needs and interests are likely related to social categories that we all occupy—as men and women (gender), as our position in the life cycle (age) and life events (marital status)—by our achievements (level of education and income) and by our heritage (ethnicity). Thus, we will first examine how these factors explain people's media use decisions, though we will defer relationships with genre preferences for a later chapter.

But the decision to consider options also is a multifaceted affair. If the gratification needing fulfillment is sufficiently broad that it can lead to multiple options, including non-media options, then we need to look at how people fill their free time. Our 2015 study did ask respondents for the things they like to do in their leisure time, so we'll examine those preferences, as well as the frequency with which they use a host of media, and see how they're related to preferences for the various film and TV genres.

Leisure-time Activities—the Moving Image and Other Options

Respondents in the 2015 survey were asked for some of the things they like to do in their leisure time. We know from previous research that there are patterns to how we fill time when we don't have to work or have other obligations, and these can help us understand people's affinity for the moving image. Some folks are "addicted" to screens, while others gravitate toward the printed page, via hard copies or mobile devices. An accounting of our 543 respondents shows how popular television, films, and print media are as leisure activities. More than 303 citations of television viewing were recorded—some mentioning specific programming, others just the medium itself. Some 153 mentioned watching movies and 20 mentioned going out to see movies.

But surfing the Internet was cited almost a hundred times, and some three-dozen mentioned social media, e.g., Facebook, Twitter, Pinterest. Watching the moving image one way or another thus remains a popular pastime. More than 300 citations of reading as a leisure-time activity were recorded, and, lest we view our sample as homebound and completely mediacentric, respondents identified other interests as well.

This profile suggests that our 2015 sample reflects the diversity of American adults. So how do the affinity for viewing moving images and attachment to media as leisure interests translate into genre preferences? First, we pulled out selected media use variables for comparison with genre preferences. Almost 56% of respondents cited television as a leisure activity, 28% cited watching movies, about 4% cited going out to see movies, 16% cited surfing the Internet, and 48% mentioned reading. We added socializing and communication, cited by 18%, gaming or playing games—much of it online—cited by about a fourth of respondents. Also, outdoor activity—including exercise and playing sports—cited by a third of our sample.

When someone has a strong affinity for watching movies as a leisure-time activity, we'd expect a preference for more genres since they are likely to have a broader base of experiences, and our data confirm precisely that. Those who watch movies as a favorite leisure-time activity also say they watch 12 different film genres more often than those who prefer other leisure pursuits, including: Westerns, horror films, science fiction, detective films, film noir, action films, mystery/suspense films, dark comedy films, biographical films, film parodies, slasher films, slapstick films, fantasy films, gangster films, samurai films, epic films, historical films, superhero films, and war films. They also watch TV dramas and TV animal/nature programs more often.

Those who say watching television is a favorite leisure-time activity watch the following TV genres more often than those citing other leisure interests: Situation comedies, TV dramas, detective programs, and children's programs. They also watch several film genres more often—chick flicks, drama films, romantic dramas, and romantic comedies—but western films less often.

Using Mass Media (2015 Users Survey)

Table 3.1 shows frequencies for a range of leisure activities in the 2015 Users Survey. Our sample is composed of active media users, with daily television viewing. Reading is a much less frequent behavior, with a quarter of respondents seldom reading magazines or newspapers but, relative to the general population, our sample opens a book more often than most.

Weekly film viewing in theaters is rare, but a quarter of respondents go out to see films in theaters every couple of weeks. However, some two-thirds of respondents see films on some device such as phones or tablets.

Surfing the Internet for pleasure and checking emails or scrolling through Facebook are ubiquitous activities that dominate the lives of our sample, with half checking Facebook and two-thirds surfing the web for pleasure several times each day. More than half also text family or friends rather than call them on the phone each day and more than 40% play video games each day.

Going out to see live musical concerts or plays in a theater are only occasional activities so in-home media behaviors fill more of our free time, as technologies link us to screens more and more often. Jeffres et al. (2000) previously found that media use was positively related to participation in other public leisure activities such as attending professional sports events, visiting museums, or going out to theaters or concerts.

The 1993 study had also found that people's affinity for new technologies was related to likelihood one would use new technologies to send messages but not to the traditional audience role for receiving messages. The 2015 study returns to these sender-receiver roles with items that find out how often people engage in communication activities that reflect the potential promised more than two decades ago. The following items used in the 2015 survey give us an

TABLE 3.1 Audience Use of Media and Technologies (2015 Users Survey): Traditional Media Audience Processor Role—Viewing the Moving Image and Using Mass Media

	Several Times Each Day	Once a Day	Several Times Each Week	About Once a Week	Every Couple Weeks	Less Often than That	Almost Never	Never
Legacy Media								
Watch television	**46.0%**	**30.0%**	10.5%	4.0%	1.3%	3.5%	3.5%	1.1%
Listen to the radio	**26.3%**	**21.0%**	19.2%	8.5%	5.9%	4.2%	9.8%	5.2%
Read a magazine	2.0%	6.6%	12.0%	**17.7%**	**16.8%**	16.0%	**19.7%**	9.2%
Read a book	10.3%	**18.2%**	**20.1%**	12.5%	14.5%	14.2%	8.1%	2.0%
Read a newspaper	2.8%	10.1%	11.2%	**15.7%**	9.2%	**16.0%**	**21.7%**	13.3%
See films in theaters	0.6%	0.7%	2.0%	5.0%	**24.3%**	**40.1%**	**21.7%**	5.5%
Media on Technology								
See films on phone, tablet	5.7%	9.9%	**27.8%**	**27.8%**	15.3%	8.5%	3.7%	1.3%
Surf Internet for pleasure	**67.6%**	**16.9%**	9.8%	2.4%	1.7%	1.1%	0.6%	0.0%
Check my email	**77.9%**	**15.7%**	3.9%	1.1%	0.4%	0.9%	0.2%	0.0%
Go on Facebook	**49.5%**	**16.8%**	7.9%	5.5%	3.3%	3.5%	4.4%	9.0%
Play video games on device	24.7%	**17.1%**	15.1%	9.6%	7.4%	6.4%	7.9%	11.8%
Watch videos on smartphone	13.6%	13.3%	**17.3%**	10.1%	9.0%	6.6%	11.0%	**19.0%**
Text family or friends rather than call on phone	**46.8%**	14.4%	**15.1%**	5.3%	4.4%	4.1%	4.1%	5.9%
Live Entertainment Activities								
See live musical concerts	1.7%	1.1%	1.8%	1.8%	10.1%	**36.8%**	**29.8%**	16.8%
See live plays in theater	1.3%	1.1%	1.1%	1.8%	4.4%	**28.0%**	**36.1%**	**26.2%**

Note: The most frequently reported categories are in **bold.**

idea of the extent to which people are technology-digital fans, have traditionalist preferences, and/or have a preference for mobile and social media. We can use these together with actual media use to describe people's patterns.

Technology-Digital fans (Tech Enthusiast Scale, Cronbach's alpha=.70)

> "I love the options at my finger-tips today, watching videos on my phone, texting in a car, streaming films."

> "I can hardly wait to see what technology comes next."

> "I think I'm getting less patient and am glad I have a smart phone or other digital options to fill the time."

Traditionalist preferences (Communication Traditionalist Scale, Cronbach's alpha=.61)

> "I'm more a traditionalist, preferring to read physical copies of books, magazines and newspapers rather than digital versions."

> "I'd still rather talk to people over the phone than text."

> "I think that the new technologies have begun to dominate our lives, occupying too much of our time."

> "I like the variety of entertainment available today but sometimes feel it's too much."

Preferences for mobile media (Mobility/Social Media Enthusiast Scale, Cronbach's alpha=.70)

> "I often watch videos on my cell phone."

> "I often search for videos on YouTube to watch."

> "I often share videos via Facebook."

> "I often share videos on Instagram."

We constructed the three scales and then looked at relationships between them and how people use the media (see Table 3.2), with results linking use of several legacy media to the Com Traditionalist Scale and use of media on technology to the Tech Enthusiast Scale. But there are no relationships for going to live entertainment activities, watching TV, or listening to the radio, so those variables are omitted from the table. Going out to see films is only marginally related, negatively, to the traditionalist scale. Unfortunately, Twitter—which reached only 23% of the population in 2021–wasn't as popular when this study was mounted, or it would have been included (Wojcik & Hughes, 2019).

TABLE 3.2 Significant Relationships between Media Use and Two Scales: Tech Enthusiast and Com Traditionalist Scales (2015 Users Survey)

	Tech Enthusiast Scale	Com Traditionalist Scale
Legacy Media		
Read a magazine		.10#
Read a book	-.10*	
Read a newspaper		.09#
See films in a theater		-.07#
Media on Technology		
Surf Internet for pleasure	.20***	
Go on Facebook	.14**	-.11*
Play video games on device	.27***	-.17***
Watch videos on smartphone	.40***	-.11*
Text family or friends rather than call on phone	.39***	

Note: #.05<*p*<.10; *p<.05; **p<.01; ***p<.001

Social categories often are strong predictors of how people use the media. Going out to see a film in a theater is related to all social categories other than education. Thus, males, younger people, higher income people, Whites, and Blacks all go out to see a film in a theater more often. Younger respondents, Whites, and Blacks watch videos more on a smartphone, while more educated folks are less likely to watch a film on newer technologies. Older respondents are less likely to surf the Internet for pleasure rather than work, to go on Facebook, play video games, or text, compared to younger respondents, but they do check their emails more often. Women are less likely to go out to see films in a theater, relative to men, but they check their emails and go on Facebook more often. Education is positively related to surfing the Internet for pleasure and checking email. Those with higher incomes go on Facebook less often, compared to those with less income, but they check email more often, surf the Web for pleasure and go out to see films in a theater more often [Table available online].

Watching Genres of the Moving Image

Table 3.3 shows the average viewing frequency, in order according to the most popular film and television genres. The five most popular film genres are comedy, action, drama, adventure, and animated films, while the least popular are samurai, film noir, and mockumentary films. However, the low rated genres also are those with which audiences are least familiar (see Table 2.1). Television dramas and situation comedies are the most popular TV genres, with soap operas least popular of the 11 rated.

We wanted to see what film viewing patterns were related to people's enthusiasm for new technologies or to traditionalist media views. Table 3.4 shows correlations between those attitudes and reports of how often one

TABLE 3.3 Popularity of Film and Television Genres (2015 Users Survey)

Film Genre Viewing	Average Frequency of Viewing (1=Never; 5=Very Often)
Comedy films	4.22
Action films	3.95
Drama films	3.81
Adventure films	3.77
Animated films	3.58
Mystery/suspense films	3.58
Science fiction films	3.53
Fantasy films	3.48
Documentary films	3.35
Romantic comedies	3.24
Superhero films	3.21
Detective films	3.20
Romantic dramas	3.04
Chick flicks	2.95
Dark comedy films	2.93
Biographical films	2.91
Historical films	2.87
War films	2.83
Horror films	2.79
Epic films	2.77
Gangster films	2.54
Foreign films	2.54
Slapstick films	2.34
Musicals	2.33
Sports films	2.33
Film parodies	2.32
Slasher films	2.14
Westerns	2.13
Mockumentaries	2.04
Film noir films	2.03
Samurai films	1.98
TV Genre Viewing	*Average Frequency of Viewing (1 = Never; 5 = Very Often)*
TV dramas	3.53
Situation comedies	3.40
Detective shows	3.23
Science fiction shows	2.92
Animal/nature shows	2.82
Reality TV shows	2.57
Late-night talk shows	2.47
Children's programs	2.44
Music or talent competitions	2.30
TV News magazine shows	2.22
TV soap operas	1.76

TABLE 3.4 Significant Relationships between Viewing Film and Television Genres and People's Enthusiasm for Mobility/Social Media, New Technologies, and Traditional Media (2015 Users Survey)

Genre Viewing	Mobility/Social Media Enthusiast	Tech Enthusiast	Com Traditionalist
Film Genre Viewing			
Genres related to all three			
Musicals	.19★★★	.11★	.09#
Detective films	.17★★	.19★★★	.19★★★
Film parodies	.19★★★	.11★★★	.11★
Romantic dramas	.10#	.11★	.17★★★
Genre viewing related to mobility/social media and tech enthusiasm			
Horror films	.21★★★	.17★★★	
Animated films	.13★	.21★★★	
Mystery/suspense films	.14★	.18★★★	
Dark comedy films	.17★★	.11★	
Slasher films	.27★★★	.17★★★	
Mockumentaries	.14★	.11★	
Chick flicks	.10#	.18★★★	
Slapstick films	.23★★★	.18★★★	
Fantasy films	.15★★	.13★	
Adventure films	.17★★	.17★★★	
Gangster films	.17★★	.11★	
Samurai films	.10#	.10#	
Genre viewing related only to mobility/social media enthusiasm			
Foreign films	.14★		
Sports films	.10#		
Superhero films	.10#		
Genre viewing related only to com traditionalist			
Western films			.13★
Biographical films			.09#
Historical films			.10#
Genres related only to tech enthusiasm			
Science fiction films		.12★	
Comedy films		.26★★★	
Action films		.14★★	
Epic films		.10#	
Genre viewing related to both tech enthusiasm & com traditionalist			
Drama films		.10#	.22★★★
Romantic comedies		.12★	.11★
Genre viewing related to both mobility/social media enthusiasm & com traditionalist			
Film noir	.18★★★		.18★★★
War films	.15★★		.14★★
Genre viewing unrelated to any of the three			
Documentary films			
TV Genre Viewing			
TV genre viewing related to all 3			
Soap operas	.26★★★	.12★	.11★
Music or talent competitions	.26★★★	.18★★★	.12★
Children's programs on TV	.23★★★	.10#	.10#

(Continued)

TABLE 3.4 Significant Relationships between Viewing Film and Television Genres and People's Enthusiasm for Mobility/Social Media, New Technologies, and Traditional Media (2015 Users Survey) (*Continued*)

Genre Viewing	Mobility/Social Media Enthusiast	Tech Enthusiast	Com Traditionalist
TV genre viewing related to mobility/social media and tech enthusiasm			
Situation comedies	.10#	.15★★★	
Detective shows	.13★	.25★★★	
Reality TV shows	.12★	.15★★	
Late-night TV talk shows	.18★★★	.15★★	
TV genre viewing related to mobility/social media enthusiasm only			
Animal/nature shows	.14★		
TV genre viewing related to both tech enthusiasm and com traditionalist			
TV dramas		.17★★★	.12★
TV genre viewing related to both mobility/social media enthusiasm and com traditionalist			
TV news magazine shows	.20★★★		.09#
TV genre viewing related only to tech enthusiasm			
Science fiction programs		.10#	

Note: #.05<*p*<.10; ★*p*<.05; ★★*p*<.01; ★★★*p*<.001

watched particular film or television genres. Both enthusiasm for mobility/social media and technology are related to more genre viewing than is the measure of communication traditionalism. The only viewing measure not related to any of the attitudinal variables is documentary film viewing.

Social categories also may be related to genre preferences. Some of these seem intuitive, with, for example, older members of the audience preferring documentary films compared to younger viewers. Similarly, women prefer chick flicks more than men, and men prefer westerns more than women.

Extensive industry research has produced segmentation analysis revealing preferences for various genres among distinctive audience segments. The Independent Cinema Office (2022) reports that each "category has established consumer, lifestyle and economic behavior patterns and these can be used to investigate the potential strength of cinema going in any defined catchment. Cinema going is generally more popular with prosperous and educated audiences..." (para 22).

Table 3.5 shows the relationships between social categories and how often respondents report watching the various genres. Only the correlations that are statistically significant are included. We see that older respondents watch western films, detective films, documentary films, biographical films, and drama more often than do younger respondents. Similarly, tastes in television genres show a preference by older people for news magazine shows and animal/nature shows, while younger viewers watch children's shows more often, likely because they're viewing with children at home. Younger viewers show a preference for horror films and slasher films, animated films, dark comedies, foreign films, and samurai films. Education generally is a strong

TABLE 3.5 Significant Relationships between Film/TV Genre Preferences and Social Categories (2015 Users Survey)

Age	Education	Income	Gender (0 = Male, 1 = Female)	White	Black
Film Genres					
Westerns .23***			Musicals .16**		
Horror films -.14**	Horror films -.14**		Westerns -.22***		
			Horror films -.11*		
			Science fiction -.19***		
Detective films .17***			Film noir -.21***		
Documentary films .12*					
Animated films -.19***					
Dark comedy films -.13*		Dark comedy films -.09#	Dark comedy films -.09#		Mystery, suspense films .12*
Biographical films .14**					Biographical films .11*
			Film parodies -.14**		
Slasher films -.18***			Slasher films -.10#		Slasher films .11*

(Continued)

TABLE 3.5 Significant Relationships between Film/TV Genre Preferences and Social Categories (2015 Users Survey) (Continued)

Age	Education	Income	Gender (0 = Male, 1 = Female)	White	Black
	Mockumentaries .12*		Mockumentaries -.21***		
			Chick flicks .37***		
Slapstick films -.09#			Slapstick films -.11*		
Drama films .13*	Drama films .10#		Drama films .17***		
			Adventure films -.09#		
Foreign films -.11*		Foreign films -.15**	Foreign films -.18***	Foreign films .12*	
			Romantic dramas .21***		
			Romantic comedies .22***		
			Gangster films -.19***	Gangster films .12*	
Samurai films -.14**			Samurai films -.27***	Samurai films .17***	
	Epic films .09#		Epic films -.16**		
	Historical films .13*		Sports films -.23***	Sports films .18***	Sports films .18***
			Superhero films -.18***	Superhero films .18***	
		War films .10#	War films -.24***		

(Continued)

TABLE 3.5 Significant Relationships between Film/TV Genre Preferences and Social Categories (2015 Users Survey) (Continued)

Age	Education	Income	Gender (0 = Male, 1 = Female)	White	Black
Television Genres					
	None correlated	None correlated	Sitcoms .10# Dramas .16**	Soap operas .16**	
TV news magazine shows .14**			Detective shows .22***	Detective shows .13*	Detective shows .11* TV news magazine shows .09#
			Music, talent competitions .14** Reality TV shows .21***	Music, talent competitions .09#	Music, talent competitions .16***
			Children's shows .11*		Children's shows .13*
				Science fiction .10#	
Children's shows −.14** Animal/nature shows .11*					

Note: #.05<p<.10; *p<.05; **p<.01; ***p<.001

predictor of media use, but here the number of years of formal education only predict a preference for mockumentaries, drama films, epic films, and historical films, and a dislike of horror films. None of the television genre preferences are related to education. The second status variable, household income, shows a similar pattern of few relationships. Those with higher incomes show a slightly stronger preference for war films and a dislike of dark comedies and foreign films.

The strongest pattern of preferences is found for gender, where women are more likely than men to like musical films, chick flicks, drama films, romantic dramas, and romantic comedies, while men show a preference for westerns, horror films, science fiction, film noir, dark comedies, film parodies, slasher films, mockumentaries, slapstick, adventure films, foreign films, gangster films, samurai films, epic films, sports films, superhero films, and war films. We also see women preferring situation comedies on television, along with dramas, detective shows, music and talent competitions, reality TV shows, and children's programs. A few preferences related to race also appear.

Shaping Genre Preferences—One's World View

Past work underscores the importance of extending the focus beyond demographic correlates of visual media use. Research by the Independent Cinema Office (2022), for instance, indicates that attitude may produce a more useful way of categorizing audiences than simply using age groups. Our own results suggest that while some of the social categories are important predictors of media use and genre preferences, surely there are a host of attitudes and perspectives that help to shape those genre preferences as our experiences pile up over time. In the 2015 survey we included items that help us look at people's "world view." The concept of "cosmopoliteness" has proven useful in capturing this notion.

The concept of "cosmopoliteness" comes from a Greek term, "kosmos," that conveys the idea of a universe of order and harmony (Moulla, 2002). During the period of city-states, the "polis" or "city" was the center of people's lives. People who were "cosmopolitan" acted consistent with universal values rather than pursuing personal ends. Within the philosophical origins of the concept of "cosmopoliteness" lie the kernels that subsequent social scientists have cultivated to apply the concept in more recent times. The literature on cosmopoliteness includes a number of dimensions (Jeffres et al., 2004): (1) diversity of interests—greater interest in local, national, and international news or information about different cultures, peoples, ideas; (2) cosmopolitan identification—identifying with a larger, international culture rather than one's national culture; (3) appreciation of different cultures—greater interest in or more experience with different cultures and a corresponding attitude of openness to learning about different cultures; (4) tolerance of different cultures and religions; (5) knowledge of different cultures and religions; (6) knowledge of current events and international affairs; and (7) cultural diversity of media content—greater exposure to media from different cultures and countries.

Jeffres et al. (2004) conducted two surveys in a major metropolitan area of the Midwest in 2000 and 2001 to examine the concept of cosmopoliteness. They found access to technology related to several cosmopolite measures, including an international focus, a cosmopolite attitude, cosmopolite Internet use, diversity of interests, and a summary scale of cosmopoliteness across dimensions.

The figures in Table 3.6 are the bivariate correlations between how often people watch a genre and the two measures of cosmopoliteness: World citizenry and how much they like to see films and television programs from other countries, as measured in the 2015 Users Survey. Controlling for social categories makes little difference (and is therefore not reported).

Is the pattern of generally positive relationships between viewing film genre and the cosmopolite measures replicated when we look at television genres? To the contrary, people who see themselves as more cosmopolitan have a preference only for detective shows, late-night talk shows, animal/nature shows, and science fiction programs, as shown in Table 3.7. Moreover, controlling for social categories, as well as frequency one watches television, does not change the pattern. However, those who like to see films and television programs from other countries seem to watch only animal/nature and science fiction shows more often. They also watch children's shows less often. Two TV genres omitted from the table because there were no statistically significant correlations include: TV news magazine shows and reality TV shows.

Assessing the Moving Image—Quality and Representation

When audiences expose themselves to the moving image, some of the time they're trying to escape from reality, while at other times they seek images that comfort them. The 2015 survey included three items that indicate whether our respondents see television as portraying the world pretty much as it really is, whether the fictional stories told on TV today are more realistic than they used to be, and whether television reflects the moral values of our culture. Table 3.8 shows a strong pattern of relationships between a belief that television portrays the world pretty much as it is and how often people watch eight TV genres: Sitcoms, dramas, soap operas, detective shows, news magazines, musical talent, reality shows, and late-night talk shows. Only frequent viewers of animal/nature shows and science fiction do not see such a congruence between the TV world and "real world." Similar patterns are found between watching the same genres (excepting detective shows) and a belief that fictional TV stories are more realistic than they used to be and a belief that television reflects the moral values of our culture. Controlling for social categories and how often one watches TV makes little difference in the pattern of relationships.

TABLE 3.6 Significant Relationships between Film Genre Preferences and Cosmopoliteness (2015 Users Survey)

Film Genre Viewing	See Myself as Citizen of the World	Like to See Films, Shows from Other Countries
Musical	.12★	.15★★
Western	.09#	.18★★★
Horror	.14★★	.12★
Science fiction	.22★★★	.33★★★
Detective	.24★★★	.14★★
Comedy	.13★	
Film noir	.22★★★	.39★★★
Documentary	.12★	.24★★★
Action	.14★★	
Animated	.12★	.13★
Mystery	.23★★★	.12★
Dark comedy	.24★★★	.30★★★
Biography	.10#	.19★★★
Parodies	.09#	.14★★
Slasher	.11★	.11★
Mockumentary	.20★★★	.30★★★
Chick flick	.12★	
Slapstick	.15★★	.11★
Drama	.16★★	
Fantasy	.20★★★	.24★★★
Adventure	.18★★★	.17★★★
Foreign	.33★★★	.68★★★
Romantic drama	.14★★	
Romantic comedy	.11★	
Gangster	.18★★★	.22★★★
Samurai	.12★	.28★★★
Epics	.13★	.22★★★
Sports		.14★★
Historical	.11★	.23★★★
Superhero		.11★
War	.10★	.11★

Note: The figures are the bivariate correlations between how often people watch a film genre and two measures: Perceived world citizenship, and how much they like to see films and television programs from other countries. #.05<p<.10; ★p<.05; ★★p<.01; ★★★p<.001

Our attitudes towards the media can impact genre preferences in a couple ways. First, those who disdain television or current film offerings are less likely to even sample what's available. They likely do not subscribe to as many if any of the commercial platforms, cable, or satellite television, or streaming services. Thus, we'd expect less familiarity and preferences based on little experience. Our 2015 survey included two items asking respondents if the quality of films was higher today than in the past and whether prime time TV programs are better than they've been in years. Table 3.9 shows the correlations between measures of attitudes and assessments and how often people

TABLE 3.7 Significant Relationships between TV Genre Preferences and Cosmopoliteness (2015 Users Survey)

TV Genre Viewing	See Myself as Citizen of the World	Like to See Films, Shows from Other Countries
TV sitcoms	.09#	
TV dramas	.09#	
TV soap operas		.09#
TV detective shows	.14★★	
TV musical talent	.10#	
TV late-night talk shows	.13★	
TV children's shows		-.11★
TV animal/nature shows	.24★★★	.33★★★
TV sci-fi shows	.24★★★	.33★★★

Note: The figures are the bivariate correlation between how often people watch a television genre and two measures: Perceived world citizenship, and how much they like to see films and television programs from other countries. #.05<*p*<.10; ★*p*<.05; ★★*p*<.01; ★★★*p*<.001.

TABLE 3.8 Significant Relationships between Perceived Reality and TV Genre Preferences (2015 Users Survey)

TV Genre Viewing	TV Portrays World Pretty Much as It Is	Fictional Stories on TV More Realistic than Used to Be	Television Reflects the Moral Values of Our Culture
TV sitcoms	.25★★★	.16★★	.15★★
TV dramas	.26★★★	.24★★★	.14★★
TV soap operas	.38★★★	.18★★★	.16★★
TV detective shows	.19★★★		
TV news magazines	.27★★★	.12★	.10#
TV musical talent	.31★★★	.19★★★	.14★★
TV reality shows	.29★★★	.20★★★	.13★
TV late-night talk shows	.14★★		
TV children's shows	.10#		
TV sci-fi shows		.10★	

Note: There were no significant relationships with animal/nature shows so it is omitted from the table. The figures are the bivariate correlations between how often people watch a television genre and the three measures of perceived reality. #.05<*p*<.10; ★*p*<.05; ★★*p*<.01; ★★★*p*<.001

watch film genres; controlling for age, level of education, income, and gender makes little difference. Film genres omitted from the table because the correlations were not statistically significant include: Westerns, biography, parodies, samurai, horror, science fiction, film noir, documentary, dark comedy, slasher films, mockumentaries, and foreign films. And Table 3.10 shows that those who believe today's prime time television shows are better than they've been in years also watch eight of the 11 television genres more often.

TABLE 3.9 Significant Relationships between Genre Preferences and Assessments of the Quality of the Moving Image–Film (2015 Users Survey)

Film Genre Viewing	Quality of films today is higher than ever
Musical	.12*
Detective	.16**
Comedy	.16**
Action	.19***
Animated	.13*
Mystery	.13*
Chick flick	.29***
Slapstick	.16**
Drama	.22***
Fantasy	.22***
Adventure	.20***
Romantic drama	.26***
Romantic comedy	.28***
Gangster	.16**
Epics	.10#
Sports	.10#
Historical	.09#
Superhero	.23***
War	.18***

Note: #.05<p<.10; *p<.05; **p<.01; ***p<.001

TABLE 3.10 Significant Relationships between Genre Preferences and Assessments of the Quality of the Moving Image–Television (2015 Users Survey)

Television Genre Viewing	Prime Time TV Shows Today Are Better than They've Been in Years
Sitcoms	.25***
Dramas	.34***
Soap operas	.22***
Detective shows	.26***
News magazines	.21***
Musical, talent shows	.29***
Reality TV shows	.31***
Late-night talk shows	.33***

Note: Children's shows, sci-fi, and animal/nature shows were omitted because the correlations were not statistically significant. ***p<.001

A Concluding Note

This chapter explores the ways in which diverse audience roles can determine genre preferences, amidst other media use behaviors. We draw from past work conceptualizing digital media uses in three domains: (1) the traditional media audience processor role, (2) the message sender role, and (3) the consumer role. Traditional media use behaviors were tapped by our 2015 user survey involving viewing the moving image and using mass media. Study data highlight the decision process for viewing the moving image.

Two scales were developed for the analysis, one focused on digital media (The Tech Enthusiast Scale) and the other on legacy media uses (the Com Traditionalist scale). The Tech Enthusiast scale is related to level of media use—encompassing five of seven measures of media technology use—providing broad support for the U&G Theory's assumptions that such enthusiasm motivates heavier media use. Neither scale was significantly related to live entertainment or legacy media attendance measures, however. The Com Traditionalist scale was only related to a pair of technology-intensive media (Facebook and mobile gaming), and in a negative direction.

Our data also identify consumption patterns for popular genres, the five most popular of which are comedy, action, drama, adventure, and animated films. These patterns of results broadly echo those uncovered in segmentation analyses conducted by the film industry, confirming the Independent Cinema Office (2022) finding that "different types of films appeal to different audiences" (para 22).

The linkages between film and television use and social connection uncovered here reinforce L'Pree's (2021) call to consider the important role that film—alongside other media such as radio, video gaming, and Internet—has played in changing our culture and socio-psychological expectations that we apply to other technologies.

4

A PROFILE OF CREATORS OF MOVING IMAGES AS AUDIENCE ROLES EVOLVE

Once upon a time, and not that long ago, audiences were seen as a collection of passive individuals who could be herded, in the case of television, into viewing slots for advertisers through scheduling and other strategies. Even producers of films timed releases to capture as many viewers as possible, or to bury films not expected to do well. But, while strategies are still available to maximize audience size and composition, the audience is no longer treated as passive, and more importantly, now they are content creators as well.

Research on uses and gratifications over the years has shown that viewers of moving images and users of all mass media were more active than once portrayed (e.g., Hunt et al., 2014). The kernel idea behind uses and gratifications is that audiences seek and derive gratifications from and find uses for their media behaviors, in our case watching film and television genres. But as the technology changed and new platforms emerged, audiences became creators too. Emmanouloudis (2015) analogizes this emerging media influence to a bazaar: "Let's imagine a bazaar. A bazaar is a place where multitudes of sellers stand, each demonstrating his/her merchandise, while shouting loud to attract customers. Enter today's age, and the digital bazaar. YouTube and other video sharing platforms function like a digital bazaar" (p. 9).

As people become creators by filming videos and posting them on social media, they often begin to interact with their audience. In this process uses and gratifications takes on a second dimension, where the gratifications are derived from the creative process and feedback from others rather than solely from being in the audience and receiving the moving image. Neenan (2018) observes that "YouTube creators listen and interact with their fans, resulting in communities that look more like friendships than fanships" (para 3).

DOI: 10.4324/9781003264828-4

O'Neil-Hart and Blumenstein (2016) found high levels of trust between the creator and their audience. Google's own work reports 70% of teenage YouTube subscribers indicating that they relate to the platform's creators more than to traditional celebrities (O'Neil-Hart & Blumenstein, 2016). Google's research also suggests that 60% of YouTube subscribers would follow purchase recommendations from a favorite creator rather than a favorite TV or movie personality, as millennials regard YouTube stars as more influential than celebrities. Google suggests that 40% of millennial subscribers indicate that their favorite creator understands them better than their friends. Another 70% of YouTube subscribers contend that YouTube creators change and shape culture (O'Neil-Hart & Blumenstein, 2016).

Producing Moving Images

Our studies included items that help provide a profile of creators of the moving image. Since this book has evolved over several years, we've been chasing a moving target. In 2015, some social media were available for posting short videos—Facebook and YouTube—but within a couple years TikTok and Twitter and other social media options added capacity and even economic incentives with the growth of "social influencers." In this chapter, we'll take a look at the creative side of people as audiences' roles evolve, first in the 2015 Users Survey data set and then the 2021 Users Survey and 2021–22 Creators Surveys.

Although our respondents in the 2015 Users Survey were active consumers and processors of messages, they were much less frequent contributors and senders of video messages, according to their responses to the items shown in Table 4.1. However, texting also is a sender activity (see Table 3.1), so the individual sender role that involves one-to-one (or a small group) messages is important. And, though our measures don't capture it, the frequent attention to Facebook is also likely to entail sender roles through "liking" activity, small but ubiquitous behaviors.

To start our profile of creators, we examined relationships between social categories—age, education, income, gender, and ethnicity—and the sender

TABLE 4.1 Contributing to the Media in Sender Role (2015 Users Survey)

	Mean Response on 7-Point Scale (1 = Not At All Like Me; 7 = Very Much Like Me)
I often share videos via Facebook.	2.85
I often share videos on Instagram.	1.77
I like to make short videos that I can share with others.	2.12

role in the 2015 Users Survey. We found that more educated people were less likely to share videos on Facebook or enjoy making videos they can share with others. Although females were more likely to share videos on Facebook, males were more likely to share videos on Instagram or to enjoy making videos they can share with others. African Americans were more likely to share videos on Facebook and Instagram than other people, and older people were less likely to engage in any of the sharing activity. Those with higher incomes were less likely to share videos on Facebook [Table available online].

The two basic roles that people inhabit in mass communication behaviors are as senders (creators) and receivers (viewers, processors) of messages. While some folks are solely viewers or consumers of film genres, others also produce videos or share them via social media. First, we note that the three producer/sender roles are strongly related in the 2015 Users Survey: sharing videos on Facebook and Instagram (correlation $r=.49$, $p<.001$); making short videos to share with others correlated with Facebook sharing ($r=.51$, $p<.001$) and with sharing on Instagram ($r=.70$, $p<.001$).

To what extent are these roles linked? Our 2015 Users Survey asked how often each genre was viewed, and also asked how often sharing or producing short videos characterized them. Table 4.2 gives the correlations between these two sets of variables.

While there are some differences, in general the three producing/sharing variables are similarly related to genre viewing, so that those who see themselves as producers and sharers of videos also tend to watch the following film genres more often: Detective films, film noir, dark comedies, parodies/spoofs, slasher films, slapstick films, dramas, adventure films, romantic dramas, gangster films, and war films. In addition, sharing videos via Facebook and Instagram is related to viewing musicals, horror films, mystery/suspense, chick flicks, and romantic comedies. In five cases, producing videos and sharing on Instagram (but not Facebook) are related to viewing of westerns, biography films, mockumentaries, foreign films, and sports films (see Table 4.2).

Looking at relationships between viewing of television genres and sharing or producing, we find five instances where viewing is related to all three, sharing videos on Facebook and Instagram and making short videos to share with others: TV soap operas, TV news magazine shows, TV musical talent or competition programs, late-night TV talk shows, and children's shows on television. In addition, sharing videos on either social media platform is related to watching TV dramas, and sharing on Facebook alone is related to viewing detective shows and animal/nature shows on television. Watching situation comedies, reality shows, and science fiction shows are related to none of the sharing or producing variables (see Table 4.3).

TABLE 4.2 Relationships between Viewing Film Genres and Sharing/Producing Videos (2015 Users Survey)

Film Genre Viewing (1 = Never; 5 = Very Often)	Often Share Videos on Facebook	Often Share Videos on Instagram	Like to Make Short Videos I can Share with Others
	(high = describes me, low = not like me)		
Musicals	.20***	.12*	
Westerns		.11*	.11*
Horror films	.15**	.09#	
Detective films	.20***	.15**	.13*
Film noir films	.18**	.29***	.28***
Mystery/Suspense	.16**	.10#	
Dark comedy films	.14**	.19***	.18***
Biography films		.14*	.11#
Parodies, "spoofs"	.12*	.17**	.21***
Slasher films	.22***	.25***	.17**
Mockumentaries		.19***	.22***
Chick flicks	.17**	.10#	
Slapstick films	.14*	.31***	.26***
Drama films	.14*	.12*	.12*
Adventure films	.09#	.14*	.18***
Foreign films		.17**	.19***
Romantic dramas	.16**	.19***	.14**
Romantic comedies	.14*	.12*	
Gangster films	.16**	.22***	.22***
Samurai films		.23***	.20***
Epic films		.12*	
Sports films		.21***	.15**
War films	.10#	.15**	.13*

Note: Only statistically significant relationships are included in the table; excluded are science fiction, comedy, documentary, action, animated, fantasy, historical, and superhero films. #.05<p<.10; *p<.05; **p<.01; ***p<.001

Entrepreneurship—When Audiences Switch Roles

Why do people decide to devote time to producing videos for posting? Essentially, they are becoming entrepreneurs in an area requiring little capital other than a cell phone and, perhaps, some software. In general, the number of people interested in being entrepreneurs has grown, and in recent decades, schools have offered courses in entrepreneurship. Even programs such as *Shark Tank* popularize the idea.

Though much of this content is disseminated through business schools, communication is a fertile field for entrepreneurship given the interest in mobile technologies and media in general. In an early study, Jeffres and Dobos (1989) surveyed 344 adults in a large Midwestern city for their awareness of

TABLE 4.3 Relationships between Viewing TV Genres and Sharing/Producing Videos (2015 Users Survey)

TV Genre Viewing (1 = Never; 5 = Very Often)	Often Share Videos on Facebook	Often Share Videos on Instagram	Like to Make Short Videos I can Share with Others
	(high = describes me, low = not like me)		
TV dramas	.14*	.11*	
TV soap operas	.23***	.32***	.27***
TV detective	.13*		
TV news mag	.19***	.27***	.17**
TV musical talent	.23***	.22***	.12*
TV late-night talk shows	.16**	.13*	.13*
TV children's shows	.24***	.16**	.17**
TV animal/nature shows	.14*		

Note: Only statistically significant relationships are included in the table; TV sitcoms, reality shows, and science fiction were not related to any of the three variables. *$p<.05$; **$p<.01$; ***$p<.001$

and interest in entrepreneurship. They found that more than 40% had considered starting an enterprise and 5% had done so. Study results suggest that opportunities from the mass media, and audience interest in becoming entrepreneurs, were linked to not only money-making reasons, but life-style factors, e.g., to get more control over their lives, for artistic freedom, and for excitement and challenges. Today, those who post videos to be "influencers" or monetize their efforts, likely share similar goals.

Jeffres, Kumar, et al. (2014) note that communication majors are witnessing a host of opportunities to start their own enterprises as technologies allow them to do what once would have required large amounts of capital. In that study of applied communication professionals and students from two American universities, younger people were most likely to start video or film enterprises. Results suggested that younger people—"digital natives"—are oriented to an increasingly digitized visual culture. The survey of entrepreneurs found that their satisfaction with their decision to start an enterprise was positively related to creativity as well as risk-taking. Interestingly, it was found that student likelihood to become entrepreneurs was positively related to the number of films in entrepreneurship viewed.

Clearly, opportunities to become video entrepreneurs have increased with the appearance of outlets such as TikTok, and our current studies may offer some clues about the situation, where "influencers" represent a fairly new entrepreneurial entry. Reasons people become entrepreneurs include a desire to be one's own boss, and to have more control over one's life. Reasons found in recent studies for becoming or wanting to become entrepreneurs include opportunity, freedom, confidence and self-expression. Cromie (2000) found that entrepreneurs are often creative, innovative, restless, imaginative, and adventurous. Armstrong and Hird (2009) found that entrepreneurs are less analytic than those who aren't entrepreneurs but are more intuitive.

Our recent surveys focus on respondents as active producers of moving images. Respondents were asked how often they post videos on Facebook, YouTube, and TikTok. We also asked whether the videos posted are those they produced themselves or were videos produced by people they knew or were merely found online and shared. In addition, we asked for the gratifications derived from posting videos.

As Table 4.4 shows, our respondents in the 2021 Users Survey actively post photos and videos on social media, documenting a substantial increase since the 2015 survey. In fact, half of respondents post photos or videos on Facebook once a day or more often, and half post several times a week or more often on YouTube and on TikTok.

What drives all this posting activity? Just as watching a film or television program provides some gratifications or serves some use for members of the audience, so does posting behavior. Table 4.5 shows that the 2021 Users sample exhibits a consensus that posting videos makes people feel a sense of achievement, satisfaction, and feel one is productive, competitive, and connecting with other people. There's also a political element to some activity, as some posts add to the representation of ethnic, racial, or LGBTQ+ groups on social media.

Elaborating on the profile of creators, how is this increased activity related to social categories in our broad sample of users? Education and African American ethnicity are the only two social characteristics related to posting activity in the 2021 Users Survey, as shown in Table 4.6. Educated people engage in more posting behavior across the social media platforms, as do African Americans. There are a couple of other relationships with gratifications—educated respondents indicate feeling more competitive and satisfied from their posting behavior and they also are motivated to provide more ethnic or sexual/LGBTQ+ representations through posting. Because our sample in this case is only about 200, our power to detect relationships is somewhat limited.

Focusing In On Creative Posting Activity

To get a clearer image of creators, we mounted two surveys that include only people who said they post videos on social media, then did a more thorough review of their activities and perceptions of the current situation. The first was the 2021 Creators Survey, a general survey mounted on MTurk in fall of 2021. The second, the 2021–22 Young Creators Survey, was a sample of college students, the group most likely to be interested and involved in social media,

TABLE 4.4 Frequency Posting Videos on Social Media (2021 Users Survey)

Social Media	Mean Frequency	Never	Almost Never	Less Often Than Every Couple Weeks	Every Couple Weeks	About Once a Week	Several Times Each Week	Once a Day	A Couple Times a Day	Many Times Each Day
Facebook (photos)	5.4	3%	3%	4%	7%	12%	15%	23%	21%	12%
Facebook (videos)	5.1	6%	4%	6%	8%	6%	16%	23%	18%	13%
YouTube (videos)	4.8	9%	7%	3%	7%	10%	14%	17%	20%	11%
TikTok (videos)	4.7	15%	4%	3%	3%	9%	16%	23%	16%	11%

Note: The mean (average) frequency of the posting activity in the first column is based on a range from 0 = never, to 8 = many times each day.

TABLE 4.5 Gratifications from Posting Activity (2021 Users Survey)

Gratifications from Posting Activity	Mean Response (1 = Strongly Disagree, 4 = Neither Agree nor Disagree, 7 = Strongly Agree)
I feel a sense of achievement when I post a video on social media.	5.32
I feel like I'm connecting to other people, often a large audience when I post a video on social media.	5.53
I feel productive when I post a video on social media.	5.52
I feel like I'm competitive, competing with others when I post a video on social media.	5.29
I feel a sense of satisfaction when I post a video on social media.	5.43
I feel creative when I post a video on social media.	5.53
I post videos to social media to provide representations with more ethnic/racial diversity.	5.26
I post videos to social media to provide representations with more sexual/LGBTQ+ diversity.	5.00

TABLE 4.6 Social Media Activity and Social Categories (2021 Users Survey)

Frequency of Social Media Activity	Education	Black Ethnicity (1 = Black; 0 = not Black)
Post videos on Facebook	.28***	.15*
Post videos on YouTube	.23***	.16*
Post videos on TikTok	.33***	.14*
Gratifications from Posting Videos		
Feel sense of achievement		.14#
Feel competitive	.17*	
Feel sense of satisfaction	.15#	
Post to provide representations of ethnic diversity	.16#	
Post to provide representations of more sexual/LGBTQ+ diversity	.29***	

Note: There were no significant correlations between social categories and feeling like I'm connecting to other people, feeling productive, or feeling creative. # .05<p<.10; *p<.05; ***p<.001

and the survey stretched from late 2021 into February 2022. Profiles of the two samples were provided in Chapter 1.

So how active are these two self-identified groups of people who actively post videos on social media? First, the broader sample of creators are heavy media users. The young creators student sample is almost the opposite, showing little use of legacy media and using other media options infrequently, which fits with busy students living in a college town. Table 4.7 describes the

TABLE 4.7 Creators' Media Use (2021 Creators Survey and 2021–22 Young Creators Survey)

Media Use Type	2021 Creators Survey Midpoints of Media Use	2021–22 Young Creators Survey Midpoints of Media Use
Watch TV	6 once a day	5 several times each week
Listen to radio	5 several times each week	1 almost never
Listen to podcasts	5 several times each week	2 less often than every couple weeks
Read a magazine	5 several times each week	1 almost never
Read a book	5 several times each week	2 less often than every couple weeks
Read hard copy of newspapers	5 several times each week	0 never
Read newspapers online	6 once a day	2 less often than every couple weeks
Surf the Internet for pleasure, not work	7 a couple times each day	7 a couple times each day
Check my email	7 a couple times each day	7 a couple times each day
Go on Facebook	6 once a day	2 less often than every couple weeks
Browse YouTube for videos to watch	6 once a day	6 once a day
Browse TikTok for videos to watch	5 several times each week	7 a couple times each day
Play video games	6 once a day	4 about once a week
Watch film on tablet, phone, computer	4 about once a week	4 about once a week
Watch TV on tablet, phone, computer	4 about once a week	4 about once a week
Go out to see a film in a theater	3 every couple weeks	2 less often than every couple weeks
Stream a movie on home TV	5 several times each week	3 every couple weeks
Stream a TV program on home TV	5 several times each week	4 about once a week
Posting Activity		
Post photos on Facebook	5 several times each week	0 never
Post videos on Facebook	5 several times each week	0 never
Post videos on YouTube	4 about once a week	0 never
Post videos on TikTok	3 every couple weeks	1 almost never

Note: 0 = never; 1 = almost never; 2 = less often than every couple weeks; 3 = every couple weeks; 4 = about once a week; 5 = several time each week; 6 = once a day; 7 = a couple times each day; 8 = many times each day. For Creators Survey, *n* = 336. For Young Creators Survey, *n* = 557.

activity of the 2021 Creators sample and 2021–22 Young Creators sample as viewers, readers, and listeners in general.

Now that we know our Creators are also active users, let's see what they post. Respondents in the 2021 Creators Survey were asked how often they post videos on social media, whether they were originals, videos produced by people they know, or videos found online that they wanted to share. Some 12% post videos every day and 19% several times each week. Another 29% post several times each month and the rest post once in a while, once a month or so. The overwhelming majority—71%—post original videos that they create, while 46% post videos produced by people they know, and 40% report posting videos they find online that they want to share. While a little over a quarter of the sample had been creating videos for posting on TikTok, Facebook, YouTube, or other social media for less than three months, 17% had been doing so for five years or longer, 11% for three to four years, 13% for one or two years, 15% for six months to a year, and 17% for three to six months. So, clearly, this is a fairly "new" phenomenon as these things go. Age is negatively associated with how often one posts videos on social media ($r=-.20$, $p<.001$), so it's younger creators who are most active. The older one is, the more likely they are to post videos found online that they want to share ($r=.11$, $p<.05$), and the less likely they are to post videos produced by people they know ($r=-.11$, $p<.05$). Those with the highest formal education post most often ($r=.15$, $p<.01$), but household income and African American or White ethnicity are unrelated to posting activity. Males are more likely to post original videos they produce themselves.

Respondents in our 2021–22 Young Creators Survey were asked the same questions, and some 34% said they never post and 46% said they post once in a while—once a month or so. Only 12% post several times a month and 8% post several times a week or every day. Some 64% said they post original videos they produce themselves, 18% videos produced by people they know, and 31% videos found online they want to share. Since this is a young group, 37% have been creating videos for posting on social media less than three months, while 6% have for three to six months, 6% six months to a year, 18% one to two years, 14% three to four years, and 20% five years or longer. Females tend to post videos on social media more often than males ($t=4.1$, $p<.001$), but there is little range on the other social categories, allowing little information on how those may impact posting behavior.

Respondents in both groups were asked if the videos they post on social media featured any of the topics listed in Table 4.8. Social issues and pets, or animals in general, and beautiful images of nature and the environment capture the top three spots for the Creators. Personal images and educational videos are at the bottom. As the table shows, it would be difficult to come up with a different set of priorities for the two groups. While the broader Creators place social issues at the top, the Young Creators, students, place it and political ideas at the bottom. Younger people post their own image and lifestyle at the top, while the broader group place that at the bottom.

The fourth study, 2021–22 Young Creators, was conducted largely for additional information on the types of videos created by the young age cohort, ages 19 to 24. Since this survey was composed of college students living in a

TABLE 4.8 Topics Featured in Creators' Videos Posted on Social Media (2021 Creators Survey and 2021–22 Young Creators Survey)

Topics Featured in Social Media Video Posts	Percent Citing
2021 Creators Survey	
Social issues	44%
Pets, animals in general	43%
Beautiful images of nature, the environment	42%
Stories I hope make people smile or laugh	40%
Political ideas	36%
Things in the arts	34%
Things that feature me and my lifestyle	32%
"How to" (educational) videos	26%
My own image	19%
2021–22 Young Creators Survey	
Things that feature me and my lifestyle	47%
My own image	42%
Stories that I hope make people smile, laugh	39%
Pets, animals in general	30%
Beautiful images of nature, the environment	30%
Things in the arts	19%
Social issues	13%
"How to" (educational) videos	9%
Political ideas	6%

Note: For Creators Survey, $n = 336$. For Young Creators Survey, $n = 557$.

non-metropolitan area, a small college town, we expected that TikTok and similar social media would be the major draw. They were asked about the types of videos they post on social media and where they typically post them. First, as busy college students, 34% said they never post videos on social media. The specific social media volunteered reveal TikTok at the top, with 55 mentions, followed by Instagram, with 26, Snapchat with 23, YouTube with 11, and only 2 mentioning Facebook, the social medium most widespread around the world and the favorite of adults who post and use it to keep in touch with family and friends.

The students, who come from fairly affluent backgrounds at a university on the East Coast of the United States, do use social media to connect with friends, and 34 respondents mentioned posting videos with friends or for friends. "I sometimes make short funny things to post on TikTok with my friends for fun. I also post short films on YouTube, which I also add to my portfolio to find an audience for," one respondent said. "Dumb videos of my friends," offered another. "I only post on TikTok and Instagram…on tiktok sometimes I'll do like a trendy dance with my friends (typically never by myself) and on Instagram I usually post pictures that I like every probably like 1-3 months. I post with my friends, or family." Another student said, "Silly videos of me and my family/friends dancing usually…nothing too serious and I never take the time to actually produce them."

Specific types of videos follow three major themes that feature prominently on TikTok—funny videos or comedy, dance and music (often with comedy) and personal accounts of one's life. More than a fourth of the sample (53) mentioned producing or posting amusing videos featuring comedy, or that the creators thought were funny, e.g.:

- I rarely post videos on social media but I share ones that others have created that I think are funny.
- I usually post dancing videos or trendy things I find funny on TikTok
- short usually funny things from my life
- funny videos on tik toks that are a trend and relatable to my life

Dancing and music are also prominent themes; some quotes:

- Dance or music related videos; usually on TikTok
- I post videos on TikTok of dances, trends, or original comedy
- On TikTok it is normally just me and my friends lip singing an audio

Finally, one's personal image and things happening in one's life are important subjects of the young creators' posts. The students said they post personal pictures, motivational and life experience, "things that I like," "pictures of my life," of myself, my pets, "short videos of what I might be doing at the moment—restaurant, vacation. etc.—on Snapchat," "videos of things I am doing, usually posted on Snapchat," "sometimes videos of a cool scenery or event that I am at," "videos of myself and artsy videos," and "videos of me talking, posted to private story."

In contrast to the broader sample of creators, there were fewer specific subjects mentioned by our students, but there were several: Video projects for school, workouts, weight training, animals, cooking videos, art, business, car videos, fashion, the outdoors, sports, and social issues. One respondent said, "Nowadays I mostly post musical content on Instagram, Facebook, and YouTube, since I am an aspiring rap artist. Back in my younger days I would make stuffed animal adventure videos, as a form of entertainment as well, or taste testing/challenge/gaming."

In the 2021 Creators Survey, we asked what their plans were for future videos they'll create and post on social media. Large numbers said they took posting videos as a hobby: "I don't have any specific plans for the future," one creator noted. "I post for myself and my friends, so I don't really care who sees it." Others said they post because they like it, have no targeted interests, or don't take posting videos too seriously. Humor is an important part of many plans. Creators said they want to "make sure they make people laugh" with their videos, and "keep being funny."

A FEW NOTES ON HUMOR...

Throughout this volume, it can be seen that comedy content is important both to receivers and to content creators. As noted in Chapter 2, a number of discrete genres share "humorous" material as a core attribute. And in our surveys of creators, intent to generate a mirth response in others is a common goal.

The creation and the reception of humorous content are both incredibly complex. The general concept of humor does not even have universally agreed-upon boundaries. As Martin and Ford (2018) note, "*Humor* is a broad, multifaceted term that represents anything that people say or do that others perceive as funny and tends to make them laugh, as well as the mental processes that go into both creating and perceiving such an amusing stimulus, and also the emotional response of mirth involved in the enjoyment of it" (p. 3). Applied to media content, which we tend to call *comedy*, the situation becomes even more convoluted.

Humor may be dissected in a variety of ways. One basic typology is that of mechanisms by which receivers find things funny. Prior research by this volume's authors (Neuendorf et al., 2014; Neuendorf et al., 2015; Neuendorf, 2020) has settled on four types:

1. Incongruity: The juxtaposition of inconsistent (or incongruous) elements in a potentially humorous stimulus. A mirthful response derives from the cognitive "solving" of a sort of incongruous puzzle. Examples include puns, other wordplay, and absurd images.
2. Superiority: A mirth response that is derived from achieving a sense of superiority over another. With roots extending to the philosophies of Aristotle, this type sees laughter as originating in malice. Examples include putdown humor, racist/sexist humor, and self-deprecation.
3. Arousal: A mirth response is linked to a release of pent-up energy related to forbidden feelings. With roots in the works of Immanuel Kant and Sigmund Freud, this type includes joy derived from observing the pain of others. Examples include slapstick, dark humor, and sick humor.
4. Social currency: Humor is generated from socially-based interplay related to building and maintaining relationships. Pleasure may be derived from playful interaction or the achievement of a sense of group understanding. Examples include in-jokes, joking to fit in a social group, and parody (which relies on a shared set of information, e.g., tropes and characteristics of a genre).

All of these types are well-represented in genre films and TV series, and also in moving image content that is created in online videos. The use of a laugh track, a characteristic of the sitcom TV genre for many years, attempts to capitalize on a sense of social belonging with its "unseen audience" (Lieberman et al., 2009; Neuendorf & Fennell, 1988). And the entire phenomenon of TikTok videos (humorous and otherwise) seems to invite social currency.

But many creators have specific topics in mind, to "share a personal story," or feature science experiment videos, videos in which they dance, videos of their kids playing sports, videos about gaming, household repair tips to help people save money, sports videos, videos about government jobs, political and social issues, cooking and baking videos, crafting videos, women's health videos, musical performances, studio clips and official music videos they produce, things they like, interesting events and facts, "top 10" lists, sleep noise videos, videos for children, Biblical and survival videos, plants and greenery, animated videos, and humorous videos.

Some said they had no plans to monetize their video posting—"I don't have any interest in trying to monetize my videos or really gain anything other than the satisfaction I feel for sharing a moment of my life." Others have business plans—"I will get back into my YouTube so that I can promote my music business and online teaching recommendations," one creator noted. There are general plans to establish a workflow and to gain more and more followers, as well as specific goals, as exemplified in the following quotes:

- I plan to build an audience and start a business through it. I intend to target Instagram.
- [I plan on] creating a production company.
- I'm in the process of building an online network complete with news, blog, online courses, etc. that I plan to use to promote my videos and services.
- The content you post on social media has the power to turn your brand into a household name and turn your followers into fans. This kind of impact only comes from having a solid social media content strategy. It's not enough to show up on every platform and sporadically update your audience when you have the time.
- I would love to become a content creator on YouTube and am working towards that, but am hesitant because I am scared knowing that EVERY youtuber has haters that post very mean comments and I am not someone that has thick skin.

Some 2021 Creators hope to improve the quality of their videos or enhance their skills. One person said they want to do more video editing and learn how to give the videos a more polished look, while others plan to audit their social networks and content, make more attractive videos, and get more likes and subscriptions. One creator set up a plan: Begin With a Strategy; Keep Videos Short and Sweet; Make the First Few Seconds Really Stand Out; If There's Talking, Include Subtitles; and Aim For Natural Lighting.

Specific social media platforms are targets for some of our 2021 Creators. Some said they "post on each account and likely will continue to use them"—"I was planning to post my videos on all social media platforms. I currently post videos on Tik-Tok, Youtube and Instagram. In future post my videos on Facebook and Twitter also." Others noted favorites:

- I would love to stick with Facebook and then add in TikTok.
- YouTube is all I need.
- I mainly post on Youtube and that's where I'll likely remain.
- Am focusing on Twitch and Twitter
- I only post on Facebook because I'm just making them for my family.
- My focus is on Youtube, Snapchat, TikTok, and Facebook

As noted earlier, people receive some sense of gratification or see a use to their posting behaviors. We asked our 2021 Creators sample how important each of several uses and gratifications were for posting behavior.

As we see in Table 4.9, the one gratification associated with posting all the topics is feeling a sense of achievement. And the topics associated with all gratifications are political ideas and social issues. Those who see themselves as a "social influencer," likely the best indicator of entrepreneurial activity, are most likely to post videos about politics, social issues, "how to"/educational topics, beautiful images of nature and the environment, and "my own image." The topics linked to the fewest uses and gratifications are pets and animals in general and stories that make people smile or laugh.

We now know that uses and gratifications are associated with topics posted, so let's see if social categories such as age, level of education, household income, gender, and ethnicity are linked to gratifications. Youth is associated with most all of the gratifications, and education isn't far behind, as shown in Table 4.10. Those with more education cite all but four gratifications as more important than those with less schooling. Income and White ethnicity are relatively unimportant, but African Americans see themselves as sharing their aesthetic, providing diversity, and see themselves as social influencers with lots of followers.

Both of our creators surveys (2021 Creators Survey, 2021–22 Young Creators Survey) included items to measure narcissism (introduced in Chapter 1), a concept that captures a focus on the self and a need for admiration. As one

TABLE 4.9 Relationships between Topics Shared in Videos and Uses and Gratifications Received (2021 Creators Survey)

	Political Ideas	Things in the Arts	Social Issues	How to/edu Videos	Beautiful Images of Nature, Environment	Pets, Animals in General	Stories I Hope Make People Smile or Laugh	Things that Feature Me and My Lifestyle	My Own Image
Feel sense of achievement	.20***	.10#	.22***	.20***	.12*	.12*	.12*	.13*	.21***
Feel I'm connecting with other people	.19***		.22***	.21***	.16**		.11*	.16**	.25***
Feel productive	.20***	.14*	.20***	.20***	.13*	.13*		.18***	.16**
Feel competitive	.35***		.40***	.13*	.11*	.11*			.16**
Feel sense of satisfaction	.17***	.14*	.14**	.16**	.13*			.18***	.20***
Feel need to express myself	.19***		.22***	.21***	.11*		.13*	.12*	.19***
To share my aesthetic with others	.21***	.12*	.24***	.18***	.15*			.16**	.18***
Want to share with family	.18***		.16**		.22***	.16**	.18***	.15**	
Want to share with friends	.12*		.11*	.11*	.18***	.11*	.15**	.19***	.15**
A lot of folks follow my posts	.30***		.28***	.11*	.13*	.10#		.13*	.20***
Like process of making videos	.20***	.16**	.23***	.18***	.12*			.20***	.19***
My posts are role model	.27***		.34***	.20***	.12*			.13*	.17**
Want to share political message	.50***		.47***	.16**	.17**	.12*			.11*
I plan videos out well in advance	.29***	.11*	.33***	.20***	.12*				.16**
I want to influence others	.32***	.12*	.39***	.21***				.09#	.18***
I see myself as social influencer	.37***		.43***	.12*	.14*				.15**
Post videos to provide representation of ethnic diversity	.40***		.52***	.15**	.15**				.11*

(Continued)

TABLE 4.9 Relationships between Topics Shared in Videos and Uses and Gratifications Received (2021 Creators Survey) (*Continued*)

	Political Ideas	Things in the Arts	Social Issues	How to/ edu Videos	Beautiful Images of Nature, Environment	Pets, Animals in General	Stories I Hope Make People Smile or Laugh	Things that Feature Me and My Lifestyle	My Own Image
Post videos to provide representation with LGBTQ+ community	.34***		.49***	.12*	.14**				
People like to know about me, what's going on in my life	.27***		.26***	.11*	.14**	.11#		.15**	.20***
People like to look at me, find me attractive	.32***		.36***		.21***	.09#			.17***
People find me entertaining	.26***	.10#	.33***	.18***	.17**			.11*	.24***

Note: Only those correlations that are statistically significant or approach significance are included in the table. $n = 336$. # $.05 < p < .10$; * $p < .05$; ** $p < .01$; *** $p < .001$

TABLE 4.10 Relationships between Social Categories and Uses and Gratifications Related to Video Posting Activity (2021 Creators Survey)

	Age	Education	Income	Gender (0 = Male; 1 = Female)	White Ethnicity (1 = White; 0 = Not White)	Black Ethnicity (1 = Black; 0 = Not Black)
Feel I'm connecting with other people		.10#				
Feel productive	-.11*	.13*		-.11#	.12*	
Feel competitive	.29***	.18***		-.14*		
Feel sense of satisfaction	-.11*	.12*		-.13*		
Feel need to express myself	-.11*		-.09#	-.12*		
To share my aesthetic with others	-.14*			-.14*		.10#
Want to share with family		.14*	.10#			
Want to share with friends						
A lot of folks follow my posts	-.18***	.14**		-.09#		.10#
Like process of making videos	-.18***	.11*		-.12*		
Feel a sense of achievement	-.14**	.11*		-.13*		
My posts are role model	-.19***	.20***	.10#	-.18***		.11#
Want to share political message	-.21***	.20***		-.18***		
I plan videos out well in advance	-.16**	.14*		-.16**		
I want to influence others	-.21***	.16**		-.14*		.14*
I see myself as social influencer	-.26***	.20***		-.20***		.10#
Post videos to provide representation of ethnic diversity	-.29***	.23***		-.16**		.13*

(Continued)

TABLE 4.10 Relationships between Social Categories and Uses and Gratifications Related to Video Posting Activity (2021 Creators Survey) (*Continued*)

	Age	Education	Income	Gender (0 = Male; 1 = Female)	White Ethnicity (1 = White; 0 = Not White)	Black Ethnicity (1 = Black; 0 = Not Black)
Post videos to provide representation with LGBTQ+ community	-.30***	.18***		-.19***		
People like to know about me, what's going on in my life	-.21***	.19***		-.16**		.09#
People like to look at me, find me attractive	-.23***	.22***		-.14*		
People find me entertaining	-.24***	.16**		-.21***		

Note: Only those correlations that are statistically significant or approach significance are included in the table. The sample size is 336. # .05<*p*<.10; **p<.05; **p<.01; ***p<.001

of the most widely predictive personality factors to help explain media use, narcissism has been linked to the kinds of self-centered behaviors that drive expressive behaviors on the media (e.g., Krishnan & Atkin, 2014; Ryan & Xenos, 2011). We would expect that creators whose personalities reflected this characteristic would also post videos more often and feature images of themselves. And the data support our expectations.

Positive correlations mean that those higher on the narcissism scale also engage in posting behaviors more often. Narcissism is positively related to posting videos more often on social media for the broader 2021 Creators ($r=.45$, $p<.001$) and the 2021–22 Young Creators ($r=.18$, $p<.001$). But the two groups diverge when it comes to the types of videos produced. Narcissism is positively related to posting original videos for the young creators ($r=.13$, $p<.01$) but not the broader creators; but posting videos produced by people they knew is related to narcissism for both the young creators ($r=.10$, $p<.02$) and the broader creators group ($r=.27$, $p<.001$). We also had asked how often they posted their "own image" and "things that feature me and my lifestyle." Narcissism is related to both measures for young creators but only one item for the broader group. Posting one's "own image" more often is correlated with narcissism for the broader creators ($r=.14$, $p<.02$) and the young creators ($r=.17$, $p<.001$). Posting "things that feature me and my lifestyle" is correlated with narcissism for the younger creators ($r=.16$, $p<.001$) but not the broader group.

The survey instruments included a list of 23 items tapping "reactions one might get from posting videos on social media," asking how much each applied to them on a 7-point scale ranging from strongly disagree to strongly agree. The items include gratifications from posting, motivations for posting, the nature of videos posted, and other self-perceptions. And it appears that narcissism in the broader 2021 Creators Survey is positively related to all of the reactions listed in Table 4.10. For the 2021–22 Young Creators, narcissism is positively related to all but sharing with family, planning ahead, posting political messages, seeing oneself as an influencer on social media, and posting to provide ethnic/racial or LGBTQ+ representation [Table available online].

To obtain a more nuanced view of social media video posts, where they've been and where they're going, we asked the respondents in both of our Creators Surveys a series of open-ended items. These also help us to understand the quantitative results presented in the tables.

First, though this is a relatively recent phenomenon in the history of media and the moving image, we asked our creators how videos on social media have changed since they started watching, and their responses provide an interesting snapshot of the past few years.

We asked our 2021 Creators how videos on social media have changed since they started watching, and as one respondent noted, the quantity has changed more than anything. The 2021–22 Young Creators agreed, noting increased professionalism, higher quality of videos, more scripted videos, and better editing. But there were several other themes running through their responses. With more people involved, lots of folks "want to become famous" and some "have a need to overshare their lives—I really don't care what you had for lunch." One creator noted that "there are far more people trying to make their 15 minutes of fame happen via social media now to the point where they're practically flooding the market and becoming stale and predictable." Again, the young creators noted the same impact of commercial interests, with more ads and sponsorships as platforms become advertising vehicles with "less genuine content." As a couple young creators noted, "it's all about creating your 'brand'" and "influencers have taken over." More and more videos have "changed from actually trying to entertain the viewer to just click baiting," one young creator noted.

One young creator noted that "people will do just about anything to go viral" and videos seem to follow trends. Videos "have become less fun and expressive," one respondent noted, and "more of a business trying to gain viewers and appeal to an audience." Many people seem to "throw out so much random content and hope something catches," one young creator noted. Some of what one young creator saw as a growing "sameness" was attributed to the impact of social media algorithms seeking to maximize viewers.

While some said that videos on social media have gotten dumber and more superficial, far more comments referred to better production values, more creativity, and higher quality videos. Here's a short selection of observations by study participants:

- They have become more reality based, more creative, and more focused on your emotions.
- They have become far more professional, and quality of video has vastly improved.
- They have advanced over time in terms of quality and content creation.
- They have become technically more proficient.
- The editing technology has improved and there are more filters.
- They have gotten longer and better quality. There's hardly any grainy uploads because nowadays most phones have 1080p.

Noting that YouTube has evolved into a much more sophisticated medium, one creator noted that "Videos there are now more planned, more produced, and generally a higher quality. We also see the evolution of full brands which wasn't happening even 5 years ago. They have become more of a business than ever." The improved quality is due in part to "people…investing in better equipment" but also "learning what viewers are interested in," one creator noted. And some of the higher quality may be due to fear of stepping on others' copyrights, as this person noted:

> Narration quality is getting significantly better. Visuals matter less than they used to–when used they are often higher quality–but not all channels bother with visual content. This is especially true of creepy pasta channels, but also in sci-fi analysis or fan theory videos–the visuals tend to be generic screenshots of games being played, so that they have something related to the franchise that isn't copyright protected. I guess a lot of the changes come down to fear of copyright strikes actually.

Fear of the competition is another force driving improved production values. As one creator noted about videos, "They've gotten better. Video/sound quality is better. Material covered is more in-depth, informative. Competition for eyeballs is greater so the video quality needs to be bumped up a notch to keep up with the rest." Getting crowds is essential, but keeping them is even much more a challenge, one creator noted, adding, "to do so your video should look, sound, and feel incredible." One informed creator pointed out that, "You need content that engages, entertains and informs the audience, and the video content just happens to be the best medium to achieve that. Statistics show that 55% of people watch videos online every day, and social media videos generate up to 1200% more shares than texts and images combined."

The greater quality also is part of the effort to monetize social media videos. "Everyone's trying to monetize now," one person noted, and "Many more [are] just doing videos in hopes of getting rich from them" another added. "I feel like the production quality of videos has vastly improved from 10 years ago. Now, content creators are expected to have high quality videos." "So many people are trying to be influencers that they're copying each other, especially on TikTok," one creator noted. The videos went from being personalized realistic home videos to everybody attempting to be an influencer.

References to changes in content and style were numerous, and here's a sampling of participant comments:

- Videos use shock humor more.
- I see much more political commentary and rants.
- They seem to be more socially correct than before.
- Some people have gotten too personal!
- [Videos are] more risqué and violent.
- It's more and more about drama
- It seems like it used to be more pranks and funny videos just to pass time, now it seems like they are more tips, lifestyle hacks, and real videos people want to see for reviews and help on certain topics, they have become more serious in a way.

- More science and technology videos
- More ads and more sex aimed at younger crowds
- More about life style
- There are more "me" type videos than showing something else.
- They have gotten more staged and trying to advertise products

Concerns over censorship also came in for scrutiny by our creators. "It's also become common recently for some people with differing views from others to unfairly have their content taken down, or get shadow banned," one creator noted, while another provided a lengthy commentary on the subject:

> Video content was removed very rarely when I first engaged with social media beginning in 2006, and it seemed like "community guidelines" were less confusing back then as well. Today, these social media giants have taken it upon themselves to unilaterally (and ham-fistedly) police their platforms at the ostensible behest of the government to "prevent misinformation" and "potentially harmful" "fake news" from reaching viewers and circulating. Of late, both human "fact checkers" and error prone algorithms are employed to roam the social media landscape in search of alleged community guideline "violators" and other ambiguously defined "offenders," resulting in rampant illogical and arbitrary censorship, demonization, and de-platforming on the flimsiest of pretenses. Indeed, today's social media reserve the right to promote, demote, or outright "disappear" content sharing political views it deems "unsuitable" and bans are enforced on videos whose content is reported by malicious or spiteful and/or vindictive viewers claiming to have had their fragile sensibilities "offended" by imaginary, made-up or innocuous content that has somehow failed to adhere to "community guidelines." Once banned, content posters have little or no recourse or ability to appeal. Hence we see the beginnings of a mass exodus of high-quality content creators moving away from abusive legacy social media platforms to less abusive competitors.

Our creators in the 2021 survey were asked what types of videos they see on social media that look like they're trying to build an audience. One set of responses noted that "opinion videos" seem to "try to gain a following to make a difference." Another noted that "educational related videos seen on social media look like they're trying to build an audience over time," as do videos about celebrities that build for more views. One creator said that videos with several parts seem to build an audience, as do those that give something away. "I see ads for getting a credit card exclusive for gay people on Facebook. I think they are trying to build an audience only for certain types of people," one respondent noted. Videos where people specialize in specific skills, such as "make-up tips," seem designed to build an audience over time, one observer noted. Similarly, travel blogs seem to build up an audience in order to increase monetization—"to increase eyeballs"—as they add more and more ads to their content.

One creator noted that the full design points to audience building:

> When they talk to the camera, address the audience, and ask them to engage or react/respond. Videos that have frequent or weekly follow-ups, and continue a storyline that will leave the audience wondering what is coming next. Informational videos that explain technologies, so that people will come back later and subscribe in order to keep up with the latest technology. Videos that keep users up to date on what the creators are up to, leaving the audience wondering what is going to take place next in a person's life.

The full set of responses included many more specifics nominated as audience building attempts, including:

- Animated videos and anime, "a fantastic way for small businesses on a budget" to try video content since "you can create them on your laptop."
- Gaming and video gaming videos—People who stream video games are always trying to build an audience so those videos are more about getting numbers and less about true expression.
- Inspirational social media platforms like Pinterest and YouTube are well-optimized for search, which means your posts should include keywords.
- Live action videos—"recording of either still or moving objects"
- Music and dance videos—filled with people singing and dancing, some lip-syncing and dancing to music and comedy skits. Most TikTok videos use dance and express their skills.
- News, and videos showing daily aspects happening in the world.
- Opinion videos—people talking about social issues.
- Prank videos, often of kids, young adults

User-Generated Content (UGC): Video Genres

This book focuses primarily on film and television genres. Earlier we compared audience expectations with those of academics and professional observers. But the growing field of videos through social media deserve attention too, and our studies provide some clues about what "video genres" are emerging in the realm of largely user-generated content. Clearly, as is the case with film and television genres today, we're observing a fluid environment, with competing platforms that appear to be attracting specific audiences but which are open to innovation as well as the pressures from commerce. This chapter seems to be the appropriate place for such a task since we're looking at creators who also are active members of the social media audience.

It's probably almost impossible to develop an exhaustive list of "online video genres" given the volume of traffic on social media. And browsing through the various lists of available videos on YouTube leads one to the conclusion that few topics are absent, and most film and television genres are accessible, with subscriptions available for music, sports, gaming, movies, and shows. Similarly, as many have noted, with cell phones not much that happens in life goes unrecorded, and much of it appears at some point on social media, and these can form the kernel of videos that evolve into recognizable genres. Google goes so far as to suggest the top half dozen types of videos to make on TikTok are: Videos based on trending sounds, TikTok challenges, videos based on trending hashtags, influencer collaboration videos, lip-syncing videos, and tutorials. Similarly, popular types of YouTube videos include: Commentary videos that express the thoughts or opinions of a creator, product review, how-to (tutorials), "top" lists, comedy, "challenge" or meme, reaction videos, question and answer videos, interview videos, docuseries that follow a particular event or subject, educational videos, music videos, narrative videos that take the viewer through a story, gaming, videos that capture the sounds of everyday experiences (ASMR—autonomous sensory meridian response—videos), and sport videos. To start our own typology, let's look at the answers the 2021–22 Young Creators gave when asked what types of videos they expect to find when they check out social media like YouTube, Facebook, TikTok, and others, supplemented with observations from others. First and foremost in the list of video genres is comedy—expressed in so many ways, as we found with film and television genres.

Typology of Online Video Genres

Comedy Videos: More than half of the 2021–22 Young Creators mentioned comedy videos, funny videos, "videos that make you laugh." The key concepts are comedy, comedic, humorous, funny, fun to watch. In the case of videos, the length of the video is an important element, since "short clips" appeared very often in descriptions. While there were references to the type of comedy—satiric, negative stuff, stupid videos—the lengthier film and television genres drew many more sophisticated references to the nature of the comedy expected. As is the case with film and television, the "gratification" derived from viewing comedy, and occasionally the "uses" to which it's put— to enjoy with friends—is a major defining factor for this video genre.

Format-centric Video Genres: Television has its "situation comedy," a quite specific, recognizable genre that audiences can describe without much trouble. Although "epics" are not solely a film genre, the wide screen and expansive story are best displayed in the physical theater than in the home. And both film and television have their "serials," "series," and "sequels." Videos also have their forms, although they're shared with the Internet as well. Our young creators cited podcasts, blogs and vlogs, often appearing daily. Those genres were expected in some accounts to provide advice or tips, or personal accounts.

Educational, Instructive, and Informative Videos: Television has its Food Channel and Home & Garden Television (HGTV) channel, focusing not just on the topics but providing information and fulfilling a host of uses and gratifications. For videos, we have several video sub-genres. While many young creators said they expect to find educational or informative videos that teach them something or provide interesting content, there were many more specifics:

Fashion and Beauty Videos. More than a dozen young creators said they expect to find videos that teach them about beauty and fashion, makeup, and different styles. Perhaps not far afield, wedding videos and babies also seem to fit here.

Food and Cooking Videos. While the lessons are abbreviated compared to the matching television genre, cooking videos seem to grab viewers with interesting images. As noted with the broader 2021 Creators survey analysis, several folks indicated an interest in creating their own food videos featuring pasta or particular interests.

Fitness and Workout Videos. It's the "instructive" element that places fitness videos in this genre niche, because, while the videos are brief for the most part, they often have targeted goals—e.g., working on one's abs.

Do-It-Yourself Videos. Several young creators said they expect to see "how to" videos when they turn on social media, including "tricks on how to do things easier," as well as tutorials and professional advice. YouTube would appear to be the social medium most popular for this video genre.

Stories and Mini-Docs. It's a challenge telling a short story in the time most viewers devote to individual social media videos, particularly on TikTok, but lots of folks try and the legacy social media provide libraries of accessible content. There are two types of video genres here, akin to the fiction and documentary categories.

Mini-Docs. Several young creators said they look for mini-documentaries on people's lives, interesting story videos, which, for example, tell about a day in the life of someone. Fitting in this genre are motivational/inspirational videos, which one young creator said she expects to see on Instagram. The briefer form of mini-docs are a version of "reality TV," allowing the audience a look into someone else's life. Sometimes, police or surveillance cameras provide "mini-crime videos" with a little editing.

Slices of Life and Nature. Among the video clips that appear often on TikTok are those that capture dramatic moments in nature, when tsunamis or tidal waves reach an unsuspecting shore, "near death" escapes, collapsing buildings, and struggles in nature—animals pursued by predators.

Routine Clips of Life. All of the social media, but especially Facebook and TikTok, feature brief videos capturing a moment in time that the creator found interesting, unique, confirming, expressive, or illustrative of a cultural, social or personal artifact. Some are mini versions of those appearing on the TV show, *America's Funniest Videos* (1990-). But others showcase fragments capturing daily routines in the community, at home or at work. The latter offer general audiences a glimpse of how products are made, buildings are constructed, trees are felled, artisans create their wares, what happens on the assembly line or on the farm.

Dramas and Fiction Videos. While not mentioned often, the drama video is also found on social media.

Amateur Talent Video Genres: Among the most popular video genres are those fitting under this category, and they include talent videos as well as "physically expressive" videos, and what at one time would have been a vaudeville act. The most viewed content category on TikTok was "entertainment content," which accumulated 535 billion hashtag views collectively as of July 2020.

Outdoors and Animal Videos: Many creators, young and old, cited funny animal videos, pet and funny stories, but some also noted outdoor settings and *National Geographic* videos.

Prankster or Trickster Videos: One Young Creator said they used to film such videos, which can best be described as the video version of *Jackass* television that made a splash in the early 2000s, as performers carry out stunts and pranks on each other for the public viewer's surprise or amusement. Very clever "image-switch" videos on TikTok and other social media appear now and then (following in the tradition of very early film, e.g., the films of Georges Melies).

Music Performer Videos: This can include both talented, amateurs, as well as lip sync versions of popular tunes. Many of the last feature good looking people, men and women, mostly young but not always, in various stages of dress or undress. Successful videos breed competition and copycats.

Dance Performer Videos: An almost endless stream of dance videos features "average" people doing brief dances, as individuals or groups, to the accompaniment of popular music. TikTok is filled with such videos.

Lifestyle and Influencer Videos: While many of our respondents in both of the creators surveys bemoaned the rise of the "influencer," they nevertheless represent an important genre, where "real" people act out some aspect of their life, showcasing products that sponsor their videos. Numerous creators said they expect to find lifestyle videos on social media.

Commercial Entertainment Videos: These include everything from household product advertising to "forthcoming film clips" and edited segments from television programs or concerts, posted by commercial enterprises.

Comedy Video Clips: Performances of well-known entertainers in concert or from television shows populate much social media "air time." When Betty White died, the number of clips from *Golden Girls* (1985-92) and her earlier TV shows multiplied on social media, featuring brief segments edited for maximum impact in the least amount of time.

Professional Performers Videos: Similarly, clips of singers and other performers in concert are edited to attract viewers. In addition to the professionals, the "surprise" performances on talent shows are edited to showcase talent and audience's surprise reactions, e.g., Susan Boyle's performance on *Britain's Got Talent* (2007-) show. And both YouTube and TikTok as well as other social media make it easy to follow the exploits of favorite performers.

Film and Acting Video Clips: The most memorable lines from classic movies appear in film video clips on social media.

Niches and Topical Interest Videos: Both our creators groups note their special interest in various topics featured in videos. Many, in fact, noted that they expect the social media algorithm to feed them videos on their favorite interests.

Politics and Social Issues Videos: Least cited among the young creators are social issues, which are more popular among older adults.

Business and Finance Videos: As one young creator put it, "When I open YouTube I expect to know how the stock market is doing."

History and Geography Videos: While history and geography videos abound on YouTube, even TikTok has a historical video genre that features 30-second clips of "life" in various cities and countries through time, many from the early 20th century. This is also called actuality programming.

Sports Videos: Sports probably fits into its own category since it ranges across so many sports, features not only amateurs "in action," but also sports highlights, commentaries, historical segments, and gaming.

News Videos: Like sports, news videos include segments featuring current events as well as historical accounts.

Gaming Videos: Gaming actually uses online connections for competitive and joint playing, but there also are videos featuring specific games.

VIDFICS...

One type of user-generated content (UGC) that did not emerge in our thematic analysis of responses regarding online video types by creators is that of *video fanfiction* (or "vidfics"). Fanfiction may be defined as a story written within an already published and established universe (Waggoner, 2012). Online written fanfiction has been popular since the dawn of the Internet. Although often associated with sexually explicit content that has been extrapolated from more standard content (e.g., "kink memes," Jamison, 2013), fanfiction also includes non-sexual narrative variations on such story worlds/canons/universes as Sherlock Holmes, *Star Trek*, *The X-Files*, Harry Potter, Japanese anime, and the *Twilight* Saga (Black 2006, 2007). When placed online for wide availability, all are what Fiske (1992) would call "textual productivity," the ultimate stage in his tripartite model of fan culture activity. Fandom, Fiske notes, results in the accumulation of "popular cultural capital" that can, on occasion, be convertible to economic capital (as in acquiring sponsorship for fanfiction).

The very notion of fanfiction is grounded in intertextuality and the type of melding that is also typical of contemporary film and television genres. As Jamison (2013) describes the phenomenon with regard to online textual fanfiction: "Most fan readers read around in fandoms; some read around in taste groupings similar to genres (hurt/comfort, slash, gen, fluff, BDSM, PWP, plot-driven, etc.), but they read *around*, often following many unfolding stories simultaneously...Plot threads cross, become confused, create patterns...[fanfiction] experienced this way is more like a web...than a series" (p. 13).

Video fanfiction has not been as prominent on the web as has textual fanfiction, which enjoys thousands of fan communities online. Copyright issues have hampered the development of vidfics. Video fanfiction is, however, represented by videos on YouTube and fan-made video games. An early and enduring example is *Angry Video Game Nerd* (2006-), a web series of retrogaming reviews by James Rolfe (available on YouTube). Although not precisely fiction, reviews and critiques have been accepted as a type of textual productivity (Fiske, 1992) on a par with other forms of fanfiction.

A Concluding Note

This chapter recounts the ways in which conceptions of media uses and gratifications have been transformed by emerging platforms, notably the production of and consumption of moving images on social media. Our focus, in particular, involves the merging roles involving users as creators of content.

Developing items profiling creators of the moving images, we've examined how these user roles have grown less passive, including the use of technology to create moving images and entrepreneurial roles. These trends were tracked from the 2015 Users Survey through the 2021 Users Survey and the two Creators Surveys in 2021–22. The latter focused on active producers of moving images, finding that half of respondents post photos or videos on Facebook daily or more often, a marked increase from 2015. Half post several times a week or more often on YouTube and TikTok. Most of the 2021–22 Young Creators post comedy videos, funny videos, and/or "videos that make you laugh."

Looking at the gratifications that drive this activity, key motivations uncovered in the surveys include feeling a sense of achievement, connecting to people, and feeling productive. Differences were uncovered between the general population and young creators in the topics featured in posts. The latter prefer posting images or features about themselves and their lifestyles, while the more general group favors pets and animals, social issues, and beautiful images. Both groups favor posting stories that make people smile or laugh. Drawing from these data, the chapter closes with an exhaustive typology of genres into which online video postings can be classified.

5

AUDIENCES COPING WITH AN ERA OF CONTENT ABUNDANCE: NOVELTY SEEKING AND INTEREST MAXIMIZATION

When audiences had only a couple theaters in town to watch films, and likely only a few possibilities during a month of leisure activity, there was little need to spend a lot of time thinking about what films to go see. Audiences could select from the few genres available on the basis of what actor or actress was in, and whether the story seemed interesting. Similarly, three television networks and limited viewing time offered a similar situation at home, so audiences could use few cues for decision-making, including the schedule. Today, with the "media of abundance," audiences need strategies for coping with "content overload." In this chapter, we will take a brief look at changes in the media environment and then review strategies that audiences can employ in response to the diverse selection of film, television, and video genres.

The New Media Environment—The Age of Media Abundance

The history of media abundance reflects the impact of new technologies (e.g., Lin & Atkin, 2002, 2007). Multiplex movie complexes maximized out-of-the house options, and first laser discs, then DVDs and Blu-rays expanded ownership and rental options. Satellite and cable systems then multiplied both film and television menus. The Internet and online services added to the mix, and mobile devices expanded the locations for viewing the moving image. Now streaming and on-demand delivery produce an almost unlimited abundance. Moreover, the number of streaming services has grown dramatically in recent years, with one list citing some 200 services. Industry research suggests that the average US household subscribes to four streaming services while others cite five to seven. With churn, the number is a moving target. In the US,

DOI: 10.4324/9781003264828-5

surveys have shown that a majority of consumers have a subscription to some sort of streaming service (Watson, 2020), and the number is growing, but some suggest the number of streaming services and platforms will drive many back to cable or more niche-based platforms (Munson, 2021). One thing is certain: The growth of streaming services adds flexibility for audiences seeking out and watching the moving image (Karrer, 2021).

This growth in options for viewing the moving image likely affects how viewers sample film and television genres. In this chapter, we will introduce the concepts of *film and television genre repertoires*—the range of genres viewed with some regularity. The next chapter will dig deeper into the audience's experiences with "screens" in this age of abundance and the relationship with film and television genre perceptions and viewing.

Impact on Audience Choices

There are several points at which audiences have to make choices that broaden or narrow the selection they have of moving images. Some are made for them—the number of theater multiplexes available is dependent on where one lives. Even the availability of cable and satellite systems and sufficiently speedy online access are due in part to where one lives. These environmental choices exist alongside the constraints of one's personal finances and availability of time.

But within the constraints that audiences face, people can make choices of which film or television genres to watch, or which videos to consider via a multitude of delivery systems. Several key concepts underpin these choice dynamics; they include the need for stimulation, situations where one feels boredom, openness to new experiences, level of curiosity, one's range of interests, and novelty seeking.

Boredom is a concept important as a stimulator for seeking behaviors. Mikulas and Vodanovich (1993) define boredom as "a state of relatively low arousal and dissatisfaction which is attributed to an inadequately stimulating environment" (p. 1). Vodanovich (2003) notes that the concept is usually measured with single items and has been assumed to exist in or be equated with monotonous or repetitive activities, though this approach neglects the individual's perception of the environment and an individual's emotional state (Mikulas & Vodanovich, 1993). Geiwitz (1966) suggests that monotony, defined as characterizing a situation, is less important than the subjective feeling of repetitiveness (p. 593).

In attempting to provide such explanations for viewer behavior, we rely both on long-established theory and literature, as well as our own contributions. We will acknowledge an inherent tension between the new and the familiar in human experience. It's possible to draw overarching conclusions about humans' need to categorize, and to develop expectancies based on past experiences with media content. Audience members routinely engage in novelty seeking within comfort zones provided by the familiar. In the age of media abundance, spectators confront an ever greater need to develop tools to navigate this environment.

The environment in this case is the media environment, or in particular, the choices of films or television programs for viewing. Clearly, someone who engages in "binge watching," for example, is seeking redundancy, maximizing one's interest rather than seeking novelty. While we have a tendency to seek predictability in our lives, we also need diversity or novelty. Sometimes, despite dozens, even hundreds of available videos, films, or television programs, nothing seems interesting or stimulating in the moment. Vodanovich (2003) notes that boredom has been linked to such negative factors as depression, hostility, and aggression but also to lower scores on need for cognition, to lower attentiveness, and to greater procrastination. Furthermore, people who score higher on boredom proneness habituate more quickly to repeated exposure to the same stimuli, in our context, particular film genres (Bornstein et al., 1990).

Openness to experience involves being receptive to novelty—new ideas, experiences, and approaches (McCrae & Costa, 2003, p. 46). Eisenberger et al. (2010, p. 602) say this includes a preference for variety, an active imagination, aesthetic sensitivity, and intellectual curiosity (see also McCrae, 1996). Openness has been found to be strongly related to the need to be different (Joy, 2004) and to sensation seeking (Garcia et al., 2005). There is some conceptual confusion about novelty seeking that might stem from viewing the behaviors as almost the same as curiosity, interest, sensation seeking, change seeking, arousal seeking, and the need for stimulation. Using correlational studies, researchers have indicated that these constructs overlap but are not the same. Reio and Choi (2004) note that novelty seeking is too often considered to be unidimensional, despite evidence of its multidimensionality (see also Litman & Spielberger, 2003; Pearson, 1970).

Novelty seeking refers to the tendency to explore unfamiliar things. Novelty seeking is associated with greater sensation seeking (Mallet & Vignoli, 2007), impulsivity (Wills et al., 1994), risk taking, and a greater orientation toward independence (Wills et al., 1994) as well as greater extraversion and openness to experience (Gordon & Luo, 2011). "Novelty constitutes, at least in some situations or for some individuals, an intrinsically rewarding stimulus" (Gocłowska et al., 2019, p. 252).

Novelty seeking as a quantifiable dimension of behavior has been studied by numerous investigators. A preference for novel rather than familiar stimulation has been postulated by Berlyne (1951, 1960) and by McReynolds (1956). Berlyne (1951) reports some evidence for such a preference in a choice situation. Gocłowska et al. (2019) found novelty seeking linked to two personality traits, openness to experience and extraversion, and to divergent thinking performance—creativity in performance.

As a short-term motivational state, novelty seeking (Duckworth et al., 2002) arouses environmental exploration and learning (Cahill-Solis & Witryol, 1994). Novel aspects of phenomena and activities stimulate learner curiosity and interest, and maintain exploratory activity (Litman & Spielberger, 2003).

Reio and Choi (2004) note that novelty seeking is associated with new experiences, "with the degree of novelty being a function of the discrepancy between previous and current experience" (p. 120). Thus, applying this to film genres, we'd expect the level of novelty being dependent on comparisons with one's past viewing. Berlyne (1960) notes that individuals have optimal levels of novelty that arouse curiosity and exploration, with lower levels less likely to arouse curiosity. Higher than optimal levels lead to being overwhelmed and anxious, deterring curiosity and exploration (Sussman, 1989; Wentworth & Witryol, 2003). So "genre-bending" that goes "too far" for some in the audience would discourage viewing.

There's even some evidence from genetic researchers that a novelty seeking gene has been located (Ekelund et al., 1999), suggesting that this personality trait has a genetic component (Reio & Choi, 2004, p. 120). That cross-sectional study found examples that novelty seeking was lower among women older than 40 and among men older than 50.

Reio and Choi (2004) looked at stereotypes that novelty seeking declines in adulthood, that as adults age they become ambivalent about trying new things (Bevins, 2001; Camp et al., 1985; Stoner & Spencer, 1986). They conducted a study examining men and women aged 17 to 59 who worked in the service industry and administered four novelty subscales. Interestingly, the 17- to 20-year-old age group in that study demonstrated noticeably less preference for novel experiences in a number of cases, and the group's scores were either similar or lower than were the scores of those in the other age groups. These results are counterintuitive, because one might expect this age group to have the highest novelty seeking scores (Lightfoot, 1997; Steinberg, 2003). Clearly, we need to be careful about how we view various segments of the viewing audience. This next section builds on novelty seeking and related concepts to show how it's relevant to the selection of genres in the age of media abundance.

Audience Film and Television Genre Repertoires

Ferguson and Melkote (1997) define channel repertoire as the "number of channels that a viewer chooses to watch, without much regard to the total number of channels available" (p. 190). Noting how the introduction of cable systems expanded the number of channels available, Neuendorf et al. (2001) expanded the concept to accommodate the changing and increasingly diverse media environment with weightings reflecting frequency of channel use and two types of channel repertoires: Primary repertoires (those sets of channels used regularly and frequently) and specialized repertoires (those sets of channels used by particular audience segments on a regular but infrequent basis). They found younger people to have a larger "primary channel repertoire" (the number of channels viewed at least daily), but differences were not significant for "secondary channel repertoire" (the number of channels viewed weekly) or "tertiary channel repertoire" (the number of channels viewed weekly or less but at least occasionally). With blurring boundaries on what constitutes "channel" and viewing of the moving image on various platforms and mobile devices, we propose shifting from channels to film and television genres to see how audiences cope with limitless possibilities. Thus, we advance the notion of "*film genre repertoire*" and "*television genre repertoire.*"

With an abundance of both classic, newly emerging, and experimental genres, audiences can become confused, facing a situation analogous to "information overload." We introduce the concept of "*genre repertoire*" as an opportunity to understand how audiences are coping with the film and television of abundance. "Genre repertoire" here refers to the number of different genres watched with varying degrees of regularity.

When distinguishing between "film genre repertoire" and "television genre repertoire," we need to emphasize that the latter is similar to but not equivalent to the channel repertoire studied previously by Neuendorf et al. (2001) because many individual networks and cable/satellite channels offer more than a single genre. Sampling different film genres and television genres in a home setting is a fairly simple process requiring minimal effort. Sampling different genres by going out to theaters is a costlier endeavor, in terms of both money and effort, though some of the sampling can be achieved at home watching films on television.

First, we will conduct a descriptive analysis of how audiences are coping with the availability of so many film and television genres. The multiplex may offer 20 to 40 different films and television delivery systems (cable, satellite, and online streaming) may offer channels and options numbering in high three digits, but how many different options are audiences exposing themselves to? What is the size of audience repertoire? The following research questions are offered:

Research Question 1: How many film genres do audiences expose themselves to?
Research Question 2: How many television genres do audiences expose themselves to?

Our survey in 2015 included 31 different film and 11 television genres. Our analysis in Table 5.1 includes the means and medians (50/50 cut point) for both cumulative and discrete measures of repertoire. Thus, for example, we see that the mean or average number of film genres watched very often or all the time was 4.99, and half of the sample had four or more frequent film genres and half

TABLE 5.1 Descriptive Measures of Film and TV Genre Repertoires (2015 and 2021 Users Surveys)

Film and Television Repertoires	2015 n = 368 2021 n = 207	Mean No. of Genres	Median No. of Genres
Cumulative Measures of Film Genre Repertoire			
Frequent Film Repertoire (no. of film genres watched very often or all the time)	2015 Users	4.99	4
	2021 Users	13.10	14
Often Film Repertoire (no. of film genres watched often, very often, or all the time)	2015 Users	10.37	10
	2021 Users	22.30	25
Film Sampling Repertoire (no. of film genres watched once in a while, often, very often, or all the time)	2015 Users	18.42	19
	2021 Users	27.60	31
Cumulative Measures of TV Genre Repertoire			
Frequent TV Repertoire (no. of TV genres watched very often or all the time)	2015 Users	1.69	1
	2021 Users	4.60	5
Often TV Repertoire (no. of TV genres watched often, very often, or all the time)	2015 Users	3.21	3
	2021 Users	7.70	9
TV Sampling Repertoire (no. of TV genres watched once in a while, often, very often, or all the time)	2015 Users	5.48	5
	2021 Users	9.60	11
Never Film Repertoire (no. of film genres never watched)	2015 Users	6.46	5
	2021 Users	1.60	0
Never TV Repertoire (no. of TV genres never watched)	2015 Users	3.39	3
	2021 Users	0.68	0

had fewer. So, on average our viewers watched five different genres most often or all the time. If we add in those genres that are watched often, the average jumps up to 10.4, almost double, with half above or below 10 genres. And, finally, if we add in those viewed once in a while, what we're labeling our "sampling repertoire," the number jumps to more than 18. Thus, our respondents claim to see almost two-thirds of our film genres at least once in a while, which makes them a group with a fairly catholic set of tastes. At the other end of the scale, we see that, on average, there are more than six film genres that they never watch. When we dig into the actual frequencies for the frequent film repertoire, we find 50 people who say they never watch any film genre very often or all the time, and these folks are likely those who seldom go out to see films. But we also find that a couple folks say they see every film genre very often or all the time, and these clearly are film fans for whom novelty is a way of life. The 2021 Users Survey shows much larger film and television repertoires. This is a much different sample in terms of demographics, but it was also during the pandemic, leading perhaps to greater sampling under quarantine conditions.

Turning to television genres, we have a smaller pool to select from, and the average number of TV genres watched very often or all the time is less than two (mean of 1.69), with a median of one, meaning the most frequent number of TV genres watched frequently is one. Adding in the TV genres watched often, very often or all the time, the average increases to 3.2, and the sampling repertoire raises the figure to 5.5, meaning that almost half of the television genres get at least an occasional viewing by our sample. Again, digging into the data, we find that 150 people say they watch no TV genres very often or all the time—likely those watching little television. But five respondents say they watch all 11 TV genres very often or all the time; clearly, these are novelty seekers, or folks who love to watch television, the proverbial couch potatoes, perhaps.

Research Question 3: How are social categories related to film genre repertoire and TV genre repertoire?

Correlations were computed for relationships between the measures of film and television genre repertoires and social categories—age, education, income—and none of the correlations were statistically significant in the 2015 Users Survey. Breaking down the repertoire by ethnicity (White, Nonwhite) there is only one statistically significant difference, where Whites watch an average of 4.70 film genres very often or all the time, compared with 6.05 for Nonwhites (t=2.4, p<.05). In the 2021 Users Survey, there was only one difference as well, with Whites having a larger TV genre sampling repertoire than Nonwhites (t=2.3, p<.05)

However, a number of gender differences appear. While there is no difference in the 2015 Users Survey for the frequent film genre repertoire between males and females, the males have a larger often film genre repertoire—watching genres often, very often, or all the time (males 11.32; females 9.87; t=2.19, p<.05)–and the film sampling repertoire—watching genres once in a while or more often (males 19.35; females 7.79; t=2.10, p<.05). Differences also appear for television genre repertoire, but in the reverse direction, with women having larger television genre repertoires than men: Frequent TV genre repertoire, females 1.97; males 1.28; t=3.2, p=.002; often TV genre repertoire, females 3.51; males 2.79; t=2.4, p=.02; and the sampling TV genre repertoire approaches statistical significance, females 5.70; males 5.11; t=1.8, p=.07. There were no gender differences in either film or television genre repertoires in the 2021 Users Survey.

We found no relationships between age and film and TV genre repertoires in the 2015 Users Survey. In the 2021 Users Survey, income also was not related to any of the film or TV genre repertoires, but age was negatively related and education positively related to all three film genre repertoires and to the often and sampling repertoires for television. Age was negatively related to: Frequent film genre repertoire (r=–.17, p<.05), the often film genre repertoire (r=–.24, p<.001), the film genre sampling repertoire (r=–.18, p=.02), the often TV genre repertoire (r=–.15, p=.04), and the TV sampling genre repertoire (r=–.15, p=.04). The reverse pattern was found for the repertoire variables for level of education, but all three TV repertoire variables were positively related: Frequent film genre repertoire (r=.26, p<.001), often film genre repertoire (r=.36, p<.001), film genre sampling repertoire (r=.35, p<.001), frequent TV genre repertoire (r=.21, p=.003), often TV genre repertoire (r=.31, p<.001), and the TV genre sampling repertoire (r=.39, p<.001).

Film and TV Genre Repertoires—and Novelty Seeking

People with broader interests are likely to seek out novel experiences. In this case, that might mean sampling more film or television genres, leading to larger genre repertoires. Our 2015 survey of audiences included three items measuring concepts that should be positively related to larger genre repertoires. First, one item asked our respondents whether they see themselves as a person who loves variety, watches new shows on TV and sees lots of different films in theaters—in other words, seeks variety in their diet of moving images. A second asked to what extent they are interested in seeing films and television programs from other countries, a measure of their interest in other cultures' media. A third measure tapped cosmopoliteness, which was introduced in Chapter 3, focusing on whether people see themselves as "a citizen of the world" (see also Earle & Cvetkovich, 1997; Jeffres, Atkin, Bracken, et al., 2004; Robinson & Zill, 1997).

Based on prior research, we chose to focus on cosmopolitan identification and an interest in seeing films and TV programs from other countries, a measure of an appreciation of different cultures. Jeffres, Bracken, et al. (2014) found that cosmopolitan identification, appreciation of different cultures, and diversity of interests were correlated with how often people went out to see movies in a theater. Similarly, frequent moviegoing was related to the cultural diversity of media content to which one is exposed. Thus, we pose the following research questions:

Research Question 4: Are novelty seeking perceptions related to film and television genre repertoires?

Research Question 5: Is an interest in films and TV programs from other countries related to film and television genre repertoires?

Research Question 6: Is cosmopoliteness positively related to film and television genre repertoires?

Before examining the expected relationships with genre repertoires, we looked at how novelty, cultural interests, and cosmopoliteness were related to media use in general. Analysis shows that people who see themselves as novelty seekers also watch television more often, go out to see films in theaters and on TV or other devices more often, play more video games, and watch videos on smartphones more often. And the relationship with going out to see live musical concerts or events approaches statistical significance. Cosmopoliteness is unrelated to any of the media use variables and those who say they like to watch films and TV programs from other countries actually watch less TV, listen to the radio less often, and go on Facebook, check their email or text family or friends less often in the 2015 Users Survey. A marginal relationship with watching more films on TV or other devices approaches statistical significance in the 2015 survey. But the reverse is found for the 2021 Users Survey, where cosmopoliteness is positively related to all of the media use variables, suggesting a much different sample than the earlier one [Table available online].

When we turn to film genre repertoires and television genre repertoires, we find a strong pattern of positive relationships with novelty seeking, interest in other countries' film and television offerings, and cosmopoliteness (see Table 5.2). Thus, those who seek novelty have larger repertoires of film and television genres that they visit regularly for both the 2015 and the 2021 users. But the picture is more complex for the items measuring an affinity for media from other cultures and cosmopoliteness. While cosmopolites also have larger film and television genre repertoires, no relationship was found between TV genre repertoires and liking media from other cultures in the 2015 Users Survey. Still, positive relationships were found for the most recent, 2021 Users Survey, suggesting that the expansion of time at home in the pandemic experience expanded viewers' tastes.

In the 2021 Users Survey, we added a variety seeking variable, as described in Chapter 1, and we find those who seek variety in their lives and media also have larger film repertoires (frequent film repertoire, $r=.40$, $p<.001$; often film genre repertoire, $r=.36$, $p<.001$; film sampling repertoires, $r=.26$, $p<.001$). Those who seek novelty and those who like a lot of variety also have larger film genre repertoires. The same pattern emerges for television genre repertoires, where variety seeking is related to the same three TV genre repertoires (frequent film repertoire, $r=.39$, $p<.001$; often TV genre repertoires, $r=.38$, $p<.001$; sampling TV repertoires, $r=.24$, $p<.001$).

Film and TV Genre Repertoires—and Interest Maximization

The "age of media abundance" allows for people to not only seek variety and novelty, but also to seek redundancy, to maximize their interests. In fact, the two are not mutually exclusive. Whether one is bored, or satisfied with their viewing experiences is likely to be a situational state, rather than a personality trait. In the process of expanding one's genre repertoires, you might encounter a new genre or subgenre that you then seek out again and again. Donohew

TABLE 5.2 Correlations between Film and TV Genre Repertoires and Measures of Novelty Seeking, Interest in Other Cultures' Media, and Cosmopoliteness (2015 Users Survey, 2021 Users Survey)

Film and TV Genre Repertoires	Novelty Seeking	Like Media from Other Cultures	Cosmopoliteness
Cumulative Measures of Film Genre Repertoire			
Frequent Film Repertoire (no. of film genres watched very often or all the time)			
2015	.32★★★	.22★★★	.24★★★
2021	.49★★★	.48★★★	.43★★★
Often Film Repertoire (no. of film genres watched often, very often, or all the time)			
2015	.36★★★	.26★★★	.26★★★
2021	.40★★★	.44★★★	.37★★★
Film Sampling Repertoire (no. of film genres watched once in a while, often, very often, or all the time)			
2015	.37★★★	.31★★★	.23★★★
2021	.28★★★	.32★★★	.28★★★
Cumulative Measures of TV Genre Repertoire			
Frequent TV Repertoire (no. of TV genres watched very often or all the time)			
2015	.23★★★		.11★
2021	.47★★★	.49★★★	.41★★★
Often TV Repertoire (no. of TV genres watched often, very often, or all the time)			
2015	.25★★★		.11★
2021	.39★★★	.41★★★	.36★★★
TV Sampling Repertoire (no. of TV genres watched once in a while, often, very often, or all the time)			
2015	.23★★★		.13★
2021	.22★★	.28★★★	.28★★★

Note: Only significant correlations are included in the table. ★$p<.05$; ★★$p<.01$; ★★★$p<.001$

and Tipton (1973) suggest that an individual operates between the boundaries of variety and redundancy, at one time tuning out the monotonous in favor of something new, while at other times seeking new content as the individual oscillates between the need for a predictable environment and the need for arousal and stimulation. During the COVID-19 pandemic, many have engaged in "binge watching" of particular television programs. One friend on Facebook asked for recommendations for other television programs to binge watch because her family had just completed several seasons of another program and were looking for something new.

So what is "interest maximization"? Utility theory is helpful for predicting how people will react when facing abundant content (Miller, 1972). Essentially, the individual facing available options is expected to maximize one's perceived utility by choosing the one most highly evaluated. Thus, a person seeking a useful way to "kill time" would gravitate toward familiar sources. Interest maximization is defined as the tendency for an individual to increase one's viewing of a film or television program among preferred genres and to decrease viewing of less preferred genres (see Jeffres, 1978).

Neuendorf et al. (2000) looked at cable subscribers, finding support for an interest maximization perspective. That analysis found "evidence of interest maximization manifested in complementary viewing of certain functionally similar channels." Fans of one channel generally tended to seek redundant programming in particular patterns.

These earlier studies took place before streaming became an option and audiences exercised more control over not only their viewing times but, with recording capabilities, content selection itself. So today, we have "binge watching" but also more opportunities for repeat viewing, since films and programs are repeated on cable and satellite systems and also available as DVD purchases or streaming online. In our 2015 survey, we posed several items that help us see to what extent people maximize their interests in viewing film and television genres. Respondents were asked to indicate to what extent each of these statements described them, with responses from 1 = not at all to 7 = very much like me. The two negative items were reversed and a summary score computed, so a higher score indicates greater preference for repeat viewing. This scale, labeled Interest Maximization, had a mean of 40.25, with a median of 40, and a range from 9 to 63.

- I often watch a favorite film again and again.
- Sometimes I buy films I've seen in the theater so I can watch the movie again later.
- When summer reruns start on TV, I find myself watching programs I've seen before.
- I don't like to watch films at home that I've seen before in a theater (R).
- I don't like to watch TV shows I've seen before (R).
- I watch TV programs with my family that we've seen before, often several times.
- When I like a TV show, sometimes I buy the complete season on DVD or other media.
- I've seen some films so often that I know much of the dialogue.
- I have a collection of DVDs and/or Blu-rays.

Note: "(R)" indicates reverse-worded items.

TABLE 5.3 Correlations between Film and TV Genre Repertoires and Interest Maximization (2015 Users Survey, 2021 Users Survey)

Film and TV Genre Repertoires	Interest Maximization Score
Cumulative Measures of Film Genre Repertoire	
Frequent Film Repertoire (no. of film genres watched very often or all the time)	
2015	.22★★★
2021	.45★★★
Often Film Repertoire (no. of film genres watched often, very often, or all the time)	
2015	.18★★★
2021	.39★★★
Film Sampling Repertoire (no. of film genres watched once in a while, often, very often, or all the time)	
2015	.15★★
2021	.31★★★
Cumulative Measures of TV Genre Repertoire	
Frequent TV Repertoire (no. of TV genres watched very often or all the time)	
2015	.24★★★
2021	.39★★★
Often TV Repertoire (no. of TV genres watched often, very often, or all the time)	
2015	.23★★★
2021	.33★★★
TV Sampling Repertoire (no. of TV genres watched once in a while, often, very often, or all the time)	
2015	.10#
2021	.23★★★

Note: #.05<p<.10; ★★p<.01; ★★★p<.001

As Table 5.3 shows, interest maximization is positively correlated with all three cumulative film genre repertoires and with the top two cumulative television genre repertoires in the 2015 Users Survey and all three TV genre repertoires in the 2021 Users Survey. However, when we look at the discrete components, the relationship is strongest with the genre repertoire tapping viewing very often or all the time. When we look only at the repertoire for viewing often, or only once in a while, the relationship drops out. This underscores support for the maximization hypothesis since it's only with the heaviest viewing that one can maximize one's interests or preference for a genre. Occasional viewing may add to novelty seeking but heavier viewing reflects interest maximization. To put it more clearly, watching a lot of different film or television genres most often reflects interest maximization, but watching a lot once in a while or occasionally does not.

Finally, we would expect people's novelty seeking and interest maximization of the moving image to depend on their overall assessments of the quality of film and television genres available today, however abundant they are. Our 2015 Users Survey included two items asking respondents to assess that quality by indicating how much they agreed with the following statements on a scale where 1 = completely disagree and 7 = completely agree:

- Quality of films today is higher than ever.
- Prime time TV shows today are better than they've been in years.

We find that people who think the quality of films today is higher than ever also think prime time television shows today are better than they've been in years. The correlation between the two is .55 (*p*<.001). Both of these are positively related to all the cumulative film genre repertoires and TV genre repertoires, as shown in Table 5.4. Again, it's the frequent viewing that's related to quality assessments, as it was with interest maximization.

TABLE 5.4 Correlations between Film and TV Genre Repertoires and Assessments of Films, TV Shows (2015 Users Survey)

Film and TV Genre Repertoires	*Quality of Films Today Is Higher than Ever*	*Prime Time TV Shows Today Are Better than They've Been in Years*
Cumulative Measures of Film Genre Repertoire		
Frequent Film Repertoire (no. of film genres watched very often or all the time)	.23★★★	.22★★★
Often Film Repertoire (no. of film genres watched often, very often, or all the time)	.22★★★	.22★★★
Film Sampling Repertoire (no. of film genres watched once in a while, often, very often, or all the time)	.20★★★	.22★★★
Cumulative Measures of TV Genre Repertoire		
Frequent TV Repertoire (no. of TV genres watched very often or all the time)	.24★★★	.32★★★
Often TV Repertoire (no. of TV genres watched often, very often, or all the time)	.25★★★	.33★★★
TV Sampling Repertoire (no. of TV genres watched once in a while, often, very often, or all the time)	.21★★★	.31★★★

Note: ★★★*p*<.001

A Concluding Note

This chapter examines changes in the media environment and the strategies that audiences can employ in response to the diverse selection of film, television, and video genres. In particular, we develop and test the concepts of *film and television genre repertoires*—the range of genres viewed with some regularity. This framework draws from literatures addressing novelty seeking, interest maximization, and related concepts and how they're relevant to the selection of genres in the age of media abundance. We stress the utility of explicating novelty seeking to inform our understanding of genre selection in the age of media abundance, introducing the concept of *"genre repertoire"* to understand how audiences are coping with the film and television of abundance.

Several key concepts are related to genre repertoires. Those who seek variety in their lives and media have larger film repertoires. Novelty seeking and variety seeking are also related to larger film and television genre repertoires. Those who evaluate the quality of films today as higher than ever also evaluate prime time television shows today as better than they've been in years. Both of these are positively related to all of the cumulative film genre repertoires and the TV genre repertoires. The fact that frequent viewing is related to quality assessments and interest maximization reinforces the utility of these content utility measures in the emerging media environment. We found that interest maximization also was related to film and television genre repertoires. While occasional viewing may add to novelty seeking, heavier viewing reflects interest maximization.

6

THE NEW VIEWING ENVIRONMENT—MATCHING GENRES WITH SCREENS

A Short History of Screen Options

The story of the moving image is also the story of matching audiences with "screens" where they can view these images.

The first screens with moving images that audiences encountered were in Magic Lantern shows. These immersive spectacles used light-projected painted images that were crossfaded to create the illusion of simple motion, accompanied by music, sound effects, oral narration, and sometimes pyrotechnics. Magic Lantern shows had existed since the 17th century, but during the 19th century they became a prominent form of large-audience entertainment. These screen-based attractions set the stage for group viewing of the moving image—these were the first large audiences watching moving images together in the dark.

By the late 19th century, a shortened exposure time for photographic film had paved the way for true moving pictures, and the tiny screens of the kinetoscope parlor provided audiences with individualized choices. The kinetoscope, patented in the US by Thomas Edison and developed by his employee William Dickson, was an enclosed projection device into which an individual would "peep" to see a very short silent 35 mm film. Content varied with what Edison's people thought would satisfy a variety of paying spectators—from salacious dancing women to muscle men flexing to cockfights. Edison's prognostication that the future of the moving images would be the individual-view kinescope was not to hold true at that time, however.

A turning point for the moving image on large screens was the December 1895 showing of "animated photography" at the Grand Café in Paris by the Lumiere brothers. Their program of ten brief "actualities" created a furor,

DOI: 10.4324/9781003264828-6

particularly *Train Arriving at La Ciotat*, which showed, simply, a train pulling into a station, moving toward the camera. The French newspaper *Le courrier du centre* reported that "spectators draw back instinctively, fearing they'll be run over by the steel monster" (July 14, 1896, as quoted in Bottomore, 1999, p. 213). The immersive nature of the large screen and darkened room is thought to have created a "presence effect"—the illusion of non-mediation, the feeling of "being there" or being part of the diegetic action (Neuendorf & Lieberman, 2010).

Gunning (1990) has identified a dividing line between the early "cinema of attractions" (c. 1895–1905), when the simple phenomenon of moving images was enough to garner spectators' attention, and the subsequent creation of films that told increasingly complex stories—i.e., the development of real narrative structure in movies. With the latter would come the development of recognizable genres. Interestingly, the moving images of the "cinema of attractions" era had a bit in common with short videos on TikTok and other modern social media, featuring non-professionals engaging in sometimes clever activities. These moving images often featured regular people engaged in fairly commonplace daily activities.

After the Lumiere brothers demonstrated that audiences would indeed co-view a movie at a specified time, moving image exhibition moved back to the Magic Lantern norm of theatrical seating (Musser, 1991). Named for their low (five-cent) cost of admission, nickelodeons flourished from 1905–1915. Nickelodeons were set up both in full theaters and, for smaller municipalities, in converted storefronts. The latter typically seated fewer than 200—the patrons often sat on hard wooden chairs, with the screen hung on the back wall (Bowser, 1990). The 3,300-seat Strand Theater opened in 1914 in New York City, marking the end of the nickelodeon era and the beginning of an age of luxurious movie palaces, as nickelodeons were gradually replaced by such theaters showing full-length films in the 1920s. These palaces were architecturally ornate and exotic, but given their typical dual purposes of movie exhibition and live performances, the screens were often a small portion of the proscenium space (Allen, 2002). By 1920, there were more than 20,000 movie houses operating in the United States. Weekly attendance at movie theaters increased by 40% between 1920 and 1926, with attendance exceeding once per week for the average American (Koszarski, 1990).

During the Golden Age of Hollywood (c. 1920s–1950s), eight movie studios dominated American film production, distribution, and exhibition. In the congenial competition that characterized this oligopoly, genres became the norm, and certain genres were identified with particular studios that invested in their development (Mordden, 1988; Schatz, 1988a). What are now considered the classical US horror films were a series of lower-budget movies produced at a minor studio, Universal. Studio mogul Carl Laemmle gave his son "Junior" control over the production side of the studio for his 21st birthday, and Junior Laemmle predictably facilitated an emphasis on horror, a genre that to this day is particularly enjoyed by young males. The first wave of classical musicals came out in the 1930s, produced at one of the majors, RKO, with a focus on the dance skills of Fred Astaire and Ginger Rogers. A second wave of musicals was produced by the (Arthur) Freed Unit at MGM, spanning from *The Wizard of Oz* in 1939 to *The Light in the Piazza* in 1962, with dozens of huge hits in between, starring such performers from the MGM stable as Gene Kelly, Cyd Charisse, and Judy Garland.

Such sets or series of films were seen by the studios as good business practice, building on the success of proven forms and popular stars, promising audiences a reliable experience. Of course, the Golden Age studios didn't call their films "genres." That term was applied retrospectively after French scholars, writing for the film journal *Cahiers du Cinéma*, focused their analyses on popular movie types such as the western and the thriller (Hillier, 1986). In addition to also contributing the concept of auteur theory to the lexicon of film studies, these writer/critics demanded the recognition of and provided the first serious consideration of film genres. (An interesting note: These writers did much of their film watching at the Cinémathèque Française, which included screenings in stairwells during busy evenings, perhaps among the most creative modes of film exhibition (Richard, 2004).)

As the 20th century marched on, the history of the moving image is one of added options for viewing. The cinema faced competition with other media, initially radio, which appealed to audiences with audio stories and content, and eventually television. But theaters persisted and multiplied their options with the introduction of sound, drive-in theaters, widescreen formats and the curved screen of Cinerama that engage peripheral vision, 3-D, and surround sound, keeping audiences engaged throughout the years (Belton, 2002; Ijsselsteijn, 2003). A number of other less-successful multisensory adjuncts have been attempted: Olfactory interfaces such as Odorama and Smell-O-Vision (Ijsselsteijn, 2003), and tactile add-ons such as Percepto were introduced and discontinued in the 1950s. Their clear offspring are the 4-D installations at major amusement parks, such as Disney World and Universal Studios.

Multiplexes were built beginning in the 1960s, providing movie houses of varying capacity. Screens became both larger and smaller, as more screens were crammed into smaller spaces or older theaters were reconfigured to fit modern tastes. Seating was revamped for comfort to match or exceed the home environment, and XD (extreme digital cinema) screens extended from ceiling-to-floor and wall-to-wall. Expanding the screen size even further, the IMAX system was introduced circa 1970, using horizontal-feed 65 mm film to produce the largest projected film image to date. The IMAX corporation introduced the companion curved-screen OMNIMAX system in 1973 with its anamorphic 180° field of view.

Ultimately, moviegoing waned from its peak in the mid-20th century. Ironically, while the drive-in eventually nearly disappeared from most communities, there was at least a momentary resurgence in interest during the COVID-19 pandemic, when the "outdoor" movies allowed folks to feel safe in a public viewing space.

Pautz (2002) summarizes the dramatic shifts in movie attendance as the 20th century unfolded. In 1930, weekly cinema attendance was 80 million people, approximately 65% of the resident US population (Koszarski, 1990). However, by 2000, that figure was only 27.3 million people, which was a mere 9.7% of the US population (Pautz, 2002). Although factors like the Great Depression and advent of television in the 1950s are commonly credited with this decline, Pautz's own analysis conveys a more complicated picture. She notes the influence of increases in the number of films released, display screens, and households with TVs, as well as inflated admission prices.

According to the National Association of Theatre Owners (NATO), there were 5,477 indoor cinema sites and 321 drive-ins for a total of 5,798 theaters and 40,998 movie screens in 2020. As multiplexes proliferated, the number of movie theater sites dropped as the number of screens rose (NATO, 2020).

With the diffusion of television, a new type of screen was added to the viewing repertoire. In 1948, there were only 35,000 television sets and 37 stations broadcasting in the US (Elert, 2009). By 1950, there were 3,880,000 TV households, or 9% of American homes, increasing to 45.7 million TV households (87.1% of US homes) in 1960, to 59.6 million (95.2% of US homes) in 1970, and almost 73 million (98% of US homes) in 1978 ("United States – Households with Television," tradingeconomics.com). By 2015, US households averaged 2.3 television screens, with a whopping 31% of American households having more than four TV sets in 2019.

Television networks provided the competition needed to develop television genres, whose forms can be seen with the appearance of situation comedies reflecting urban life and later more rural settings (see Chapter 2). Television genres in some cases moved over from the medium of radio, particularly variety shows, but also comedies, musical talent shows, and talk shows.

In the 1950s and into the 1960s, it's television that expanded the number of screens available for viewing the moving image, but cable and eventually satellite technologies dramatically provided larger menus of film and television genres to select from. Satellite television grew out of the cable industry, since they were used to distribute TV programming to remote cable systems, but by 1980 satellite TV was well established in the US and Europe. The cable TV market is just under 50% worldwide, and the US has 1,775 TV stations, with 5,200 cable systems run by 660 operators that pass 90% of the population. By 2019, only 14% of US television homes had the capability to receive TV only "over the air" (Perez, 2019).

Starting in the 1970s, as physical media copies of film and television content on videotapes and discs became available, it wasn't just the appearance of a new set of screens that increased the menu of film and TV genres available, but other technologies that provided mobility, time-shifting, and control over viewing. The Internet and cell phone technology have unhooked the viewing experiences from stationary locations to mobile viewing and put more control into the hands of audiences. In some senses, Edison's plan for the individualized viewing of content (with his kinetoscope) has proved to be viable. Indeed, today's spectators are often "viewing alone."

Technology also contributes by allowing for manipulation of forms and altering content in a variety of ways and allowing audiences to also be creators. And creative artists and producers have responded by developing new film and television genres (see Chapter 4). Further, video gaming and computer gaming developed in a parallel fashion to film, with emergent genres (e.g., action, adventure, fantasy, horror, and science fiction), and ultimately a variety of delivery systems, with the arcade vs. home play with online options mirroring the choices for film (Skalski et al., 2008).

At the end of the day, there are three major ways that moving images reach audiences at home or some other mobile location—through wires (cable and Internet), over the airwaves or through satellite/cell phone signals, and through "hard copies" that can be kept, transferred, stored (e.g., discs, tapes). These are in addition to the original option, watching in a theater with all its amenities (which now may include recliner seating and meals and drinks served by waitstaff).

The competitive atmosphere generates numerous streaming services that invite "a la carte" viewing as well as subscriptions to legacy social and mass media services. This growth of options provides the volume necessary for development of different film, television and video genres as providers try to capture viewers with traditional genre forms but also innovative options. The research tracking winners and losers among providers misses the larger picture that the pie has grown ever-larger and is highly unstable as the roles of users/viewers and creators blur.

Audiences can buy home televisions that are limited in size only by their finances and wall space. The largest home theater setups, which only the wealthy can afford, might include Samsung's gigantic 292-inch television screens, but the merely affluent can enjoy screens of 146 inches, or 75-inch touch screens. In a competitive streak for bragging rights, a British company in 2014 created what was the world's biggest TV at the time—370 inches diagonally (at a cost of more than a million dollars), leapfrogging the previous champ by almost 20 feet but requiring the TV be put together by hand (NBC News, 2014). Across the more than a century of exhibition of moving images, we see a wide variety of technologies and systems introduced, and even with the abandonment of some, there is a steady increase in the range of options for film and television "screenings" (Waller, 2002).

The Nature of the Screen

A number of characteristics of the screen upon which spectators view the moving image are pertinent to critical thought about how important screen type is to access to and enjoyment of genres: The size of the screen, the location of the screen, and the means of access to content filling the screen.

Screen Size

Does size matter? The assumption from the early days of the moving image was, "the bigger, the better." Nickelodeons with their wall-sized screens replaced the small screens of the kinetoscope parlors. Movie palaces provided screens as tall as 30 feet. When television challenged the dominance of theatrical movies, screens in theaters got larger, via the introduction of widescreen formats that would dazzle the moviegoer, and would result in aspect ratios (e.g., 2.35:1 for CinemaScope starting in 1953) that were incompatible with the 4:3 format of TV (Belton, 1992; 1996; 2002). Such films would "never" be shown on television, it was thought. Of course, what followed were decades of format/aspect ratio wars, with letterboxing, pan and scan, pillarboxing, and other adaptations making images "fit" (see Neuendorf et al., 2009). And while home television screens grew larger during the late 20th century and early 21st century, other very tiny screens were added to the viewing toolset. Handheld viewing via a smartphone became a common option.

Studies of the impact of screen size have focused on two quite different areas: Learning outcomes, and perceived sense of presence (including immersion). For learning outcomes, researchers have looked at whether small screens impinge upon people's ability to read, comprehend, and/or organize information. The results have been mixed, with no clear signal that smaller screens are particularly disadvantaged. For example, Al Ghamdi et al. (2016) found that mobile phone screens increase reading time but do not reduce comprehension or retention of information.

In presence research, larger screens have generally been found to result in a greater sense of physical immersion. Some research on television screen size supports the notion that viewing on a larger screen results in a greater sense of physical movement, greater feelings of excitement and enjoyment, and more physiological arousal (Lombard et al., 2000). Bracken et al. (2003) found that larger images increased viewer sensation of presence. Rigby et al. (2016) discovered that very small screens, such as a 4.5" phone screen, lead to reduced immersion.

Perhaps the ultimate "screen size" might be that of the virtual reality system. In VR, viewers/players are immersed in a 360-degree "computer-generated world" (Slater, 2018). The study of VR genres is just beginning; Foxman et al. (2020) have identified the most commonly featured VR genres from the

Steam platform as Action (45%), Shooter (30%), Simulation (22%), Adventure (13%), and Puzzle (12%). Rodríguez-Fidalgo and Paíno-Ambrosio (2020) have identified the nascent "immersive social documentary" as a novel form or genre on the WITHIN VR platform.

Screen Location

To what extent do audiences prefer watching film and television content in the home, or on a personal device? Does some subset of the audience limit viewing of the panoramic blockbuster film with special effects to brick-and-mortar theaters but watch less "visual" or more "cerebral" films on laptops or cell phones? Foreshadowing Hollywood's shift away from theater releases during the COVID-19 pandemic, the horror thriller *Bird Box* was released directly to streaming in December of 2018. The film attracted an audience of 89 million viewers during the first month, ranking as Netflix's 2nd highest-grossing release (McClintock, 2019).

A *New York Times* analysis focuses on the reported "take over" of Hollywood by on-demand streaming services. "The digital forces that have reshaped music and television have been chipping away at cinema for a long time… The pandemic accelerated the disruption. Traditional studios like Paramount, Universal, Sony, Warner Bros. and Disney rerouted dozens of theatrical films to streaming services or released them simultaneously in theaters and online…The worry is that, as streaming services proliferate—more than 300 now operate in the United States, according to the consulting firm Parks Associates — theaters could become exclusively the land of superheroes, sequels and remakes" (Barnes & Sperling, 2022). This recognizes that theatrical exhibition is still particularly amenable to content that will capitalize on special visual effects and surround sound and/or will draw a reliably large audience to co-view because it is part of a franchise. At the same time, 2022 saw the first Best Picture Oscar granted to a streaming-only film (*CODA*, from Apple TV+).

Obviously, a main tradeoff seems to be theatrical viewing vs. home viewing (including the control offered by streaming). This will be explored further in the present chapter through a series of analyses of our studies.

Access to the Content on the Screen

The current viewing environment is competitive and complicated, and each new commercial opportunity—e.g., video on demand, subscription-based video, advertising-based video on demand—has its own strategy. With flexibility in viewing times and a competitive streaming environment, what is the relationship between viewing preferences and viewing patterns?

The streaming options are categorized according to the nature of the "VOD" (Video on Demand). TVOD, Transactional Video on Demand, follows the original model of "on demand" cable TV offerings—a given piece of content (a movie or a series) is paid for by the viewer for a one-time window of viewing (rental) or a more permanent purchase. SVOD, Subscription Video on Demand, involves the viewer paying a monthly fee, for which they are granted access to a playlist of content, both films and series (think Netflix). AVOD, Advertising-based Video on Demand, grants free or inexpensive access to content to the viewer, with the insertion of must-view commercials (e.g., Hulu, Tubi). Some services are a hybrid of VODs—e.g., Amazon Prime Video is an SVOD service that also has some content available only via TVOD. And HBO Max has both an SVOD service, and a somewhat cheaper AVOD subscription version. While the various VODs afford the audience member/consumer almost unfettered ability to gain access to content they seek, there are complex tradeoffs for the viewer in terms of money and time.

Adjuncts to the Screen, i.e., "Beyond the Screen"

Moving image products—movies and TV shows—have never existed in a vacuum exclusive of related messages and information such as promotions, source materials (e.g., a book from which a film is adapted, which might bring with it a fandom), and possible sequels and spin-offs. But in the digital and Internet age, additional adjuncts such as online fan groups, video game spin-offs of films, and websites devoted to movies and TV series may extend the narrative beyond the original content. As Creeber (2006) notes, "Knowing where a 'text' [i.e., film, series] starts and ends seems increasingly difficult to ascertain, a problem clearly heightened in the multi-media age" (p. 82).

Atkinson (2016) has considered "emerging cinema," characterized by an "expansion of cinematic and spectatorial spaces" (p. 1). Drawing on her earlier work on interactive cinema, Atkinson explores the concept of "omnidiegetic," the world of the materials, rhetorics, and discourses by creators that surround the main content (p. 7). A film's back-story, post-story, and parallel-story plot extensions might be provided. Paratextual content might engage audiences prior to the release of a film or TV program, as occurred with *The Hunger Games* (2012). A 100-clue puzzle was created and released 100 days before the film debut, which assured early engagement by participating audience members (Atkinson, 2016).

She also notes that certain genres have predominated in emerging cinema—sci-fi, detective murder mysteries, thrillers, and horror—while others such as comedy are notably absent. It is proposed that those genres that are associated with the gaze/narrative mode of spectatorship are more amenable to emerging cinema systems in which "opportunities for involved audience encounters are engendered and conspiratorial digressions are facilitated" (p. 208).

Beyond the primary screen experience, spectators may also employ "second screens," whereby smartphones, tablets, or computers are used "in synchronization and in subordination with" the primary screen experience

(Atkinson, 2016, p. 79). Deleted scenes, live chats, and other supporting materials might be available online via an app while viewing, inviting such possibilities as "social television" (Cunningham & Eastin, 2017; Gil de Zúñiga et al., 2015; Jenkins et al., 2013; Weimann-Saks et al., 2020).

Another interesting possibility that extends beyond the screen is the role of crowdsourcing for the creation and/or marketing of content. At Cleveland's Transition Studios, the editor/director of a religious documentary networked via social media for several years before completing his film, *American Gospel* (2018), sharing photos, clips, and updates on the progress of the film. Thus, an audience was already waiting for the doc when it was first released on TVOD. And, the expectations of both audience and filmmaker were met, because both sides had already engaged in a lengthy dialogue online. The type of "contract" between spectator and creator that is usually implicit (and supported by the predictability of genre content) can be explicit, as in cases such as this, made possible by social media.

A Note About Sound and Music

The emphasis in this chapter—and throughout this book—has been on narrative and visual aspects of image content, i.e., what is conveyed via a screen. Indeed, genres seem to be defined primarily by these aspects. But the critical role of sound and music should not be forgotten. Our studies have found that some genres bring with them audience expectations of certain types of music (e.g., musicals, horror films). And whether the audience knows it or not, some music scholars have contended that many genres have their own signature music conventions for non-diegetic scores, although with greater genre hybridity has come greater musical hybridity (Brownrigg, 2003; Neuendorf & Baumgartner, 2022). While key music scholars have ignored the delineation of film genre (e.g., Gorbman, 1987), other scholars have recently used computer analyses (supervised neural network modeling) to successfully predict film genres from technical characteristics of the musical scores (Ma et al., 2021).

Concerning sound more generally, Neuendorf and Lieberman (2010) laid out a history of sound and music for film, with a focus on the role of sound in evoking a sense of presence. Further, Skalski and Whitbred (2010) found that surround sound was more important than image quality (i.e., HD vs. non-HD) in predicting player enjoyment and sense of presence in a gaming study.

Audience Preferences for Viewing Film Genres—Theatrical, Home, and Mobile

Given the choices available to current audiences, what are the preferences for viewing various film genres? Are there optimal locations for viewing certain content, or do we want to watch moving images wherever we are? Waiting for an appointment, we may turn to the mobile phone or laptop to occupy ourselves with a film, TV program, or video available.

In our 2015 survey, we asked open-ended questions about what film genres respondents would like to see in the theater, and which they would like to see at home, with five entries possible for each question. Since these questions were open-ended, responses did not have to match the subsequent 31 film genres asked about. Still, the genres mentioned mapped well to our list.

Tables 6.1 and 6.2 list the top 20 genres mentioned for each of the two questions, with number of mentions shown for each of the respondents' five choices, with total mentions in the final column. The two tables show very few differences in preferred genres for in-theater and at-home viewing. Essentially, respondents are indicating their favorite genres, regardless of location of viewing. Comedies (a broad category, to be sure) are first by a wide margin, followed by action films, dramas, sci-fi, and horror. In sum, genre preferences seem to dominate over preference for mode of spectatorship.

We also asked respondents how they'd prefer to watch each of the 31 specific film genres—in a theater, at home on a TV, on a mobile device, or no preference (plus "don't care to watch anywhere"). Table 6.3 shows the results of these forced choices, ordered by preference to watch at home rather than

TABLE 6.1 Top 20 Genres Listed as Preferred to See in a Theater (Open-ended) (2015 Users Survey)

Film Genre Cited	First Choice	Second Choice	Third Choice	Fourth Choice	Fifth Choice	Total
1. Comedies	140	115	80	53	35	423
2. Action	118	64	56	44	23	305
3. Drama	51	79	77	62	35	304
4. Science fiction	50	35	37	29	28	179
5. Horror	42	21	29	33	28	153
6. Thriller, psychological thriller	7	27	37	23	27	121
7. Romance	9	33	18	28	29	117
8. Adventure	10	13	20	15	15	73
9. Animated	7	13	11	18	19	68
10. Documentary	4	7	15	13	27	66
11. Fantasy	12	14	12	15	9	62
12. Romantic comedies	13	10	17	4	12	56
13. Suspense	5	7	11	15	11	49
14. Mystery, murder mystery	3	7	12	10	2	34
15. Family, kids' film, children/family, clean movies	1	10	0	3	18	32
16. Action/adventure	11	8	4	4	0	27
17. Historical, historical drama	2	4	6	5	9	26
18. Foreign films, independent/foreign	2	3	5	7	6	23
19. Independent, indie films	6	3	5	6	3	23
20. Chick flicks	1	2	1	4	3	11

TABLE 6.2 Top 20 Genres Listed as Preferred to See at Home (Open-ended) (2015 Users Survey)

Film Genre Cited	First Choice	Second Choice	Third Choice	Fourth Choice	Fifth Choice	Total
1. Comedy	158	88	74	60	45	425
2. Action	80	82	54	66	33	315
3. Drama	51	70	85	49	37	292
4. Science fiction	49	41	32	33	28	183
5. Horror	39	28	31	21	31	150
6. Romance, love stories	7	33	20	30	31	121
7. Thriller, psychological thriller	13	23	30	22	21	109
8. Documentary	17	23	14	20	28	102
9. Animated	9	16	11	19	18	73
10. Family, kid friendly, family oriented	13	13	15	9	19	69
11. Adventure	7	7	14	17	13	58
12. Fantasy	7	14	15	9	13	58
13. Romantic comedy	12	13	10	8	8	51
14. Suspense	4	6	14	11	7	42
15. Mystery, murder mystery	5	8	13	8	4	38
16. Historical, period movies	4	6	9	4	5	28
17. Foreign films, British films	4	6	5	8	4	27
18. Action adventure	9	7	6	4	0	26
19. Independent, indie, art	4	7	6	4	5	26
20. Biography, biopic	0	3	5	3	2	13

in a theater (represented in the final column in the table, the difference in percentages for the two choices). Also included are average ages for those selecting each preference.

As the pattern shows, there is an overwhelming consensus that home is the best place to watch most film genres, and mobile devices are the "last resort." But there also are apparent preferences among some segments of the audience for viewing some film genres in theaters. And that pattern provides empirical support for what we anticipated—that it's best to view content like epics, adventure films, action films, and superhero films on a big screen in the company of others. These four genres are the last four listed in Table 6.3, each showing at least a slim preference overall by respondents for watching in the theater. Each of the four also enjoys at least a 15% segment of respondents who prefer theatrical viewing. Additional genres also have a substantial audience segment reporting a preference for in-theater viewing: Fantasy films (14.2%), science fiction films (14.0%), war films (10.7%), and musicals (10.2%).

These data provide contemporary verification of the preference for watching "blockbusters" and action on the big screen as audiences have returned to moviegoing outside the home as pandemic constraints lift. Superhero films were back to 75% of pre-pandemic levels, while adult character-driven genres were down 66% to 75% from normal and family films were off 50%, according

TABLE 6.3 Preferences for Viewing Film Genres, Including Mean Ages (2015 Users Survey)

Film Genre	Prefer to Watch in a Theater	Prefer to Watch at Home on a TV	Prefer to Watch on a Mobile Device	Makes no Difference, will Watch Anywhere	Don't Care to Watch Anywhere	Home over Theater
Documentary films	3.3% Av. age: 31.9	36.1% 35.4	2.8% 35.1	16.6% 35.0	9.0% 32.3 ns	32.8%
Biographical films	3.7% 32.4	29.3% 36.1	2.0% 34.0	20.6% 35.0	12.2% 31.6 F=2.0a	25.6%
Detective films	5.3% 30.7	28.9% 37.0	2.0% 30.4	21.0% 34.0	10.5% 32.5 F=3.5★★	23.6%
Chick flicks	4.4% 32.5	25.2% 34.6	1.7% 31.4	19.9% 34.9	16.6% 35.4 ns	20.8%
Comedy films	9.2% 31.8	29.5% 35.3	1.5% 38.1	23.6% 35.6	4.1% 31.3 ns	20.3%
Foreign films	4.2% 32.7	24.1% 32.8	1.5% 37.8	11.8% 33.0	26.2% 37.3 F=3.4★★	19.9%
Romantic comedies	5.7% 32.1	25.4% 35.6	2.8% 30.7	22.5% 35.3	11.4% 33.8 ns	19.7%
Historical films	6.8% 35.5	26.5% 35.6	1.1% 40.3	20.8% 35.2	12.5% 31.0 F=2.5★	19.7%
Mystery/Suspense films	8.7% 31.5	28.0% 36.4	1.5% 35.9	23.6% 34.4	6.1% 32.3 F=2.1a	19.3%
Romantic dramas	5.5% 33.9	24.7% 36.0	2.6% 31.7	21.7% 34.5	13.3% 33.3 ns	19.2%
Drama films	7.5% 31.3	26.2% 36.0	1.8% 33.3	24.5% 35.4	7.7% 31.5 F=2.3a	18.7%
Slapstick films	2.6% 28.9	19.5% 34.8	2.8% 27.3	14.7% 34.5	28.2% 36.0 F=2.9★	16.9%
Dark comedy films	5.0% 33.0	21.7% 34.6	2.4% 35.2	20.3% 33.9	27.2% 36.1 ns	16.7%

(Continued)

TABLE 6.3 Preferences for Viewing Film Genres, Including Mean Ages (2015 Users Survey) (*Continued*)

Film Genre	Prefer to Watch in a Theater	Prefer to Watch at Home on a TV	Prefer to Watch on a Mobile Device	Makes no Difference, will Watch Anywhere	Don't Care to Watch Anywhere	Home over Theater
Westerns	4.8%	21.0%	2.2%	10.7%	29.1%	16.2%
	31.2	37.8	33.8	36.9	32.3 F=5.0★★★	
Animated films	9.0%	24.5%	2.6%	22.8%	8.8%	15.5%
	32.6	34.7	32.2	34.6	37.6 ns	
Mockumentaries	2.2%	17.5%	2.2%	13.6%	32.2%	15.3%
	29.5	32.1	33.8	35.5	36.2 F=2.7★	
Film parodies	4.1%	18.6%	2.4%	17.5%	25.2%	14.5%
	29.9	33.7	33.2	33.8	36.9 F=2.6★	
Sports films	5.5%	19.3%	1.5%	16.9%	24.5%	13.8%
	31.4	36.4	30.1	34.6	34.4 ns	
Pornography	1.3%	14.7%	9.2%	5.7%	36.8%	13.4%
	29.3	32.5	30.3	32.9	37.1 F=5.4★★★	
Horror films	8.5%	21.7%	1.3%	12.0%	24.3%	13.2%
	30.6	33.2	33.0	33.7	38.0 F=5.0★★★	
Gangster films	6.6%	19.0%	2.0%	16.9%	23.2%	12.4%
	31.3	36.9	33.1	34.0	34.5 ns	
Film noir films	4.1%	15.1%	1.5%	12.2%	35.0%	11.0%
	32.8	33.4	37.6	33.1	35.9 ns	
War films	10.9%	21.7%	0.9%	16.8%	17.5%	10.8%
	31.5	37.2	38.2	33.0	35.0 F=3.2★	
Samurai films	5.5%	16.0%	1.1%	13.1%	32.0%	10.5%
	31.8	33.3	30.8	33.3	36.6 F=2.4a	
Slasher films	5.9%	14.0%	1.5%	11.4%	35.0%	8.1%
	32.8	31.9	37.4	31.7	37.0 F=4.5★★	

(*Continued*)

TABLE 6.3 Preferences for Viewing Film Genres, Including Mean Ages (2015 Users Survey) (*Continued*)

Film Genre	Prefer to Watch in a Theater	Prefer to Watch at Home on a TV	Prefer to Watch on a Mobile Device	Makes no Difference, will Watch Anywhere	Don't Care to Watch Anywhere	Home over Theater
Science fiction films	14.0%	21.4%	2.8%	17.9%	11.8%	7.4%
	33.1	35.7	29.6	34.9	35.5 ns	
Musicals	10.7%	18.0%	1.3%	13.3%	24.5%	7.3%
	32.8	36.1	28.3	34.5	34.8 ns	
Fantasy films	14.2%	19.9%	2.0%	19.7%	12.0%	5.7%
	33.0	36.6	39.0	33.2	35.4 F=2.1[a]	
Epic films	18.0%	17.7%	1.5%	17.3%	13.3%	-0.3%
	34.8	37.0	30.2	33.6	33.4 ns	
Adventure films	21.7%	20.6%	0.9%	20.1%	4.4%	-1.1%
	33.8	36.8	36.2	34.3	30.7 ns	
Action films	21.9%	20.6%	1.5%	19.7%	4.1%	-1.3%
	32.4	36.5	40.3	35.2	33.3 F=2.4[a]	
Superhero films	19.7%	18.2%	0.9%	17.1%	11.8%	-1.5%
	32.9	36.3	38.4	33.7	36.3 ns	

Note: n =368; [a] .05<*p*<.10; **p*<.05; ***p*<.01; ****p*<.001.

to an Associated Press dispatch (Coyle, 2021). This was attributed to pandemic level concerns among older adults, while younger viewers attracted to these genres returned to the theater for viewing their favorite genres.

The ages reported in Table 6.3 show some interesting patterns. Significant differences in age between the five types of responses are shown, tested via single-factor ANOVAs. Generally, those who report preferring to watch a genre in the theater are younger, while those preferring to watch at home tend to be older. In terms of those preferring to watch on a mobile device (which is typically only 1-3% of respondents), the age of the group varies substantially across the genres.

In order to examine the most recent evidence we have regarding theatrical vs. home viewing preferences, we examined frequency of viewing data from the 2021 Creators Survey and the 2021–22 Young Creators Survey. Although the findings do not address specific genres, they afford us a snapshot of who is going out to see films in the theater, who is watching films on a tablet or other hand-held device, and who is streaming movies on a television at home. Further, a "streaming over theatrical movie viewing" indicator was calculated by subtracting each respondent's frequency of going out to see a film at the theater from their reported frequency of streaming a movie at home.

We conducted correlational analyses between these viewership measures and demographics/social categories: Age, gender, education, race, income, and political philosophy (a five-point response scale from 1 = strong conservative to 5 = strong liberal). We found theatrical filmgoing to be significantly related to younger age, higher education, and a less liberal political orientation (in the 2021 Creators Survey). Theatrical filmgoing is related to identifying as Nonwhite and having a lower household income, along with a near-significant tendency to be male, among the 2021–22 Young Creators.

Watching films on a personal device is significantly related to younger age and higher education in the 2021 Creators Survey, and with younger age, being male, and, to a near-significant level, identifying as Nonwhite in the 2021–22 Young Creators Survey. Streaming movies at home on a TV is related to younger age, higher education, and to a lesser extent, greater household income in the 2021 Creators Survey, and, to a near-significant level, to being female and identifying as White in the 2021–22 Young Creators Survey.

The difference score "streaming over theatrical movie viewing," an indicator of a tendency to stream movies rather than go out to the theater for movies, is related to older age, a more liberal political philosophy, and, at a near-significant level, to lesser education in the 2021 Creators sample. In the 2021–22 Young Creators sample, this tendency is related to being female, identifying as White, and having a greater household income.

Content Trumps Form

Much of the discussion in this chapter has examined the nature of the screen by which spectators access the moving image, and therefore film and television genres. Across analyses, we see a tendency for the content—i.e., the genre—to be more important to the viewers than the mode of access and viewership. We see this in the lack of difference between Tables 6.1 and 6.2. Spectators report strong preferences for certain genres, regardless of the delivery mode.

Our own team has encountered this "content trumps form" theme in a range of research settings in the past. Neuendorf et al. (2012), in an experiment manipulating the delivery system of a true story about a young woman whose mother had been incarcerated, found that the modality of delivery—written transcript, audio-only narration, or video documentary—mattered much less than the sheer reception of the story (compared to a control group). Lieberman et al. (2009) found that the specific content (i.e., episode) of a sitcom determined the effectiveness of the addition of a laugh track. One study comparing 3-D and 2-D versions of the same film (*Spy Kids 3-D: Game Over*, 2003) failed to confirm greater sensations of spatial presence in the 3-D version (Bracken et al., 2004). Bracken et al. (2003) found that screen size did not relate to source credibility consistently, positing that differences between study findings may have been based on content type rather than the size of the image. In all cases, content "trumped" form, in a sense (see also Neuendorf, Skalski, et al., 2012). And in a video game study, Skalski and Whitbred (2010) found that surround sound was more important than image quality (i.e., HD vs. non-HD) in predicting player enjoyment and sense of presence, again calling into question the primacy of visual technical qualities of the moving image.

A Concluding Note

The present chapter begins by profiling the diffusion of variegated options available to audiences over the past century; this includes growth in the number of films and series, channels/streaming platforms, international interplay (e.g., *Squid Game* (2021), *Parasite* (2019), *Drive My Car* (2021)), theater screens (despite dwindling locations), online options for spectatorship, and for creation. We analyzed data from our studies to see how the nature of the screen and locations impacted preferences for viewing different genres. And the answer is very clear—that content, or genre preferences, trumps the location, and size of the screen available for viewing. As technology evolves and generations pass, we'll need to periodically revisit this question and pose more complicated questions about audiences' relationship with genres and the moving image, as both viewers and creators.

7

DEVELOPING CONTENT THEORY FOR MOVING IMAGES

How do film and television genres emerge in the creative process? In earlier literatures, film scholars argued whether films are "authored" by directors or, taking a more macro view, whether genres are the result of an interactive process over time between creative producers and audiences who react to those creations. As the moving image has developed into a more popular instrument for expression by a broader spectrum of creative producers—and by people in general—we need to bring the talents of a variety of researchers to bear on what are likely rapidly changing targets: the modern video of online streaming, film and television genres crossing national and cultural boundaries, and moving images on mobile platforms. Here we add the theoretical views of empirical scholars in communication to the dialogue, in the hopes of providing a linkage between the *arts and (social) sciences* underpinning our understandings of the moving image.

As discussed in Chapters 1 and 2, the expectations of audiences are a central factor in these discussions. When a creative product succeeds commercially with audiences, it has a feedback "loop" into this process. Genre development generally has been described as proceeding through four stages: Primitive, classical, revisionist, and parodic (Giannetti & Eyman, 2010). Later in this chapter, we present a fifth stage—Genre-bending, the combination of elements from differing genres. This includes both genre hybridity, the mixing and blending of genres that has received attention in both the scholarly and popular literature, and trope appropriation, the transgressive use of specific genre tropes to create novel narrative meaning by drawing on genre-based conventions, in general a more recent phenomenon.

Although individual members of film and television audiences develop their own expectations based on personal experiences and tastes, collectively

DOI: 10.4324/9781003264828-7

audiences differentiate among genres with their decision-making. This chapter will examine the number and types of references used by audiences to describe each film and television genre included in the datasets. Where is there genre consensus and clarity, and where are these lacking? We also consider how these contents are related to audience viewing patterns. Furthermore, are those film and television genres with clear audience expectations also those generating the highest ratings on viewing preferences? Much of this analysis will take place at the macro level of genre using the expectations of audiences captured in our surveys.

Several concepts help us to understand the genre development process through time. Our sample of audience expectations produced more than 20,000 "votes" for what constitutes the various film and television genres, in addition to thousands more decisions where audiences claimed they didn't know, weren't familiar with, or didn't like or watch particular genres. These data points allow us to determine whether the following concepts are sustained empirically and have utility in our understanding of the moving image: core genre characteristics, genre specific ingredients, universal donors, genre affinity, genre-bending, genre hybridity, and trope appropriation. We will use the datasets to examine these concepts in this chapter.

Describing Creative Processes

While film scholars can argue whether films are "authored" by directors or represent forms and structures developed over time, it makes sense as communication scholars to focus on how the message—film and television genres—is the product of an interactive process between creative producers and audiences who process and react to those creations. When applying symbolic interaction theory to TV drama, Abelman and Atkin (2011) cast communication as an interaction between content creators and audiences. For these symbols to be effective, there must be a shared meaning among all; in particular:

> The concept of *internal reality* pertains to the institutional environment of the television industry and the creative climate in which the owners and creators of television programming reside. Because commercial television programming is the end product of corporate decisions, the creative process, and financial considerations, many of the functions, premises, and structures of programs are formed within this reality. Long established programming conventions, well-defined artistic guidelines, and set budgets and barriers for creative expression emerge from this realm, and the artisans in the television industry are well schooled in them. Much of what we see on television is guided or mandated by the internal reality in which members of the television industry exist.
>
> *(p. 36)*

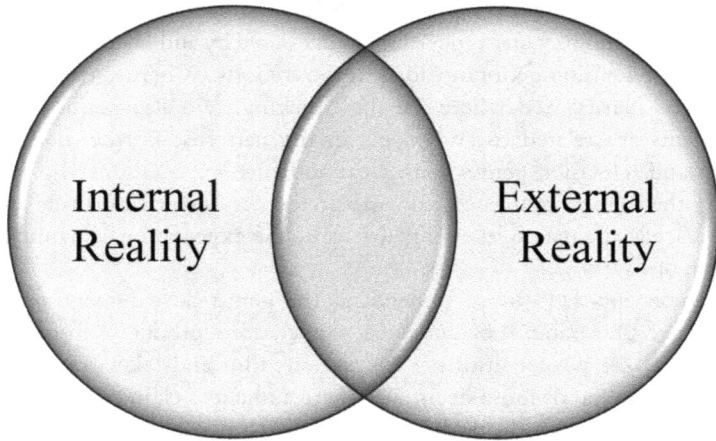

- Plot Conventions
- Conventional Settings and Trappings
- Stock Characters
- Conventional Dramatic Formats
- Conventional Narrative Structures
- Genre Tropes
- Sound
- Mise en Scène
- Time Frames
- Production Technology/Cinematography
- Institutional Influences

- Norms of Society
- Domestic Cultural Values
- Overseas Market Constraints
- Economic Factors
- Fandom
- Regulatory Constraints
- Rites and Rituals
- Media Consumption Trends
- Dominant Ideologies
- Cultural Fads and Fashions
- Audience Media Literacy

FIGURE 7.1 The Symbolic Interaction of TV and Film Content

The interaction occurs when this internal reality draws from the external reality (depicted in Figure 7.1)—which circumscribes the overlap between creators and audiences—forming a language of film and television that is derived from both an internal reality and external reality.

The authors note that the artistry of making such a creative enterprise is the creation of verisimilitude, the appearance of being true or real: "This is achieved by borrowing symbols and their shared meanings from the realm of the audience—the *external reality*" (p. 37). The shared meaning is achieved when participants perceive a symbol in the same way and attach their meaning to it. Television thus allows symbolic interaction to occur between a massive number of participants over large distances. A priori genre definitions of literary and film scholars have focused on fictional narratives, which are not applicable to mixtures of narrative and nonnarrative structures or mixes of news magazines and sitcoms or blends of soap operas and talk shows, dramatized true-story crime shows or reality television programs. Mittell (2004) notes that, unlike film, television genres "resist[s] clear authorial definition, with an episodic style of programming and production practices that are even more collaborative than for film" (p. xiii). Still, "core" features of a genre persist, and audiences and critics alike need a vocabulary to discuss the moving images offered in today's complex environment.

Biocca (1991) discusses how media professionals use forms, conventions, and structures that make media "user friendly," thus assisting audiences by guiding and limiting the types of inferences they may make. When audiences confront such "new" forms of film or TV, they use cues introducing the content to make inferences about the setting, topic, and structure, activating inferences based on their past viewing experiences. As more examples of a new form appear, audiences develop clearer and stronger expectations that direct their viewing and selection. Creative professionals in communication respond as well to audiences and their peers, copying, changing, and evolving genres that solidify a core "definition" or blurring the boundaries with others.

Over time, film and television genres represent successful compromises between creative producers (the collection of encoders—writers, directors, producers) and public expectations. New genres generally represent combinations of older genres, or subtle changes in the elements associated with an existing one (Wood, 2004). Genres from the past appear new when recast with current problems, language and popular culture (White, 1985). This processing activity by audiences ultimately must be linked to the uses and gratifications that are delivered through the viewing and sought in subsequent viewing across time; thus, content and form are linked to the sustaining functions of the genre (see Chapter 3). Minnebo (1999) illustrates the interaction between communicator and receiver in the case of reality television. Beliefs that people have about media are important in expectancy value theory for gratifications research (Palmgreen & Rayburn, 1985), where gratifications are related to beliefs about media attributes.

When audiences react in particular ways to film and television genres, their feedback to media professionals discourages or supports the use of particular conventions, styles or emphasis on particular contents. Since film producers and other creators tend to rely on symbols that the widest audience will understand and favor with subsequent patronage, a genre becomes established over time as audiences and producers react to each other. Certainly, film producers with expressive visions can follow their own drummer, but without supportive audience reactions, the path followed is likely to be a short one (see discussion in Jeffres, 1994).

A Case Example—Reality TV Genre

The emergence of a contemporary television genre provides an opportunity to ascertain audience expectations given more limited experience with the novel form. In a study conducted not long after the "reality TV" genre emerged after a hiatus of a couple decades, Jeffres et al. (2011) explored models predicting audience enjoyment of the then-relatively new genre, "reality TV." The original version of reality TV that emerged in the late 1970s featured people engaging in activities that were novel or trying to set records (e.g., *Real People* (1979–1983)) (Rushdie, 2001). That genre disappeared and differs from the one that appeared under the same label with the advent of *Survivor*, which was so successful that imitators followed and a new genre began to evolve.

The reality TV genre actually has roots in a tradition of realism dating to the 1890s, when the Lumiere brothers made films like *Train Arriving at La Ciotat*. As Giannetti (2011) notes, realistic films try to reproduce the surface reality with a minimum of distortion; the audience rarely notices production styles in realistic fare, as the artist instead concentrates on what is being shown rather than how it is manipulated. The reality TV programs that emerged in the 1990s kept the ingredients of exotic locales and competition of a cast of "real people," or non-actors—*The Amazing Race* (2001-), *Big Brother* (2000-), *The Apprentice* (2004–2017). A study that surveyed largely those in the target audience for reality television programs (ages 18–30) produced the following characteristics in a collective definition via open-ended responses (Jeffres et al., 2011):

- Competition—for participation in a game of attrition, for "end-game" prizes.
- Unscripted but planned behavior—participants follow rules but their words are not scripted in the sense that "fictional" media are.
- Participants are non-actors—most participants are drawn from a pool of "real" people considered by producers. In some versions all participants are youthful, to be consistent with the program competitive theme (e.g., "Average Joe"), but an effort toward diversity is achieved on most, allowing for more of the audience to find targets of identification.

Jeffres et al. (2011) offered an additional characteristic not reliably mentioned by survey respondents:

- Limited rather than open-ended time frames—although the length of programs varies, each is a limited run, generally a matter of weeks or months. This commits less time on the part of audiences, allows for non-actors to participate without disrupting their lives inordinately, and it allows for a tempo that sustains novelty in competition and relationships. This also means that "seasons" are self-contained, with subsequent "seasons" featuring new participants, new locales, and new activities and rewards.

Additional features of reality TV have been offered by Baruh (2009), who via content analysis of 15 programs identified characteristics that differentiate among them: private vs. public setting, fly on the wall shooting style, disclosure of personal information, negative vs. positive emotions, gossip, intimate touching, and nudity. Certainly, reality TV programs have manifested such characteristics to different degrees, and draw on different historical genre origins that may have enhanced spectators' immediate familiarity with the genre. The "fly on the wall" type of program (e.g., *Duck Dynasty* (2012–17), *Storm Chasers* (2007–12)) draws from both direct cinema documentary shooting style and soap opera sensibility. Similarly, the setup show (e.g., *Big Brother* (2000-)) draws from the same source types, but begins with a situation forced upon the subjects by the producers—e.g., strangers living together. These programs have been called "docusoaps" (Scharrer & Blackburn, 2018), in recognition of their derivation from documentaries and soap operas. The competition archetype (e.g., *Dancing with the Stars* (2005-), *Top Chef* (2006-)) has its origins in game shows. The expert intervention archetype (e.g., *Property Brothers* (2011-), *Queer Eye* (2018-)) is an offshoot of self-help media and perhaps educational television. The very specific subcategory of reality dating shows (e.g., *The Bachelor* (2002-)) have been characterized as having features of both fly on the wall shooting and competition basis (Ferris et al., 2007). According to Groombridge (2002; see also Hall, 2005), all of these types tend to rely on a reciprocal relationship between the voyeuristic needs of the viewers and the exhibitionism of program subjects.

In our 2015 survey of audience expectations, we can see that some of these characteristics of reality television cited above in the early stages of this genre's development are found among the most popular references made. The top five references included talent competition and context theme, the non-scripted nature of the show, as well as references to drama and fighting (see Chapter 2). Since its inception, the reality television genre has "spread its roots in every conceivable direction" from its germinating seed, *Survivor* (1997-), a "shrewd combination of quiz show, adventure program, and soap opera elements" (Rose, 2003, p. 3). So the data show genre hybridity in the birth of one of the most popular moving image genres of the past 30 years

Uses and Gratifications

Although Uses and Gratifications Theory (see Chapter 3) is prominent in effects studies, the functional theory also can be used to explain media behaviors. Audiences thus engage in media use for particular uses and gratifications derived (Katz et al., 1974). Numerous scholars have linked uses and gratifications to specific television genres: reality TV (Aubrey et al., 2012; Papacharissi & Mendelson, 2007); TV news (Henningham, 1985; Lin, 1996; Wicks, 1989); soap operas (Livingstone, 1988), music videos (Brown et al., 1986); and TV sports programming (Duncan & Brummett, 1989).

Jeffres et al. (2011) argued that the uses and gratifications literature has not been sufficient in predicting audience media behavior patterns because of the rather stationary level of theorizing. Hence they moved down from the major and more general dimensions (e.g., enjoyment) to more specific functions tied to the genre structure, in particular parasocial communication—the illusion by audience members that they are engaged in a relationship with someone in the program (Horton & Wohl, 1956; Rubin & McHugh, 1987)—with non-actors with whom they can identify, as opposed to unknown celebrities where there is an enormous status gap. A second explanatory concept examined was "presence," where audiences view the viewing as a non-mediated experience or as an illusion of nonmediation (Lombard & Ditton, 1997). Employing many TV genres, Jeffres et al. (2011) found enjoyment of the reality TV genre was positively related to more uses and gratifications dimensions than any of the more established genres, but it is the addition of the more focused, parasocial uses and gratifications that allow us to more accurately gauge our target—enjoyment of reality TV programming.

People's media behavior patterns are sustained because of the uses derived and the gratifications experienced. Thus, if a television program no longer provides the excitement, escape, or stimulation sought, the viewing pattern is likely to be extinguished over time. A variety of reasons may occur to increase or decrease the importance of various uses and gratifications.

Data reported here reveal that audiences repeatedly cited particular uses and gratifications as expectations in their definitions of both film and television genres. In our 2015 survey, we asked how important six uses and gratifications were for going out to see films in a theater. Table 7.1 shows correlations between how important each gratification is linked with how often respondents go out to see films and preferences for particular genres.

Two of the most general uses and gratifications refer to general entertainment—just wanting to be entertained or to waste time. Those who say just wanting to be entertained is more important for going out to see films in a theater are more frequent viewers of horror, science fiction, action, and animated films, as well as dark comedies, film parodies, fantasy, superhero, and war films. Those who say wanting to waste time or not having anything to do motivates them to go out to see films in a theater are more frequent filmgoers of westerns, horror films, film noir, dark comedies, film parodies, slasher films, mockumentaries, slapstick films, samurai films, and sports. But these audiences are less likely to be frequent viewers of dramas.

Those who express the need for more emotional gratification as a motivating force for filmgoing more often seek out musicals. But these audiences also favor darker genres—film noir, film comedies, film parodies, slasher films, mockumentaries, slapstick films, and samurai films.

TABLE 7.1 Correlations of Uses and Gratifications for Going Out to See Films in the Theater and Film Genre Viewing (2015 Users Survey)

Just Want to Be Entertained	Just want to Waste Time, Have Nothing to Do	Feel Down and Need Cheering Up	Want to See a Particular Actor	Want to See a Particular Type of Film	Want to Be with Friends
Horror .13★ Sci-fi .10#	Western .09# Horror .15★★	Musical .13★	Musical .14★★	Horror .11★ Sci-fi .09#	Musical .20★★★
	Film noir .17★★	Film noir .16★★	Detective .16★★ Comedy .12★	Comedy .10#	Detective .10★ Comedy .17★★★
Action .09# Animated .10★			Action .12★ Mystery/suspense .14★★	Action .10#	Action .12★ Animated .14★★ Mystery/suspense .10★
Dark comedy .09#	Dark comedy .12★	Dark comedy .16★★			
Parody .12★	Parody .15★★ Slasher .22★★★ Mockumentaries .19★★★	Parody .18★★★ Slasher .14★★ Mockumentaries .18★★★	Parody .12★ Slasher .13★	Slasher .12★	
	Slapstick .18★★★ Drama -.10#	Slapstick .16★★	Chick flicks .17★★ Slapstick .18★★★ Drama .15★★	Slapstick .10#	Chick flick .22★★★ Slapstick .13★ Drama .09#
Fantasy .12★			Fantasy .11★ Adventure .13★	Fantasy .10# Adventure .09# Foreign .10#	
	Samurai .14★★	Samurai .10★	Romantic drama .13★ Romantic comedy .15★ Gangster .13★	Samurai .10#	Romantic drama .18★★★ Romantic comedy .20★★
Superhero .18★★★ War .13★	Sports -.10#		Sports .16★★ Superhero .13★ War .10★	Sports .09# Historical .09# Superhero .17★★	Sports .11★

Note: #.05<p<.10; ★p<.05; ★★p<.01; ★★★p<.001

Specific actors, often associated with particular genres, are motivating factors for seekers of the longest list of genres in the table—e.g., musicals, detective films, comedies, action films, and 14 more genres. Those who say seeking a particular genre is a major reason for going out to see films are more likely to be frequent viewers of horror films, science fiction, comedies, action films, slasher and slapstick films, fantasy films, adventure films, foreign films, samurai films, sports films, historical films, and superhero films. Interestingly, two film genres are found only in the fifth column, suggesting that those who go out more often to see historical films and foreign films are fans of the genres themselves.

Lastly, when the social function of filmgoing is strongest, people are attracted more often to see musicals, comedies, chick flicks, and romantic dramas and comedies—likely preferred in a dating context. But these socially motivated viewers also favor animated films (family fare), detective films, action films, mystery/suspense films, dramas, and sports films.

If we look at the specific uses and gratifications that appear among the most frequent references in audience expectations (see Chapter 2), we see genres where such gratifying outcomes are certainly expected. Thus, for example, musicals are expected to be boring to many filmgoers (it's a frequent expectation), but not those who feel a need to be cheered up or want to be with friends, as suggested by Table 7.1. One of the most frequent expectations for detective and for mystery films is feeling suspense or intrigue, and we see in Table 7.1 that both genres are more frequently sought out by those who go out to films to see particular actors or be with friends. Comedies seem to fulfill a host of gratifications, with comedies in one form or another (dark, romantic, slapstick, or mere comedy) appearing with each motivating gratification in Table 7.1; one of the defining references to comedy films is expecting to laugh during viewing. Three film genres are absent from the table—documentaries, biographies, and epic films. If we had included a use or gratification associated with a "cognitive need," such as need to be mentally challenged, or wanted to know more about some topic, documentaries and biographies might have filled the bill.

The study being reported here is limited to data collected on audiences, and does not include data on activities of the creative people who produce films or television programs. But we can achieve some sense of genre development by examining comparisons among genres based on audience perceptions, and preferences, and the degree of consensus in defining genres.

Genre Consensus and Clarity

When respondents to the 2015 survey offered their expectations of specific genres, their responses were catalogued via thematic analysis using a codebook that spans dozens of pages and covers a range of categories that include not only the conventions, techniques, and subject matter used by scholars to define genres but also expectations about how respondents would react, be affected, or otherwise respond.

Examining these expectations, we can determine the extent to which there is a consensus on defining elements that reflect these categories. Thus, considering all the categories available, when a larger share of expectations is captured by the fewest defining elements, there is greater audience clarity on what constitutes a genre. When there is little consensus and expectations are dispersed across more categories, then a genre is more broadly defined.

In our study, twelve referential categories are broken down further into dozens of sub-categories that capture more specific agreement or disagreement among respondents in their expectations for film and television genres. Tables 7.2 and 7.3 capture this level of analysis. Thus, we see, for example, that the musical film genre generated 553 references in expectations spread over 74 specific categories, while animated films generated 586 references in expectations spread over 149 different sub-categories.

If we look at the single category with the most expectations, and the top three categories in popularity, we derive some measure of audience agreement in their expectations for the different genres. We find for musicals that almost 44% of film expectations are represented by a single category, and almost 70% by the top three categories. That's a large measure of agreement—not surprisingly, musical behaviors almost by definition come to mind by our respondents when expecting the musical. In contrast, for animated films, the single category capturing the most expectations only rises to 4.3% of references and the top three to only 16.4%. Musicals are the film genre with the highest agreement on audience expectations, followed by horror films, slasher films, foreign films, comedies, and westerns.

Not surprisingly, there seems to be the least agreement for film genres that are most ill defined by audiences—film noir (lots of don't know and don't watch responses), and those so popular in scope that expectations lead in different directions, that is, dramas.

We see a much different pattern for television genres, where the category with the highest percentage of references ranged from 5.8% for dramas to 12.5% for situation comedies and animal/nature shows, with a high level of agreement for television genres using the top three categories. Interestingly, television dramas generated the least consensus.

Genre Reactions

Clearly, one viewer's delight in watching a genre will be shared by many but also matched with distaste or avoidance by other viewers. Thus, viewers' expectations of specific genres in terms of reactions is a personal matter of taste. In addition, the survey instrument has measures of how often

TABLE 7.2 Audience Agreement on Expectations for Film Genres (2015 Users Survey)

Film Genres	Total References	No. of Different References	Category with Highest % of References	% in Top 3 Categories
Musical	553	74	44.4%	69.6%
Western	601	104	16.3%	46.9%
Horror	598	100	25.9%	44.8%
Sci-fi	565	122	18.4%	37.0%
Detective	582	108	17.5%	37.5%
Comedy	575	118	22.8%	42.4%
Film noir#	501	151	22.9%	36.3%
Documentary	561	142	8.2%	21.4%
Action	650	114	16.2%	32.2%
Animated	586	149	4.3%	16.4%
Mystery	545	123	8.1%	23.5%
Dark comedy	527	146	7.4%	26.4%
Biography	529	136	9.6%	19.1%
Parodies	511	113	14.9%	30.1%
Slasher	589	100	30.6%	42.6%
Mockumentary	481	125	9.8%	24.1%
Chick flick	579	143	15.0%	28.5%
Slapstick	501	113	12.2%	29.7%
Drama	572	157	7.7%	17.1%
Fantasy	555	154	9.2%	22.3%
Adventure	560	153	11.3%	22.0%
Foreign	528	117	28.6%	41.3%
Romantic drama	587	134	14.0%	31.0%
Romantic comedy	644	139	11.8%	30.9%
Gangster	679	134	19.6%	32.8%
Samurai	621	121	25.3%	35.4%
Epics	551	163	7.8%	20.1%
Sports	579	143	11.1%	25.4%
Historical	571	165	8.2%	16.5%
Superhero	642	144	13.6%	26.3%
War	669	135	14.1%	35.1%

Note: #-The largest category for film noir is "don't know"; with that excluded the top three categories account for only 16.2% of references.

respondents watch each film and television genre, which can be viewed as a measure of preference.

Research Question 1. What is the relationship between genre consensus and audience viewing?

As Table 7.4 shows, the top most popular film genres by frequency viewed share an average audience consensus of 28.3% in expectations, while the least

TABLE 7.3 Audience Agreement on Expectations for Television Genres (2015 Users Survey)

Television Genres	Total References	No. of Different References	Category with Highest % of References	% in Top 3 Categories
TV sitcoms	551	150	12.5%	26.3%
TV dramas	534	175	5.8%	14.4%
TV soaps	582	145	10.7%	23.2%
TV detective	598	153	9.2%	26.8%
TV news mags	493	141	8.5%	22.1%
TV musical talent	577	132	13.5%	32.2%
TV reality	536	172	8.8%	20.1%
TV late-night talk	626	103	7.8%	22.0%
TV children's	577	133	10.6%	23.2%
TV animal/ nature	633	126	21.8%	34.0%
TV sci-fi	594	173	16.3%	22.9%

TABLE 7.4 Degree of Audience Consensus among Most/Least Popular Film Genres (2015 Users Survey)

	Popularity/Frequency Viewed	Audience Consensus: % of References in Top 3 Categories
Most Popular Film Genres		
Comedy films	4.22	42.4%
Action films	3.95	32.2%
Drama films	3.81	32.2%
Adventure films	3.77	22.0%
Animated films	3.58	16.4%
Mystery/Suspense films	3.58	23.5%
Average:	3.81	28.3%
Least Popular Film Genres		
Samurai	1.98	35.4%
Film noir	2.03	16.2% (36.3% including don't know)
Mockumentaries	2.04	24.1%
Westerns	2.13	46.9%
Slasher films	2.14	42.6%
Film parodies	2.32	30.1%
Average:	2.11	32.6%

popular film genres share a higher consensus of 32.6% in shared expectations; the difference is largely due to the greater consensus for westerns and slasher films. In other words, audiences know what to expect and they don't like these genres as a result. The more popular genres appear to generate more diverse expectations and attract larger audiences as a result, each person finding what

TABLE 7.5 Degree of Audience Consensus among Most/Least Popular TV Genres (2015 Users Survey)

	Popularity/Frequency Viewed	*Audience Consensus: % of References in Top 3 Categories*
Most Popular TV Genres		
TV dramas	3.53	14.4%
Situation comedies	3.40	26.3%
Average:	3.46	20.4%
Least Popular TV Genres		
TV soap operas	1.76	23.2%
TV news magazine shows	2.22	22.1%
Average:	1.99	22.6%

they like. There are several ways to read this pattern. First, some genres appear to be "big tents," offering more things to more people, allowing for more expectations to be met and more uses and gratifications fulfilled. Secondly, some genres allow for more people to "identify" with or ascertain "meanings" that other, more "narrow" genres cannot.

Research Question 2. What is the relationship between television genre consensus and audience viewing?

A similar but less sharp pattern is found for television genres (see Table 7.5), where the two most popular TV genres—TV dramas and sitcoms—have a shared consensus of 20.4% in expectations, while the two least popular genres—soap operas and news magazines—have a shared consensus of 22.6% in expectations, a small difference.

Genre Development—Genre Hybridity

How do film and television genres emerge from the creative process? Certainly, as media historians have noted, each film and television genre has its own history of creative contributions through time, but we also can look at patterns and several concepts help us to understand the development process through time. As noted above, genre development generally has been described as proceeding through four stages: Primitive, classical, revisionist, and parodic (Giannetti & Eyman, 2010). Here, we consider content that goes beyond parody, to a stage that includes hybridity, which will be explored in greater detail later in this chapter. For now, we will discuss the basic notion of hybridity. This is not exactly a novel concept, since hybridity has been the norm for some time in film and television. The general concept of hybridity is not a simple one, and it has a history in many disciplines and fields of study. Originally coming from botany and zoology, where it described cross-breeding of separate species, hybridity has been traced back to Russian philosopher Mikhail Bakhtin (1895–1975), who defined hybridization as a blending of two social spheres. Hybridity has a longstanding presence in literature–for example, William Blake's *Marriage of Heaven and Hell* (1793), with its blend of poetry, prose, and engravings.

Hybridity in film or television blends themes and elements from two or more different genres. For some in film, hybridity refers to a blending of cultures and national traditions. It has been seen as a response to the dominance of the American film industry and Hollywood itself in a global context, where hybrid forms are the product of cultural interactions and exchanges (Ritzer & Schulze, 2016), as seen in commercial Hindi cinema ("Bollywood") that combines western influences with Indian cultural themes. Further, in East Asian and South Asian visual media generally, a type of hybridity is frequently seen in which emotional tone shifts throughout the narrative, creating a "masala" or mixture of emotions that to a Western observer would seem to present inconsistent content from varied genres. The appreciation of these co-occurring contradictory emotions has been called naïve dialecticism, and has been found to vary significantly between East Asian and US audience members (Kim et al., 2014). The variability in affective tone that is often associated with genre hybridity can be seen in such popular Bollywood films as *Kabhi Khushi Kabhie Gham…*(2001), the title of which literally means, "sometimes happiness, sometimes sorrow," and *3 Idiots* (2009), which at various points in the film presents as a slapstick collegiate comedy, a mystery of assumed identity, and a psychological drama. In such cases, the hybridity of genre conventions seems to *follow* the main goal of constructing a narrative with affective variability. That is, the emotional pastiche is planned, and various genre conventions are used to provide the winding path necessary.

Within the context of Hollywood film, there is a question of whether genres have ever been clearly defined from the start, and whether they are forever fluid creations through time with hybridity being a constant, not a new phenomenon. Staiger (1997) notes that films produced in Hollywood in the prior forty or so years are instances of genre mixing, that Hollywood films have never been "pure," or easily arranged into categories (p. 6). Indeed, as noted earlier, the term "genre" was not used by Hollywood producers and directors, nor audiences, of the Golden Age (1920s–1960s). The term was applied retroactively to bodies of American film work that showed consistent conventions and seemed to demonstrate a tacit relationship between filmmakers' goal of success and audiences' expectations of predictable entertainment. Staiger does add that Hollywood films do evince patterns, which are "valuable material for deviation, dialogue, and critique." For some, the issue is a comparison of the earliest establishment of genre forms—what were westerns or comedies in their classic forms—with recent variations. More recently, hybridity has been popular in discussions of the gaming industry and moving images, crossing media boundaries (Skalski et al., 2008). Some have given up on classifying genres, concluding it is increasingly difficult even on a common-sense level (Casey et al., 2008). The origins of specific genres are another matter, and Mittell (2004, p. xvi) notes that specific television genres can be traced to industrial practices such as scheduling, while cycles in audience tastes and segmentation have been influential as well. And cultural studies approaches ground formal analysis in historical, social, and cultural contexts.

Mittell (2004, p. 40) refers to hybridity, but prefers the term genre mixing and says that "genre mixing is a primary way that genres evolve and change throughout their history—by drawing upon the conventions and assumptions of other genres, new subgenres and fully distinct genres can emerge." He suggests that genre mixing discussions have tended to focus on exceptional rather than common practices, and that "generic boundaries are permeable, fluid, historically contingent, and subject to change, while still offering categorical coherence at any given moment" (p. 154). And he concludes that "generic mixing generally does not lead to the declining importance of genre but actually reinforces and reasserts the role of genres in media practice" (p. 155). Focusing on television genres, Mittell notes that blurring boundaries between genres can occur through "fusion," adding one genre to another, and this can occur at a variety of levels, within individual episodes (e.g., *M*A*S*H* (1972–83) blending with a newsreel in a 1976 episode), within specific programs (e.g., *The Munsters* (1964–66) blending comedy and horror) or among emergent genres (*The Walking Dead* (2010-) merging themes of apocalyptic films with drama and western themes at times).

Occasionally, hybrid films isolate the features of the contributing genres temporally. That is, the film *American Splendor* (2003) is a hybrid of documentary and comedy presented in narrative form, switching back and forth between the real graphic novelist Harvey Pekar commenting on his life, and the fictionalized Pekar (played by Paul Giamatti) navigating life as a sardonic Cleveland VA hospital file clerk. Similarly, Errol Morris' *Wormwood* (2017), a limited series on Netflix, vacillates between fact-based murder mystery narrative content and documentary interviews with surviving individuals related to the case. For both *American Splendor* and *Wormwood*, some critics refer to the narrative content as "reenactments," but these cases go far beyond the typical staged reenactment as a minor component in documentary content.

The hybridity that we have been discussing is rapidly extending to another level, with the emergence of content that knowingly violates expectations, and garners positive audience response for such transgressions. In the wake of *Parasite's* big win at the 2020 Oscars, there was much discussion of whether we are in a post-genre information environment. NPR called the film "genre-bending" (NPR, 2019). There will be a fuller discussion of this trend later in this chapter.

While individual members of film and television audiences develop their own expectations based on personal experiences and tastes, collectively audiences differentiate among genres with their decision-making. When audiences assign characteristics and expectations to their understandings of what a film genre is, they establish relationships among them as well as differentiate between them. They also identify "core characteristics" essential to their understanding of what constitutes a particular film or television genre, and they at least hint at how genres have "morphed" or split off into sub-categories through sharing.

Based on our sample's 20,000+ "votes" for what constitutes the various film and television genres, we generate the following novel concepts:

> *Core Genre Characteristics*: Are particular characteristics essential to audience definitions of specific film or television genres, and can we establish this through overwhelming consensus in identifying particular expectations?
>
> *Genre Specific Ingredients*: Are some expectations unique to individual genres and seldom if ever generate more than a stray expectation for other genres?
>
> *Universal Donors*: Are particular genre ingredients found in almost all if not all film or television genres?
>
> *Genre Affinity*: We might expect from labels alone that particular film genres should share particular ingredients. For example, romantic comedies should share some expectations of both "chick flicks" and film comedies, just as romantic dramas should share some expectations of drama films and "chick flicks." Other pairings might include: detective films and mystery/suspense films; action films and adventure films; superhero films and fantasy films.

The nature of the expectations produced include a wide variety, ranging from concrete identifiers of images (nature of setting, costumes, actors), to production and performance measures (sound, singing, acting assessments), structural "story," or thematic concepts (nature of plot, story content), and expectations of how audiences expect to react or experience the genre when exposed (be in suspense, laugh, understand, be entertained).

In Chapter 2, we analyzed the use of different expectations by genre, showing how audiences' expectations often concurred with the descriptors used by scholars and critics to define genres. The same data help us to understand issues of genre "fusion," or where audiences see genres as sharing the same features. However, the issue is not necessarily clear at this level, since some referential categories are "core" features of several genres.

First, let's pick several genres for which a "core" feature helps to define each, illustrating our notion of "*genre affinity*": comedy, romantic comedy, dark comedy, slapstick films, and, though this crosses media, situation comedies on television. We can see from Table 7.6 how "comedy" genres share

TABLE 7.6 Comparison of Expectation References for Genres Sharing Comedy Elements (2015 Users Survey)

Top Referential Categories Used by Audiences	Comedy Films	Romantic Comedy Films	Dark Comedy Films	Slapstick Films	Situation Comedies on TV
Types of activities	313 1st	289 1st	234 1st	231 1st	160 1st
	74 jokes, joking, telling jokes, humor	25 jokes, joking, telling jokes, humor	25 jokes, joking, telling jokes, humor	32 jokes, joking, telling jokes, humor	20 jokes, joking, telling jokes, humor
	39 types of jokes, humor	11 types of jokes, humor	71 types of jokes, humor	61 types of jokes, humor	15 types of jokes, humor
	14 adult jokes, humor	2 adult jokes, humor	12 adult jokes, humor	30 humor, laughs, jokes with negative connotation	1 adult jokes, humor
	13 good, smart, witty, clever jokes	3 good, smart, witty, clever jokes	14 humor, laughs, jokes with negative connotation	56 laughing, funny refs with positive connotation	10 good, smart, witty, clever jokes
	131 laughing, funny refs with positive connotation	75 laughing, funny refs with positive connotation	39 laughing, funny refs with positive connotation	6 adult jokes, humor	20 humor, laughs, jokes with negative connotation
	10 refs to funny, amusing content		26 death and dying refs		69 laughing, funny refs with positive connotation
	Only 2 refs to sexual activities	26 sexual activities			10 refs to funny, amusing content
		17 kissing, hugging			
		76 love, romance			

(Continued)

TABLE 7.6 Comparison of Expectation References for Genres Sharing Comedy Elements (2015 Users Survey) (*Continued*)

Top Referential Categories Used by Audiences	Comedy Films	Romantic Comedy Films	Dark Comedy Films	Slapstick Films	Situation Comedies on TV
Reactions, feelings	68 2nd 39 laughing in response to film/TV content 11 to have fun, be entertained	44 5th 11 laughing in response to film/TV content 9 to have fun, be entertained	64 2nd 10 laughing in response to film/TV content 6 to have fun, be entertained 4 being bored 9 dislike, disturbing	45 4th 7 laughing in response to film/TV content 6 to have fun, be entertained 10 being bored	– 11 laughing in response to film/TV content 20 to have fun, be entertained 8 being bored
People	58 3rd 17 comedians, comic actors 7 funny people/characters/actors	61 3rd 1 comedian, comic actor 11 couples	–	– 10 goofy people, goofiness	61 3rd 12 families 8 friends
Plot, story line	10 refs to comedy forms, themes	112 2nd 17 refs to happy endings 14 comedy, sitcom forms, themes 48 romantic themes, love stories	47 4th 9 good story, plot 6 plot twists, turns 5 dark, somber plots	– Nothing other than individual references to zany plot, no story, skits, formulaic	82 2nd 11 group of friends story theme 22 comedy, sitcom forms, themes
Evaluations, assessments	10 general negative assessments	57 4th 11 refs to shallow, corny, cheesy 9 cliché, tries, predictable	49 3rd 6 overall negative assessments 8 emotions, feelings 7 disliking, disgusting reactions	56 3rd 20 overall negative assessments	– 13 overall negative assessments
Don't know	–	–	–	58 2nd	–

common references in audience expectations. Since "pure" film comedies can be viewed as the senior genre in this grouping, we start with the top three referential categories: (1) types of activities; (2) reactions and feelings; and (3) people and roles. Then, as we add the other comedy genres, that is, romantic comedy films, dark comedy films, slapstick films, and television situation comedies—we retain those three categories and add in those categories more important in audience expectations of those genres, that is, plot and story line; evaluations and assessments; and don't know. It should come as no surprise that jokes, joke telling, and the many ways we can discuss humor are an identifiable "core" ingredient for these five genres. When there are deviations from the "mother genre," it is to further define elements distinctive to those genres. So, for example, romantic comedy adds expectations for sexual activities and romantic behaviors. For dark comedies, audiences expect the element of humor but also with death and dying, the "dark" element making that genre distinct from "pure" comedy films. And, while slapstick films do not deviate too far from pure comedy in their emphasis on comedic activities, they do hone in on distinctive types of humor, which we'd expect from this genre of "physical comedy." Finally the classically popular situation comedies on television merely elaborate on the types of activities in the "mother core."

The second most important category in audience expectations for comedy films is reactions and feelings—the uses and gratifications people expect from comedy—to laugh, be entertained, to have fun. But dark comedies and slapstick films, and even sitcoms, elicit more negative expectations, including boredom or being disturbed in the case of dark comedies. The third major category in audience expectations is people and roles. In particular, comedy films are expected to have comedians or funny people performing in those roles. In the case of slapstick films, these expectations extend themselves to goofy people or goofiness. However, the frequency of television programs and the need for a stable cast of characters prompts audiences to expect families and friends when they turn in.

Plot and story line, while not as important in audience expectations for comedic films, are more central for three of the other comedic genres—romantic comedy, dark comedy, and TV sitcoms. Happy endings, romantic themes and sitcom-like scenarios are among the most important audience expectations for romantic comedy films. Dark comedy films have audience expectations for good plots, dark or somber themes, and plots with twists and turns. Situation comedies are expected to focus on stories about interactions among a group of friends. Slapstick films do not seem to be defined at all by story lines. Lastly, audiences register their general dislike more strongly than their affinity for these genres, particularly slapstick films. Using the concepts cited above, within the categories of expectations by audiences, we can identify comedic activities as core ingredients of this set of genres but we can also see some genre specific characteristics (not unique to these genres exclusive of others not compared, of course), e.g., romantic behaviors for romantic comedies, death and dying for dark comedies.

Mittell (2004) says that "genres work primarily within cultural practices that are conscious and explicit, not beneath the surface" and "genre mixing brings generic practices to the surface, making the conventions and assumptions clustered within individual categories explicit through the juxtaposition of conflicting or complementary genres" (p. 157).

This perspective builds on the work of Neale and Krutnik (1990), who claim that genre parody should be distinguished from genre hybridity, which combines conventions. Parody makes audiences laugh by drawing upon and lampooning the genre's conventions, turning the genre into a comedic genre (pp. 158–159). Mittell suggests viewing parody as a particular mode of generic mixture between comedy and another genre. A popular example is *Young Frankenstein* (1974), where the horror genre's classic features are exaggerated to invoke laughter. Other examples of genre pairing for parody are *Police Squad!* (1982, police drama), and *Soap* (1977-81, soap opera).

We see in Table 7.7 that the same ingredients in comedic genres make their appearance in audience expectations for mockumentaries, but the numbers are reduced, likely because the top category besides types of activities is don't know. This supports Mittell and others who see parody as using comedy to exaggerate other genres rather than labeling mockumentaries as a distinct form of genre, as it was in our study. The one item that stands out as an added ingredient in mockumentaries is the appearance of "interviews," which are often used in parodies of historical or "true life" events paring comedy with documentary genres.

In addition to comedy, several other sets of genres illustrate genre affinity (shared features), including detective films, mystery/suspense films, and TV detective shows. As Table 7.8 shows, there is a consistency across categories of the features used most often by viewers to describe these genres. The most important category is plot, or story line, and the top reference is to mystery or mystery themes, followed by plots with twists and turns, then drama, cliff hanger endings, and problem-solving puzzles. The second and third most important categories of expectations shift a bit by genre. People and roles, and types of activities are the second or third most frequently cited category of expectations for detective films and TV detective shows, and the specific responses are almost identical: legal roles—police and courts, and crime perpetrator roles, and types of activities—criminal or crime solving activities.

Reactions place second as the most popular category of expectations for mystery/suspense films, but come in fourth for the other two genres. In all cases, however, feelings of suspense and intrigue are top of mind as expectations. Interest and excitement also are important. Special effects are important for mystery and suspense films, with citations of darkness, suspenseful music, dark colors. In all of the analyses here, the shared characteristics refer to general

TABLE 7.7 Comparing Expectations for Mockumentaries with Comedic Genre (2015 Users Survey)

Referential Categories	Mockumentaries
Types of activities	157 1st
	47 jokes, joking, telling jokes, humor
	30 types of jokes, humor
	2 adult jokes, humor
	5 good, smart, witty, clever jokes
	14 refs to humor, laughs, jokes with negative connotation
	39 refs to laughing, funny with negative connotation
	3 refs to funny, amusing content, plot
	10 refs to interviews
Reactions, feelings	46 4th
	10 refs to being bored
	6 disliking, disturbing reactions referenced
People	25 6th
	4 comedian, comic actor references
Plot, story line	37 5th
	6 refs to comedy forms, themes
	Scattered references to breaking the fourth wall, realistic story, real life, true events, documentaries, fake documentaries, talk show themes, half-truths, politics, satire, etc.
Evaluations, assessments	63 3rd
	17 overall negative assessments
	Scattered references to exaggerated stories, mockery, good/poor/flawed acting, low budget bad scripts, confusing, hard to follow, silliness, serious, controversy, weird, etc.
Don't know	85 2nd

genres, but respondents could be thinking in terms of specific television programs (*Law & Order* (1990-2010), *CSI: Las Vegas* (2000-15)) or films (*Murder on the Orient Express* (1974 & 2017), *Fargo* (1996), *The French Connection* (1971)), and even specific episodes of TV programs. A contemporary example is illustrative. The return of *Perry Mason* in 2020 might have been categorized as a TV detective show, which interestingly cast the famed lawyer as a detective who almost coincidentally evolved into an attorney in a program with film noir overtones and themes of mystery in subplots that were as important as efforts to solve a crime in 1932 Los Angeles.

Respondents were asked to identify their three favorite films of all time. If we compare these choices to expectations for specific genres, we see hints

TABLE 7.8 Comparison of Expectation References for Genre Sharing Detective/ Mystery Elements (2015 Users Survey)

Top Referential Categories Used by Audiences	Detective Films	Mystery/Suspense Films	TV Detective Shows
Plot, story line	169 1st 102 mystery, mystery themes 18 plots with twists and turns 9 drama 9 problem solving, puzzles to solve	151 1st 48 mystery, mystery themes 35 plots with twists and turns 17 cliff hanger, surprise story endings 14 drama	160 1st 55 mystery, mystery themes 31 law and order crime story themes 13 plots with twists and turns 12 good story, plot referenced
People, roles	116 2nd 66 legal roles-court & police 27 crime perpetrator roles	– 14 legal roles— court & police 7 heroes and villains 5 crime perpetrator roles	85 3rd 51 legal roles—court & police 12 crime perpetrator roles
Reactions, feelings	70 4th 26 feeling suspense, intrigue 13 level of interest referenced 8 feel excitement, thrilling 8 being bored	131 2nd 38 feeling suspense, intrigue 34 feeling scared, fear 18 feel excitement, thrilling 16 level of interest referenced 15 being surprised, uncertain	66 4th 26 feeling suspense, intrigue 11 level of interest referenced
Type of activities	95 3rd 50 criminal behaviors 13 crime solving, investigation activities	67 3rd 42 criminal behaviors 6 crime solving, investigation activities	121 2nd 54 criminal behaviors 22 crime solving, investigation activities
Special effects	–	60 4th 10 darkness, dark colors, dark shots 9 suspenseful soundtrack, music, tense music	–

of what their expectations are based on, and perhaps how expectations lead to decisions to go out to see specific films. A 32-year-old Asian male who said that the film *Gone Girl* (2014) was one of his favorite films later said he expects to see conspiracy and intrigue in mystery films. A 45-year-old female who said *Fargo* (1996) was a favorite film expects to see crime and dramatic music in mystery films. A 33-year-old White male who said *Death on the Nile* (1978) was a favorite film expects "lots of mystery" for mystery films.

Two other pairs of genres continue our examination of genre affinity (shared characteristics): Action and adventure films, and superhero and fantasy films. As Table 7.9 shows, action, and adventure films share the top category, types of actions, and the third most frequently cited category, reactions, and feelings, with differences in specifics that point to the unique features of action films—fighting in action films and traveling in adventure films. Both generate expectations of excitement, fun and thrills. Even so, audiences expect to see weapons and cars in action films, and stories of adventure and quest in adventure films. In addition, adventure films are expected to be situated in exotic locales or different cultures. The other pair of genres is expected to share fewer features. Both are expected to have superheroes or supernatural characters in the top category, people and roles, and both are expected to have science fiction plots or story themes. But they also demonstrate different emphases, with superhero films having lots of action, and people flying and fighting and fantasy films set in imaginary or magical/fantasy settings. Material culture and symbols are relatively important for both genres, but the specifics are very different. Audiences expect superheroes in outfits, with robes, capes, masks, and disguises, and fantasy films populated with imaginary animals or creatures, spaceships, saucers, and weapons.

When we look at the films that respondents said were among their all-time favorites, we see the expectations attached to specific genres. A 22-year-old male who said *The Avengers* (2012) was among his all-time favorites expects to see "magical powers" in superhero films. Many respondents identified science fiction films among their top three films. A 26-year-old White man who said *Star Wars* (1977) was a favorite expects to find aliens and spaceships in science fiction films, while a 62-year-old White woman who said *2001: A Space Odyssey* (1968) was among her favorites expects to see "out of this world aliens and space" in science fiction films.

Our final pair of film genres exemplifying genre affinity includes two very popular genres, slasher films and horror films, and as Table 7.10 illustrates, they're almost mirror images of each other, suggesting they're a single genre or slasher films are a subgenre of the broader horror genre.

A 27-year-old woman who said that *A Nightmare on Elm Street* (1984) was among her favorite films expects to see "death, scary plots, killers" in horror films. And a 26-year-old White male who said the original *Halloween* (1978) is among his favorites, expects to see "scary clowns, blood and death" in horror films.

TABLE 7.9 Comparison of Expectation References for Genre Sharing Elements: Action Films, Adventure Films, Superhero Films, and Fantasy Films (2015 Users Survey)

Top Referential Categories Used by Audiences	Action Films	Adventure Films	Superhero Films	Fantasy Films
Types of actions	308 1st 105, actions, activities, including war actions 62 chasing, chases 47 fighting	147 1st 72, actions, activities, including war actions 28 traveling, trips 13 chasing, chases	132 2nd 63 action, actions, including war actions 27 people flying 13 fighting	
Material culture, symbols	84 2nd 49 weapons 25 cars of all types		60 4th 29 black outfits, robes, capes, disguises, mask 10 leather, fabric, outfits, costumes	64 3rd 36 imaginary animals, creatures 11 weapons 6 spaceships, saucers
Reactions, feelings	71 3rd 28 feeling excitement, thrilling 18 feeling suspense, intrigue 11 to have fun, feel entertained	82 3rd 32 feeling excitement, thrilling 21 to have fun, feel entertained		
Plot, story	–	102 2nd 21 quest, journey 20 fast pace 19 adventure themes	95 3rd 22 sci-fi, science fiction themes 10 adventure themes 10 romantic, love story themes	59 4th 12 sci-fi, science fiction themes 9 good, positive plots 8 unreal situations 7 unbelievable, unrealistic plots
Settings		73 4th 10 exotic locales, culture, locations 8 positive scenery refs		118 1st 51 fantasy, magic settings 25 imaginary; created worlds
People, roles			149 1st 87 superheroes 25 villains, hero roles	68 2nd 37 supernatural characters 7 cartoon, kids characters

TABLE 7.10 Comparison of Expectation References for Genre Sharing Elements: Horror and Slasher Films (2015 Users Survey)

Top Referential Categories Used by Audiences	Horror Films	Slasher Films
Material culture	172 1st	231 1st
	155 blood, gore, dead body/parts	180 blood, gore, dead body/parts
	14 weapons of all types	45 weapons of all types
Reactions, feelings	118 2nd	62 3rd
	79 fear, being scared	28 fear, being scared
	18 feeling suspense, intrigue	8 feeling suspense, intrigue
Types of activities	92 3rd	91 2nd
	30 screaming, yelling, arguing	23 criminal behaviors
	22 criminal behaviors	19 physical violence
	19 death, dying	16 screaming, yelling, arguing
	12 physical violence	14 death, dying

We wanted to see what features audiences would expect to share among more television-specific genres, especially TV news magazines shows, TV late-night talk shows, and two "non-fiction" genres, musical talent, and reality TV shows. See Table 7.11.

The larger categories of expectations are not a perfect match for TV news magazine shows and late-night talk shows, but the similarities in specifics show parallels. Thus, while the program structure is the most frequent category for magazine shows, it places third for late-night talk shows. As we'd expect, news, reporting, and facts are frequent specifics for magazine programs, comedy, comedic skits, and comedic spin on current events describe late-night talk shows. Specific talk show themes are cited for both. Types of activities as a category place first or second in both TV genres, and while both refer to communication activities—the "talkative" nature of both genres—magazine shows are expected to have gossip and rumors while the latter feature joking, laughing, interviews, and monologues. Assessments illustrate preferences, and audiences expect to be bored or entertained, interested, educated. The final frequently cited category, people and roles, includes specifics easily fitting into the two genres—hosts (journalists and familiar characters) and guests (singers, performers, celebrities).

The final two television genres compared here illustrate how modern creations of the two genres have borrowed features of other genres. The talent competition as a genre certainly dates back to radio, where it began in 1934 as *Major Bowes' Amateur Hour*, and ran until its creator, Major Bowes, died in 1946. Ted Mack, a talent scout who had directed the show under Bowes, revived it for ABC Radio and the DuMont Television Network in 1948. The radio show

TABLE 7.11 Comparison of Expectation References for Four TV Genres (2015 Users Survey)

Top Referential Categories Used by Audiences	TV News Magazine Shows	TV Late-Night Talk Shows	Musical Talent Competition	Reality TV Shows
Plot, story structure	129 1st 27 refers to news, sources 13 talk show themes, ingredients 12 fluff, poor, sensational reporting 18 facts, factual base, data	106 3rd 37 comedy, sitcom forms, themes 20 talk show themes, ingredients 11 comedic spin on news, current events 10 comedic skits, routines	128 2nd 54 talent competition themes 54 judging in competitions	139 1st 47 drama references 22 talent competition themes 21 non scripted nature referenced
Types of activities	76 2nd 40 gossiping, rumors, remarks	225 1st 49 jokes, joking, telling jokes, humor 45 laughing, funny 44 interviews 15 monologues	146 1st 78 music, songs, singing, amazing lyrics 32 dancing 9 crying, tears	82 3rd 18 fighting of all types 10 screaming, yelling, arguing
Reactions, feelings	65 3rd 21 being bored 9 being interested 7 educational, learning, informative	53 4th 19 to have fun, be entertained 15 being bored 10 being interested	60 5th 16 to have fun, be entertained 13 being bored	57 4th 15 being bored 12 to have fun, be entertained

(Continued)

TABLE 7.11 Comparison of Expectation References for Four TV Genres (2015 Users Survey) *(Continued)*

Top Referential Categories Used by Audiences	TV News Magazine Shows	TV Late-Night Talk Shows	Musical Talent Competition	Reality TV Shows
People, roles	49 4th* 23 general or familiar characters, actors, celebrity roles 11 journalist, media roles 5 program host, guest roles	129 2nd 44 program host, guest roles 29 general or familiar characters, actors, celebrity roles 21 specific talent, performer roles of singing, performing	72 4th 48 specific talent, performer roles of singing, performing	51 5th 7 stupid, dumb people
Evaluations, assessments			77 3rd 15 good host, good guests 12 negative acting, performing	99 2nd 39 overall negative assessments 13 negative acting, performing 12 fake, unrealistic 10 representational ref as staged rather than truthful

★ *Note*: Don't know was actually 4th, with people and roles 5th, but it's omitted here.

featured singers or other musicians but on television included such vaudeville acts as jugglers, tap dancers, and baton twirlers. Later, Ed McMahon's *Star Search* (1983–1995) featured contestants competing as singers, comedy acts, vocal groups or dance, with champions and challengers judged by a panel. Today's music and talent competitions blend not only on-stage performances but filmed interviews, family stories and personal details as context and to dramatize the competition.

At the same time, the original reality TV show that some would say started it all, *Survivor* (1997-), began with "real people" but in the process created celebrities that have reappeared in subsequent competitions. Here too audiences are introduced to the participants and their back stories. The blur between "staged reality" and "real life" is illustrated by *The Apprentice* (2004-17), whose host ended up in the White House, along with Omarosa, who was a particularly combative contestant on his show. Years later, she reappeared on *Big Brother* (2000-), another reality TV show, not too long before her book reporting details from her time in Washington, DC, was released. We see aspects of these features in the expectations of our respondents. The program structure (categorized along with plot, story structure) is important in both TV genres, where respondents cite talent and competition along with drama, noting the "non-scripted nature" of reality TV shows. The type of activities is more specific to the genre—music, singing and dancing in talent competition, fighting, screaming, yelling and arguing in reality TV shows. People's preferences come across in their descriptions of the types of people they expect to find, specific talented people—singers—in talent competitions, and stupid, dumb people in reality TV shows; we know there are super fans of reality TV programs who know every contestant through the years on their favorite program. And, no surprise, the assessments and evaluations category is important in audience expectations.

It's difficult to find specific audience expectations unique to individual genres, but in the coding of open-ended responses, there was a category labeled "descriptive concepts and abstractions for content" and another "miscellaneous." We find that for each genre there are a number of expectations that overlap with only a couple of other genres. The unique expectations, found for only one genre, included "fatalism" for film noir, "strange relationships" for foreign films, "pride" for gangster films, "ideals" for samurai films, and "bad situations to be in" for comedy. For each genre, a number of expectations that overlap with only a couple other genres were found, as illustrated in Table 7.12. We do find many abstract concepts audiences expect for many genres, e.g., "silliness," which is cited for 15 different film and television genres, "truthful" for 13 different genres, and "tension" for 11 different genres.

External and Other Influences

While genre expectations and anticipated uses and gratifications are the primary influences on decisions to go out to see films, or to watch films or programs on television, there also are external influences. Some research shows

TABLE 7.12 Infrequent Expectations (2015 Users Survey)

Infrequent Descriptors in Audience Expectations	Genres for Which They're Cited
Staged	TV musical or talent competition shows TV late-night talk shows TV science fiction shows
Epic	Epics Westerns
Catastrophe, disaster, mayhem, chaos	Science fiction films Superhero films Slasher films War films Adventure films
Depth, depth in exploration of ideas	Science fiction films Documentary films Biography films
Self-importance, self-promotion	TV dramas Film noir films TV late-night talk shows
Hardship or poverty	Documentary films Gangster films TV detective shows
Winners and losers	TV musical or talent competition shows Superhero films (But add in action films and sports films for "winners" alone)
Betrayal, deceit	Mystery and suspense films Romantic drama films TV dramas TV soap operas
Honesty	Biography films Historical films TV musical or talent competition shows
Innocence	Slapstick films TV reality shows
Controversy	Documentary films Mockumentary films Foreign films
Ego	Biography films TV reality shows TV late-night talk shows
Honor, duty, codes	Samurai films Historical films War films Sports films
Patriotism	Samurai films
Jingoism	Historical films War films
Humiliation	Gangster films TV reality shows
Intimidation	Gangster films TV musical or talent competition shows TV reality shows

that reading reviews prompts people to see films or set their recorder to make sure they don't miss a program. Given the importance of the Internet and influences from social media, the "general buzz" about a film can be a motivating force, perhaps to "be in the know," to not be left behind. We know that people who see themselves as "opinion leaders" try to keep up with the topics they expect to encounter in conversations with friends (e.g., Katz, 2015). And friends still are important influences for all sorts of personal choices.

In the 2015 survey, respondents were asked to rate the importance of 10 "reasons for deciding to go out to see a film in a theater," including four representing external influences from other people or the media, using a scale ranging from often very important to almost never important:

- I've read a review and the film sounds interesting.
- I'm going with someone who picks the film.
- Because of the general "buzz" about the film.
- A friend recommended the film.

Correlations between the importance of these external influences on going out to the theater to see films and film genre viewing are in Table 7.13. Only statistically significant correlations are included, and three film genres are absent from the table—horror films, documentary films, and fantasy films; for these genres, none of the influences are important.

Patterns can be detected. It appears that going out to see particular films is less than a unanimous decision for many people, whether it's a couple of friends, or in a dating relationship or marriage. Respondents who more highly endorse "someone else picks the film" also say that they more often watch musicals, chick flicks, slapstick films, both "generic" and romantic dramas, romantic comedies and film parodies. In fact, all four types of influences are more important for those who do more viewing of film parodies, chick flicks, and romantic dramas.

In addition, we build up preferences based on past experience with specific genres, with who has directed the film, with actors who become favorites, with the origins of the film—by country, and language. Although timing is less important now that films and television programs are available via streaming and few "appointments" are necessary to see a film, there still is some value in "being in the know," being up to date; thus, the recency of a film can be a factor. Our survey instrument asked respondents how important each of four items was in making a decision on whether to watch a film or not, using a 7-point scale ranging from 1 = not important at all to 7 = extremely important.

- The director of the film.
- The recency of the film's release/how new the film is.
- The country the film is from.
- The language the film is in.

Table 7.14 shows correlations between the importance of four factors for deciding to watch a film and how often one watches the particular genres. Only

TABLE 7.13 Correlations of Importance of External Influences on Going Out to See Films in the Theater and Film Genre Viewing (2015 Users Survey)

Read a Review, and Film Sounds Interesting	Someone Else Picks the Film	General Buzz about the Film	A Friend Recommended the Film
	Musicals .14**	Musicals .15***	Musicals .13*
Westerns .12*		Westerns .11*	
		Science fiction -.13*	
Detective films .14**		Detective films .14**	
Film noir .18***		Comedy films .13*	
		Film noir .11*	
			Action films .11*
Animated films -.10#			
Mystery/suspense .13*		Mystery/suspense .15**	
Dark comedy films .12*			
Biographical films .10#		Biographical films .10#	
Film parodies .11*	Film parodies .11*	Film parodies .23***	Film parodies .12*
		Slasher films .09#	
Mockumentaries .10#		Mockumentaries .11*	
Chick flicks .09#	Chick flicks .23***	Chick flicks .25***	Chick flicks .15**
	Slapstick films .14**	Slapstick films .20***	Slapstick films .14**
	Drama films .12*	Drama films .14**	Drama films .10#
		Adventure films .09#	
Foreign films .12*			
Romantic dramas .09#	Romantic dramas .23***	Romantic dramas .23***	Romantic dramas .09#
	Romantic comedies .19***	Romantic comedies .25***	Romantic comedies .13*
Gangster films .17***		Gangster films .16**	Gangster films .11*
		Samurai films .10#	Samurai films .09#
Epic films .09#			
		Sports films .25***	Sports films .16**
Historical films .14**		Superhero films .10#	
War films .17***		War films .12*	War films .12*

Note: #.05<p<.10; *p<.05; **p<.01; ***p<.001

TABLE 7.14 Correlations of Importance of Other Influences on Deciding to Watch a Film and Film Genre Viewing (2015 Users Survey)

Director of the Film	Recency of Film's Release	Country the Film Is from	Language the Film Is in
Musicals .10★			Musicals -.10#
Westerns .18★★★	Westerns .10#	Westerns .11★	
Science fiction .20★★★			
Detective films .12★	Detective films .13★ Comedy films .10#	Detective films .11★	Comedy films .11★
Film noir .36★★★	Film noir .11★		Film noir -.26★★★
Documentary films .25★★★			Documentary films -.10★
Mystery/suspense .12★	Mystery/suspense .17★★★		Mystery/suspense .09#
Dark comedy films .30★★★	Dark comedy films .11★		Dark comedy films -.13★
Biographical films .21★★★	Biographical films .16★★		
Film parodies .11★	Film parodies .14★★		
Slasher films .13★	Slasher films .13★		
Mockumentaries .28★★★	Mockumentaries .10★		Mockumentaries -.16★★
Chick flicks -.14★★			Chick flicks .12★
	Drama films .11★		
Fantasy films .12★	Fantasy films .09#		
Adventure films .09#	Adventure films .21★★★		
Foreign films .41★★★			Foreign films -.44★★★
	Romantic dramas .15★★		Romantic dramas .12★
	Romantic comedies .15★★		Romantic comedies .14★★
Gangster films .25★★★	Gangster films .14★★		
Samurai films .25★★★	Samurai films .13★		
Epic films .18★★★	Epic films .10★ Sports films .16★★		Epic films -.13★
Historical films .22★★★			
	Superhero films .18★★★	Superhero films .10#	
War films .15★★	War films .14★★		

Note: #.05<*p*<.10; ★*p*<.05; ★★*p*<.01; ★★★*p*<.001

statistically significant correlations are included in the table, so three genres are missing from the table—action films, animated films, and slapstick films. We see that the importance of the country of origin for a film is correlated with the frequency of viewing for only three film genres—westerns, detective films, and superhero films. When the director of a film is important, respondents say they more frequently watch 21 different film genres, but the strongest relationships are found for foreign films, film noir, dark comedy films, and mockumentaries. If the recency of a film's release is important, again respondents say they watch 21 film genres more frequently, but none of the correlations are particularly strong. If the language of a film is more important to respondents, they are less likely to view foreign films, film noir, musicals, dark comedies, mockumentaries, and epic films, but more likely to watch comedy films, mystery suspense films, chick flicks, and romantic dramas and comedies. The strongest relationships are for foreign films and film noir. This may document the aversion to subtitles prevalent in a large subset of the audience (Rader et al., 2016).

Beyond Parodic: Genre-Bending, Genre Hybridity, and Trope Appropriation

From the discussion of genre affinity above, we see that separate, distinguishable genres often share characteristics. Yet, these genres maintain independent identities, and are recognizable by audience members just from their titles. We now explore a different type of blending, in which such identifiable and discrete genres are merged, or contribute elements to moving image content in more complex ways.

Recall that the four stages of genre development—primitive, classical, revisionist, and parodic—culminate in a form (parodic) that relies on the audience holding a full understanding of the elements and tropes of the genre in question. It is a fulfillment of the "contract" between content creators and spectators, whereby the audience member's long-term relationship with the genre has afforded them the ability to understand and appreciate a parody. The audience member "gets" the joke—and they have the joy of an "in-joke," by which only those in the know (i.e., with extensive knowledge of the genre) will be fully rewarded.

The utility of an audience understanding of genre conventions is not limited to humor. Moving beyond the fourth stage of parodic, at a proposed fifth stage of genre development—Genre-Bending—content creators use well-understood elements or tropes (techniques, content cues, etc.) as a type of cultural product currency. Whereas the "language of cinema" once referenced raw production techniques such as the close-up, the dissolve, or parallel editing, as popularized by U.S. director D. W. Griffith over a century ago (see, e.g., *The Birth of a Nation* (1915) and *D. W. Griffith: The Father of Film* (1993)), we may need to add to the vocabulary of the language of the moving image such genre-related tropes as "laugh track," "chiaroscuro lighting," "dissonant music," and "blood/gore." Each has particular meaning assigned by virtue of its long use within certain genre contexts. And that meaning is available to content creators to attach to any type of content. The term we have adopted, Genre-Bending, was previously employed by Abelman and Atkin (2011), with the definition: "experimentally bending the rules of established program formats to allow narrative techniques and conventions found in other genres to work their way in" (p. 68). We anticipate two types of Genre-Bending: (1) Genre Hybridity, in which a merging of two or more genres constitutes the film or TV program, and (2) Trope Appropriation, in which only discrete elements from one genre are inserted into content that is otherwise not of that genre as a method of imparting a certain meaning.

Further, while this fifth stage is conceptualized to exist post-parodic, it is of course also post-revisionist. A note about the presumed differences between content that is judged to be revisionist for a given genre, and content that is genre-bending—in revisionist content, supplementary meaning is given by the application of ideas that are not specifically from moving image genres. For example, the 1956 sci-fi film *Invasion of the Body Snatchers* was imbued with political allegory drawn from the U.S. Red Scare era. A full understanding of the film requires the spectator to be conversant in the politics of the time (or, now, in political history). The film did not pull in conventions from other genres. Genre-bending content is rich in cross-genre references and appropriations, demanding a knowledge of multiple moving image genres.

BREAKING THE FOURTH WALL

A small number of respondents to the 2021–22 surveys indicated that genre-bending involves "breaking the fourth wall." This refers to instances where characters address the audience directly, thus breaking down one wall of their diegesis (world of the film or television show) (Abelman & Atkin, 2011, p. 41). Examples given by respondents include the superhero film *Deadpool* (2016) and the TV sitcom *Central Park* (2020–21). There does not seem to be any association of this technique with particular genres. Rather, this process signifies an attempt to remind the spectator that the content is mediated, an effort that might apply to any genre.

Another clarification of note—Genre-bending may, or may not, be seen as a certain application of the concept of intertextuality. Intertextuality was originally applied to written texts, but the concept has broadened to include moving image material as text. Intertextuality is the referencing within one body of content to other content, usually intentionally. This referencing shapes the meaning of the new content, which relies on the receiver's knowledge of the older content. Intertextuality may be as concrete as an exact quotation (e.g., when characters in the film *Sleepless in Seattle* (1993) watch and react to portions of an earlier film, *An Affair to Remember* (1957)). Or, it may take the form of parody (e.g., the near-imitation of the blind monk scene from *Bride of Frankenstein* (1935) in Mel Brooks' *Young Frankenstein* (1974)), or pastiche (e.g., the technique-laden homage to Ingmar Bergman's *Persona* (1966) within Woody Allen's *Interiors* (1978)). An extreme example of quotation might be the parody film *Airplane!* (1980), which was based in substantial part on the screenplay for an earlier, non-comedy film, *Zero Hour!* (1957). Entire segments of dialogue are repeated from one film to the other—but with punchlines added.

As these examples show, intertextuality normally takes the form of referencing a specific piece of content, rather than the tropes or other characteristics of a whole class of content such as a genre. Although the process of meaning-granting afforded by intertextuality is similar to or parallel to that given by genre-bending, we would maintain that the levels are different. Intertextuality is assumed to apply to content-specific references (i.e., references to specific texts), while genre-bending is at a more aggregate level (i.e., the genre).

In all three of the 2021 and 2021–22 Surveys, we included an open-ended query asking "Can you name one movie or TV program you've seen that really 'bent' the genre by introducing aspects of other genres? Please explain." Those responses have been reviewed and summarized, as shown in Table 7.15 and Figure 7.2. Responses were so varied as to defy quantitative analyses. Instead, a thematic analysis of responses across the three surveys was executed (Neuendorf, 2019).

While some respondents claimed not to be familiar with genre-bending, citing either that they were unfamiliar or that such a phenomenon did not exist, the majority of those responding did have a viewpoint on the matter. Others had no hesitation to report exemplars of bending, and blending. As one respondent noted, "It's getting harder to really classify a movie into one single genre."

Perhaps the simplest type of "bending" identified by respondents is when a single anthology series with some overarching theme uses different genres in different episodes. A classic example of such a series is *The Twilight Zone* (1959–64), which used episodes that were comedy, dark comedy, science fiction, horror, and psychological thriller to tell tales of morality and social commentary, all with an undertone of irony and usually with a surprise twist in the end. *Black Mirror* (2011–19) provides an eclectic set of sci-fi arrangements, with episodic emphases on horror, drama, and comedy.

As anticipated, a main type of genre-bending identified by respondents was indeed hybridity. There were interpretations of hybridity as either simple (two genres blended in one piece of content) or complex (more than two genres involved). Examples of simple hybridity included the film *A Nightmare on Elm Street* (1984), in which writer/director Wes Craven merged the slasher horror film with dark comedy, and the TV series *The Office* (2005–13), which is a clear merger of situation comedy and (pseudo) documentary. Complex hybridity was represented by such exemplars as the films *Somewhere in Time* (1980) (romance/science fiction/fantasy), *Avatar* (2009) (science fiction/action/fantasy), and *Parasite* (2019) (drama/thriller/dark comedy), and the series *Stranger Things* (2006–) (horror/science fiction/drama), *Jane the Virgin* (2014–19)

TABLE 7.15 Thematic Summary of Responses to Open-Ended Prompt about Genre-Bending (2021 Users Survey; 2021 Creators Survey; 2021–22 Young Creators Survey)

Theme	Description	Examples
Unfamiliarity	Respondent is uncertain	
Denial	Respondent indicates that they have never encountered such a thing	
Anthology shift	One series with an overarching theme varies by genre across episodes	*The Twilight Zone* (1959–64) *Black Mirror* (2011–19)
Simple hybridity	The combination of two genres in one cultural product	*A Nightmare on Elm Street* (1984) *The Office* (U.S.; 2005–13)
Complex hybridity	The combination of three or more genres in one cultural product	*Somewhere in Time* (1980) *Avatar* (2009) *Stranger Things* (2016–) *Parasite* (2019) *Squid Game* (2021)
Trope appropriation (non-diegetic)	Discrete genre tropes are used/inserted to ascribe meaning; this is non-diegetic, i.e., created by producers/writers for the benefit of spectators and does not reflect what characters within the diegesis are experiencing	*Community* (2009–14) *Kevin Can F**k Himself* (2021–) *Dr. Death* (2021)
Trope appropriation (diegetic)	Discrete genre tropes are used/inserted to ascribe meaning; this is diegetic, i.e., reflects what characters within the diegesis are experiencing (e.g., mentally)	*9 to 5* (1980) *WandaVision* (2021) *Landscapers* (2021)

(telenovela/romance/drama/comedy), and *Squid Game* (2021) (drama/action/ "survival film"). In all cases, the hybridity appears to occur at the *macro*, or program, level. That is, the integration of aspects of situation comedy and documentary form occurs throughout the episodes of *The Office*, not just during limited or circumscribed sections.

In contrast is the notion of the second type of genre-bending, trope appropriation, in which specific elements of a genre are utilized in a more *"micro"* fashion—they are typically limited to one episode of a series or just one small section of a film or series. One way to distinguish the two might be to examine whether the genre characteristics are *blended* in the resultant content, or whether there is a stark, often noticeable insertion, resulting from the appropriation of genre elements. Elements from recognized genres (as painstakingly described throughout this volume) are deconstructed or extracted from their "host" content, and used for particular meaning within alternative content, not necessarily

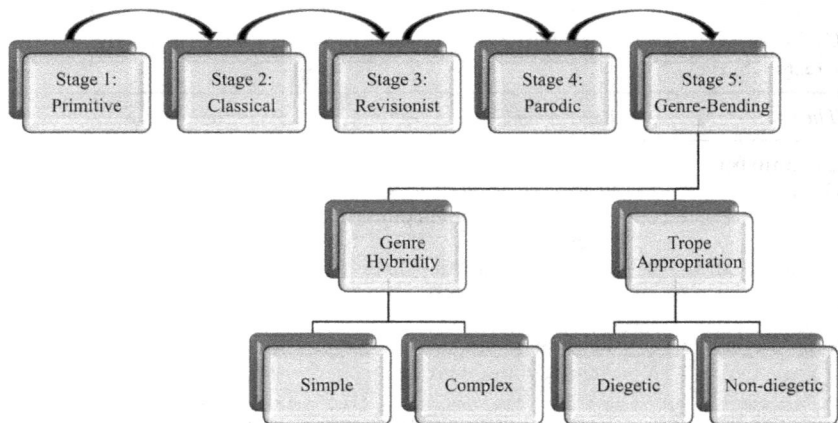

FIGURE 7.2 Genre Evolution: Breakdown of the Stage 5 Concepts

of the host content's genre. This trope appropriation acknowledges the transgressive nature of the deconstruction of genre characteristics that are used within content of all types to forge a meaning that references prior well-worn tropes.

Trope appropriation seems to be manifested widely across television and film content in the 21st century. The fan debates concerning the 2021 miniseries *WandaVision*'s genre-bending, and its validation of the notion of acceptable multiverses, can serve as a point of departure for a discussion of this additional level of hybridity. *WandaVision*'s reliance on story presentation via tributes to different eras of TV sitcoms demands a broad viewer knowledge concerning TV tropes over the years. Other examples of such increasing demands on viewer understanding of genre/format elements include the series *Community*'s (2009-14) structural parodies/homages with intertextuality and references to such well recognized genres/formats as buddy cop films, zombie movies, and Ken Burns documentaries. Other examples offered by survey respondents include the television series, *It's Always Sunny in Philadelphia* (2005–) and *Euphoria* (2019–). Another more limited example is the very discrete inclusion in the 2021 miniseries *Dr. Death* of transitions invoking specific recognizable content such as the opening credits of the 1978-91 TV series *Dallas*. And the 2021 miniseries *Landscapers* incorporated a lengthy homage-seeming section, fusing the look and feel of a revisionist western film into a true-crime story set in 2000s suburban England.

Using and extending the convention of sound in media, this trope appropriation may be thought of as either diegetic in nature, or non-diegetic. If one considers the diegesis the "world of the film" or the "world of the television series," then sounds that characters can hear and respond to are diegetic, while sounds (including a musical score) that characters do not experience in their world are non-diegetic. Applied here, trope appropriation (not limited to sound and music) that is non-diegetic is for the benefit of the spectators only. Examples include the series *Community* (2009–14), which utilized elements of various film and television genres across episodes for the engagement of the viewer, and *Kevin Can F**k Himself* (2021–), which uses a laugh track only when Kevin is with others, and includes no laugh track when Kevin is alone (see also Lieberman et al., 2009)

Diegetic trope appropriation uses elements of genres to represent the reality of character(s) within the narrative. It has been used for quite some time in isolated instances. The classic 1980 film *9 to 5* features a section in which each of the three main characters is shown in marijuana-fueled reverie, fantasizing the way in which she might dispose of their abusive boss. Judy (played by Jane Fonda) imagines stalking and ultimately shooting the boss, shown in crime film form with high-contrast lighting. Doralee (Dolly Parton) daydreams that she lassos and hogties her boss, while dressed in traditional western garb (or at least what would be worn in a Wild West show), her arrival on a white horse accompanied by the theme music of *The Lone Ranger* TV series (1949–57) (i.e., Rossini's William Tell Overture). And Violet (Lily Tomlin) thinks about getting rid of the boss by feeding him a poison apple—while dressed as Snow White and in the company of animated forest creatures. While the genre references—to crime films, westerns, and Disney animation—are certainly the brainchild of *9 to 5*'s writer/director Colin Higgins, they are received by the spectator as interior mental constructions of the three characters. The conceit of the film is that these three characters are familiar with extant genres and are prone to think in genre terms, and also there is the assumption that the film's spectators are likewise conversant in these genres.

Similar assumptions are made by recent popular limited series. In both *WandaVision* (2021) and *Landscapers* (2021), we are led to assume that the characters are knowledgeable about particular genres, and tend to daydream (or more) using their conventions. In the case of *Landscapers*, this genre familiarity is explained with a true-life reveal that the couple were big fans of westerns, especially such films as *High Noon* (1952), starring Gary Cooper. In the case of *WandaVision*, the explanation is also revealed, when it is shown that Wanda experienced her happiest days during her childhood when her nuclear family was intact, watching *The Dick Van Dyke Show* (1961–66). To seek comfort in her adult life, she supernaturally constructs a world that mimics the sitcoms of her youth. What's unique about the *WandaVision* case is, of course, that the representation of genre tropes is not just representing Wanda's inner reality; rather, she has created an objective reality via superpowers.

There is a clear tension between the new and the familiar revealed by the responses to our query about genre-bending. This tension is one that extends throughout this entire volume, based on an overarching truism about humans' inherent need to categorize, and to develop expectancies about these categories based on past experiences. As spectators' past experiences with existing genres have multiplied, spurred by the media of abundance, their palettes (and, perhaps, palates) of genre-based tropes have also increased. This creates a sort of new language of genre elements (such as those appearing in tables through-out this chapter), available for the imparting of meaning in practically any type of content. Looked at in a slightly different way, in the age of the media of abundance, spectators have an ever-expanding need to develop reception skills or tools to navigate this environment of composite content.

Some spectators acknowledge the challenge of such navigation, even look-ing upon receivership as a puzzle or game to be mastered. They may relish the transgressive or even subversive nature of *WandaVision* (which realigns a portion of the Marvel Cinematic Universe (MCU) with the norms of TV sitcoms across the decades). There may be enjoyment gleaned from having all the tools to understand a very complex set of trope appropriations and genre intermixings, as reflected in the musings of the Carlin brothers on the podcast, *Popcorn Culture*. Audience members may see the appropriation of genre tropes as an homage to (not a denigration of) their favorite genre forms, and may take a certain pride in their own stockpile of "narrative currency" made up of genre conventions. There may actually be disappointment when there are no expectations violated, no transgressions to stimulate thought. A straightforward single-genre film or TV program may not meet the needs of contemporary audiences.

Indeed, qualitative interviews with spectators that preceded our surveys revealed a sentiment among some that it's almost an "insult" for a film or series *not* to have challenging references to popular culture and genre tropes. Whereas once, specific intertextual references to such high culture as Shakespeare were seen as an admirable elite barrier to entry, today the references tend toward the popular, be they content-specific intertextuality or genre-derived trope appro-priation (see Gans, 1999, for a delineation of high and pop culture). In 2002, Jaramillo made the argument that networks started pursuing "quality" as opposed to "quantity" of audiences with more intellectually taxing fare, beginning in the late 20th century (e.g., the series *The Sopranos* (1999–2007)). Here, quality was realized via intertextual references, including coverage of psychoanalytical issues (e.g., Tony's visits to psychiatrist for hit-man stresses), liberal humanism, self-reflexivity, satire, focus on character alongside plots, and a lack of redemption at the end. More currently, the references include intertextual references in 2022 Superbowl commercials, such as a reunion of *Sopranos* actors (and theme music) in a Chevy spot that presupposes a degree of media literacy that likely evades millennials and those of Gen Z who were not in that late-90s audience.

Another interesting case, more genre trope appropriation than content-specific intertextuality, might be the 2022 Netflix series, *The Woman in the House Across the Street From the Girl in the Window*. This limited series, ostensibly a parody of the "domestic suspense genre" in popular literature and film, may actually be part parody and part genre-bending, shifting from one to the other throughout the five-plus hours of content, keeping careful viewers on their toes. As noted by critic Laura Miller (2022), the series "sometimes plays like parody, sometimes like pastiche," and Miller queries whether it is indeed "spoof" or "specimen."

A Concluding Note

In conclusion, this chapter profiles moving images by describing creative pro-cesses with the aid of several surveys. We examine the number and types of references used by audiences to describe each film and television genre included in the current datasets. Our survey data identify domains of genre consensus and clarity, as well as disfluency, including how these contents are related to audi-ence viewing patterns. This analysis is informed by macro-level conceptions of genre, including the symbolic interaction between audiences and creators. A key component of internal reality in that context helps define genres, which evolve from primitive, classical, revisionist, and parodic forms (Giannetti & Eyman, 2010). We supplement this typology by adding a fifth stage, *genre-bending*, or the combination of elements from different genres. This new stage is comprised of two components: (1) genre hybridity, the mixing and blending of genres that has received attention in both the scholarly and popular literature, and (2) trope appropriation, the transgressive use of specific genre tropes to create novel nar-rative meaning by drawing on genre-based conventions.

A case-study in genre evolution involving reality TV is also provided. Our 2015 survey of audience expectations reveals key characteristics of real-ity television cited above in the early stages of this genre's development. In particular, the top five references included competition and context featured and the non-scripted nature of the show, as well as references to drama and fighting. The data thus provide evidence of genre hybridity in arguably the most dynamically evolving genre over the past 30 years.

That survey also examined how particular audience uses and gratifications help inform their definitions of both film genres and television genres. After reviewing several patterns of audience genre preference, we conclude that two of the most general uses and gratifications refer to general entertainment—just wanting to be entertained or to waste time. Focusing on audience conceptions for genre catego-ries, the data reveal the largest level of agreement for the musical genre, with one category encompassing just under half of film expectations. This was followed, in order, by horror films, slasher films, foreign films, comedies, and western films. We see the least amount of agreement for film noir—rendering it one of the most ill-defined by audiences—and dramas, which garnered a more diffuse set of expectations. Agreement levels were rather lower for television genres, ranging from 5.8% for dramas to 12.5% for situation comedies and animal/nature shows.

On balance, the more popular genres prompt more diverse expectations and attract larger audiences as a result, enabling each person to find what they like; that is, some genres offer more things to more people, en route to fulfilling more uses and gratifications. Moreover, some genres facilitate greater polysemy, enabling more viewers to identify with them, relative to "narrower" genres that generate less shared meaning. A similar but less sharp pattern is found for television genres.

8
RESPONDING TO THE PANDEMIC IN A STREAMING ENVIRONMENT

Audience choices and behaviors do not exist in a vacuum. The pandemic's advent in 2020 challenged viewers as quarantines forced people indoors, theaters and public places closed, and work and school routines were disrupted. During the spring of 2020, the novel coronavirus (COVID-19) emerged as an unprecedented global pandemic. The US enacted stay-at-home measures, among other mitigation activities, in March of 2020. Then, as schools, theaters, and other segments of the society shut down—or assumed remote operations—audiences migrated to home-based alternatives like cable and streaming.

As theaters shut down that spring, home viewership proliferated while citizens quarantined at home. Cable news networks, for instance, emerged as the main form of evening entertainment for millions during 2020 (Bauder, 2021). Adgate (2021, para 5) details how global theater revenues dropped from $42.3b in 2019 to $12b in 2020, as audiences moved to streaming:

> With shut-downs occurring throughout the globe, consumers relied on digital (video-on-demand, streaming video and electronic sell through) for entertainment. The trend toward digital entertainment was accelerated in 2020 as revenue climbed to $61.8 billion, an increase of 31%. Digital media had accounted for over three-quarters of total theatrical, home/mobile entertainment revenue. There are now 1.1 billion online video subscribers worldwide up 26% from 2019.

In the US, digital revenue increased by a third in 2020, to $26.5 billion, while the digital media share of theatrical revenue increased from 55% in 2019 to 82% in 2020. By the fall of 2021, nations worldwide reported more than 200 million confirmed COVID-19 cases, including 4.4 million deaths

DOI: 10.4324/9781003264828-8

(WHO, 2021b). The arrival of several different vaccines in 2021 helped mitigate the viral spread, although the pandemic raged on throughout the year (WHO, 2021a) and into 2022.

Both work and leisure patterns had thus changed as we collected data through early 2022. Social interaction was also curtailed, at least for the short term. People spent more time at home, as film releases dried up and commercial actors responded with more streaming options. Restrictions lifted slowly, with theater rentals and a return to the drive-ins. During the quarantine, audiences with access to their own devices developed videos for sharing and blogs with moving images. The home-viewing context was altered, as families and friends in "safe, comfortable pods" scheduled viewing parties of films available through paid streaming at the same time the films were released for exhibition in brick-and-mortar theaters.

As society gradually reopened through 2021, movie theaters did so as well. On the two-year anniversary of the March 2020 shut-down, US box office revenues were projected to be 60% of prepandemic levels in 2019 (Freyman, 2022). As the receding pandemic freed audiences from the confines of their home theaters, Netflix experienced its first-ever decline in subscribership during the first quarter of 2022, prompting a 35% drop in stock value (Bursztnsky & Alessandrini, 2022). Still, factoring in streaming, recent data reported in *Variety* suggest that the film industry is enjoying "a return to prepandemic levels" (Rubin, 2022, para 1). Conversely, after having been buoyed during the pandemic, prime-time viewership receded; viewing declined 38% at CNN, 34% at Fox News, and 25% at MSNBC, for example, while number of unique visitors to *The New York Times* website declined 44% in the year ending in November 2021 (Bauder, 2021).

Responding to the Pandemic: How Did the Pandemic Affect Media Use Patterns?

This chapter will examine how audiences responded to the pandemic and their expectations for viewing patterns in the "return to normal." In October, 2021, we mounted a survey on audience media use patterns to paint a picture of what has happened. The 2021 Users Survey, described in Chapter 1, is fairly well balanced by gender, well educated, fairly affluent, and racially diverse.

As the pandemic continued, statewide and local restrictions and policies were uneven. For many, the pandemic seemed to end, but for many it continued through 2021 as the public was slow to return to theaters and indoor venues. Our sample is national, so we cannot specify that all had the same pandemic experiences or the speed with which things returned to "normal." Our 2021 sample also is more educated than the 2015 sample, and direct comparisons on estimating parameters are less feasible. But we know from the latest survey how people see their situations, and we have additional information about pandemic-related media use, particularly streaming.

Our 2021 Users Survey is an active group of media users, with more than half indicating they're frequent movie fans, with many going out to see films weekly if not more. They also are avid viewers across platforms, and this viewing behavior is closely related to education, with positive correlations between education and frequency one watches films on a tablet, computer, or cell phone (r=.21, p=.003), watches a TV program on a tablet, computer, or cell phone (r=.24, p<.001), streams a movie on home television (r=.13, p=.003), streams a TV program on home television (r=.16, p=.03), browses TikTok for videos to watch (r=.28, p=.07), and watches videos on a smartphone (r=.24, p<.001). In addition to being fans of the moving image, our educated sample also does a lot of reading, with positive relationships between level of education and reading magazines (r=.19, p<.01), newspapers (r=.14, p=.06), and books (r=.17, p=.02).

Education is also related to the producer role, with more educated respondents posting photos on Facebook more often (r=.28, p<.001), posting videos on Facebook more often (r=.37, p<.001), posting videos on YouTube more often (r=.23, p<.001), and posting videos on TikTok more often (r=.33, p<.001). Interestingly, going on Facebook and checking emails are not related to level of education.

While education clearly is an important predictor of film going and other media use variables, age is another factor. We find that age is negatively associated with browsing TikTok for videos to watch (r=-.19, p<.01). Age is positively related to checking email more frequently (r=.22, p<.001). There were no significant differences on viewing, posting or reading behaviors between men and women.

So how has the pandemic affected the behaviors of our respondents? Respondents were asked to what extent their media behavior increased, decreased, or remained the same during the pandemic. The results are shown in Table 8.1. Between a quarter and a third of our respondents saw no changes during the pandemic, whether using legacy media, watching films, TV shows or videos, attending live events, or their activities as producers—sharing photos or videos on social media such as Facebook, YouTube, or TikTok. Some 40–50% of respondents reported increasing their use of legacy media other than the "moving image"—reading books, magazines or newspapers, and listening to the radio or podcasts. This concurs with anecdotal evidence that people stuck at home had more time on their hands and used available outlets. We also see reports of greater attention to the "moving image, whether at home or elsewhere." For example, around half of respondents reported spending more time watching a film on a tablet, computer, or cell phone, watching a TV program on a tablet, computer, or cell phone, streaming a movie on home TV, streaming a TV program on home TV, or browsing YouTube for videos to watch. Moreover, large numbers reported spending more time browsing social media for videos to watch. Smaller increases were reported for seeing live events such as concerts or plays. Our data are consistent with results of a

TABLE 8.1 Changes Reported in Use of Media and Communication Technologies During Pandemic (2021 Users Survey)

Media Behavior	Have Done None at All during Pandemic	Have Done Much Less during Pandemic	Have Done a Bit Less Often During Pandemic	This Has Not Changed during Pandemic	Have Done a Bit More during Pandemic	Have Done Much More Often during Pandemic
Legacy Media						
Watch television	1.5%	7.6%	11.2%	23.9%	34.5%	21.3%
Listen to the radio	5.6%	8.1%	12.2%	30.5%	29.4%	14.2%
Read a magazine	4.1%	6.6%	13.7%	36.0%	25.4%	14.2%
Read a book	1.5%	4.6%	11.7%	34.5%	27.9%	19.8%
Read a newspaper	5.6%	5.6%	7.6%	35.0%	29.9%	16.2%
See films in a theater	16.8%	9.1%	15.7%	23.4%	25.9%	9.1%
Media on Technology						
Listen to podcasts	2.0%	4.1%	12.2%	35.0%	28.4%	18.3%
Watch a film on a tablet, computer or cell phone	4.6%	4.6%	14.2%	28.4%	30.5%	17.8%
Watch a TV program on a tablet, computer or cell phone	3.6%	5.1%	12.2%	27.4%	36.5%	15.2%
Stream a movie on home TV	0.5%	5.6%	9.6%	29.4%	34.0%	20.8%
Stream a TV show on home TV	1.0%	2.5%	11.2%	30.5%	37.6%	17.3%
Surf the web for pleasure, not work	3.0%	9.6%	11.7%	24.9%	34.5%	16.2%
Check my email	1.0%	3.0%	12.2%	29.9%	30.5%	23.4%
Go on Facebook	2.0%	6.6%	16.2%	25.4%	27.9%	21.8%
Post photos on Facebook	3.6%	7.1%	9.6%	33.0%	26.9%	19.8%
Post videos on Facebook	6.6%	5.6%	15.7%	29.9%	30.5%	11.7%
Browse YouTube for videos to watch	2.0%	5.6%	11.7%	25.4%	33.5%	21.8%
Post videos on YouTube	10.2%	6.6%	12.2%	29.4%	30.5%	11.2%
Browse TikTok for videos to watch	8.1%	5.1%	11.2%	28.9%	26.9%	19.8%
Post videos on TikTok	13.2%	7.1%	9.6%	26.9%	30.5%	12.7%
Play video games on some device	2.0%	4.6%	14.7%	29.4%	29.4%	19.8%
Watch videos on a smartphone	2.5%	3.6%	11.2%	29.4%	29.9%	23.4%
Attend Live Events						
Go to see live musical concerts, events	13.2%	8.1%	13.7%	29.9%	23.4%	11.7%
Go to see live plays performed in a theater	14.7%	8.1%	12.7%	25.4%	33.0%	6.1%

national survey conducted July 13–17, 2020, which asked American adults what they did to cope with the pandemic (Pew, 2020). Nine in ten US adults said they watch TV or movies at least weekly to cope with the outbreak, including three fourths (73%) who say they do so daily.

We also examined how social categories were related to reports of media use changes during the pandemic. Education is the most important of the five variables, predicting more readership of magazines and newspapers during the pandemic. Those with more formal education also say they went out to see films and watched them more often on mobile devices than did less educated respondents. The educated also report more browsing and posting behaviors—posting more photos on Facebook and more videos on all three social media, YouTube, TikTok, and Facebook. In contrast to less educated viewers, they went out to see more live theater and musical concerts or events.

The older our respondent, the less often they went out to see films in theaters. But these older audiences also did less Internet surfing for pleasure while checking their email more often—perhaps as a function of working at home. Women reported listening to the radio more often, watching TV programs on mobile devices more often, and streaming TV programs on home TV more often, relative to the men in our sample. Women also reported going out to live theater and musical concerts and events more often than did men. Race, coded here as being White, was only important for three items, posting videos less often on Facebook and TikTok, but watching videos on mobile devices more often. Several media use variables where changes were reported during the pandemic are not related to any of the five social categories—watching television, listening to podcasts, reading books, playing video games on some device, and browsing for videos on TikTok [Table available online].

The pandemic provided audiences an opportunity to engage in some activities encouraged by quarantine restrictions. Some 27.5% of our respondents said they rented a whole movie theater to see a first run film with family or friends. Nearly a quarter (24.6%) said they went to see a drive-in movie, where they could view on the "big screen" while remaining in the company of only those they trusted were safe from the virus. In addition, 41.5% said they watched a movie or TV with family or friends, again a quite safe option. Nearly 35.7% said they simultaneously streamed a TV show or movie with others at another location.

Respondents were also more active posting photos or videos on social media, with almost half reporting they posted more photos on Facebook and slightly lower proportion posting more videos on YouTube, TikTok, or Facebook.

So how did our sample access options for viewing "moving images" during the pandemic? As Table 8.2 shows, only 13% of our sample do not have access to either cable or satellite, and cable still has the broadest reach. With

TABLE 8.2 Use of Streaming and Other Subscription Services for the Moving Image During the Pandemic (2021 Users Survey)

Delivery Services	Subscribers
Cable television	60.4%
Satellite television	47.8%
Neither cable nor satellite television	13.0%
Streaming Services Used	
Netflix	81.2%
Disney+	68.1%
Amazon Prime Video	60.9%
YouTube Premium	32.4%
Discovery+	29.5%
HBO Max	28.0%
Apple TV	25.6%
Google Play	24.2%
Hulu	22.2%
Android TV	13.0%

access to streaming services "built in" to smart televisions, it should be no surprise that so many of our respondents can access so many services, though likely not all at once, with shifts from one system offering a particularly high-profile series at one moment, then shifting to another when that one ends and a more attractive option appears elsewhere. The most popular streaming services are shown in Table 8.2, where only eight streaming services are used by more than 10% of the sample, while another 11 services attract between 5% and 10% of respondents (Paramount+, Peacock, Philo TV, Vidgo, AT&T TV Now, Dailymotion, NFL Game Pass, Roku, Chromecast, T-Mobile TVision, AMC+). The other 12 services record less than 5% users.

Does Use of Services Relate to Genre Preferences?

We would expect that access to cable or satellite and various streaming services would lead to greater exposure of various genres and subsequently broader genre repertoires. First, we look at whether there is greater viewing of specific genres by subscribers vs. non-subscribers of cable and satellite. As we see in Table 8.3, subscription to both cable and satellite stimulate greater viewing of most television genres and more than half of film genres.

Use of the various streaming services should also stimulate use of various genres, so we constructed a streaming variable by adding up use across all the various services. The total ranged from 1 (9.2%) or 2 (10.1%) to an average of 4.9 and a median of 4, with three individuals claiming use of more than 15. Analyses show that all of the television genres and all but three film genres (musicals, detective films, or documentary films) are viewed more often by those using more streaming services [Table available online].

TABLE 8.3 Differences in Genre Viewing by Cable and Satellite Subscribers vs. Others (2021 Users Survey)

Genres Viewed More Frequently by Cable Subscribers vs Non-subscribers	*Genres Viewed More Frequently by Satellite Subscribers vs. Non-subscribers*
Film Genres	
Musicals	Musicals
Westerns	Westerns
Horror films	Horror films
Film noir films	Film noir films
Action films #	
	Animated films
	Mystery/suspense films
	Biographical films
Film parodies #	Film parodies
Slasher films	Slasher films
Mockumentaries	Mockumentaries
	Chick flicks
Slapstick films #	Slapstick films
	Fantasy films
	Foreign films
Romantic dramas	Romantic dramas
	Romantic comedies
Gangster films	Gangster films
Samurai films	Samurai films
Epic films #	Epic films
Sports films	Sports films #
	Historical films
	Superhero films
War films #	War films
TV Genres	
	Situation comedies #
Dramas #	Dramas
Soap operas	Soap operas
Detective shows	
News magazine shows	News magazine shows
Music or talent competitions	Music or talent competitions
	Reality TV shows
	Late-night talk shows
Children's programs	Children's programs on TV
Animal/nature shows	Animal/nature shows
	Science fiction shows

Note: Genres not related to cable or satellite subscription are omitted from the table. #$p<.10$; the other differences were all significant at $p<.05$.

Given these results, we would expect that cable and satellite subscription and use of more streaming services would be related to genre repertoires. Tables 8.4 and 8.5 confirm this expectation for cable television subscribers as well as satellite subscribers, who have larger film genre repertoires compared to nonsubscribers.

TABLE 8.4 Differences in Film and TV Genre Repertoires by Cable Subscription (2021 Users Survey)

Film and TV Repertoires	Cable Television		
	Subscribers (n=125)	Non-Subscribers (n=82)	One-way ANOVAs
Cumulative Measures of Film Genre Repertoire			
Frequent Film Repertoire (no. of film genres watched very often or all the time)	13.98	11.77	$t=1.9$ $p=.06$
Often Film Repertoire (no. of film genres watched often, very often, or all the time)	7.57	8.84	$t=2.2$ $p=.03$
Film Sampling Repertoire (no. of film genres watched once in a while, often, very often, or all the time)	4.35	7.11	$t=2.8$ $p=.005$
Cumulative Measures of TV Genre Repertoire			
Frequent TV Repertoire (no. of TV genres watched very often or all the time)	4.94	4.01	$t=2.04$ $p<.05$
Often TV Repertoire (no. of TV genres watched often, very often, or all the time)	8.26	7.01	$t=2.67$ $p<.01$
TV Sampling Repertoire (no. of TV genres watched once in a while, often, very often, or all the time)	10.10	8.89	$t=3.61$ $p<.001$

We find a similar pattern for use of streaming services, with larger repertoires for those using more streaming services (see Table 8.6).

Communication Roles and Orientations in the Pandemic Context

The 2021 Users Survey provided an opportunity to return to several concepts we thought might be related to viewing behaviors and communication roles as processors of images, as creators of images, and as consumers. These concepts were introduced in Chapter 3. The items in the 2021 survey were developed to represent the current options and technologies. First, we measured the key roles audiences fill, the processor role (viewing films and TV programs and other media content), the sender/creator role (the focus of Chapter 4, where social media videos are prominent creations), and the consumer role (using online and other technologies for our consumer needs). The three key roles were measured with the following items, which were summed up for scales tapping the strength of each concept.

TABLE 8.5 Differences in Film and TV Genre Repertoires by Satellite Subscription (2021 Users Survey)

Film and TV Repertoires	Satellite Service		
	Subscribers (n=99)	Non-Subscribers (n=108)	One-way ANOVAs
Cumulative Measures of Film Genre Repertoire			
Frequent Film Repertoire (no. of film genres watched very often or all the time)	14.98	11.38	t=3.28 p<.001
Often Film Repertoire (no. of film genres watched often, very often, or all the time)	24.76	20.10	t=4.26 p<.001
Film Sampling Repertoire (no. of film genres watched once in a while, often, very often, or all the time)	29.18	26.22	t=3.85 p<.001
Cumulative Measures of TV Genre Repertoire			
Frequent TV Repertoire (no. of TV genres watched very often or all the time)	5.52	3.69	t=4.26 p<.001
Often TV Repertoire (no. of TV genres watched often, very often, or all the time)	8.81	6.80	t=4.58 p<.001
TV Sampling Repertoire (no. of TV genres watched once in a while, often, very often, or all the time)	10.28	9.01	t=3.86 p<.001

Traditional Processor Role (Cronbach's alpha=.70)

- I love that there are so many options for finding something to watch or listen to with so many options on line or through streaming services. (mean (M)=5.33)
- There is so much available today that I sometimes feel almost overwhelmed with the choices available online or through streaming. (M=5.35)
- I enjoy just browsing through online videos or streaming options to find something that fits my personal tastes. (M=5.41)

Sender/Creator Role (alpha=.84)

- I often take advantage of the opportunities to send messages and connect with others through Twitter, Facebook posts, or other social media. (M=5.20)
- Once you had to be a journalist to "speak" to the broader audience but today I feel empowered that I can do this often via Twitter, other social media or online vehicles. (M=5.11)

- Today the only thing limiting my desire to communicate online or through social media to audiences is time and money. (M=5.09)
- I've always felt a need to express myself, to communicate with other people one way or another. (M=5.08)

Consumer Role (correlation between the two items=.52, p<.001)

- I relish being able to stay home and take care of business, to accomplish things using new technologies. (M=5.43)
- I do as much shopping and "running errands" online or through technologies as I can. (M=5.40)

How are these three roles related to the use of mass media and, in particular, viewing the moving image? Furthermore, how are social categories related to the relative importance of these roles? Analysis shows relationships between the three composite measures of the roles and how often respondents engage in the various media behaviors during the pandemic. Composite figures represent the strength of the roles for our respondents, and we found that the stronger the role, the more often respondents engage in most all these behaviors. The audience role is related to all of the media use measures, from going

TABLE 8.6 Correlations between Film and TV Genre Repertoires and Number of Streaming Services Used (2021 Users Survey)

Film and TV Repertoires	*Number of Streaming Services Used*
Cumulative Measures of Film Genre Repertoire	
Frequent Film Repertoires	.20★★
(no. of film genres watched very often or all the time)	
Often Film Repertoire	.24★★★
(no. of film genres watched often, very often, or all the time)	
Film Sampling Repertoire	.26★★★
(no. of film genres watched once in a while, often, very often, or all the time)	
Cumulative Measures of TV Genre Repertoire	
Frequent TV Repertoire	.18★★
(no. of TV genres watched very often or all the time)	
Often TV Repertoire	.21★★
(no. of TV genres watched often, very often, or all the time)	
TV Sampling Repertoire	.24★★★
(no. of TV genres watched once in a while, often, very often, or all the time)	

Note: n=207. ★★p<.01; ★★★p<.001

out to see films in a theater, to watching TV or streaming films to posting videos on social media. The sender role is related to all media behaviors except surfing the Internet, and the consumer role is related to all but listening to the radio [Table available online].

We saw in Chapter 3 that orientations toward technology are related to media use in the 2015 Users Survey, and we replicated the measures in the 2021 Users Survey, as follows.

Tech Enthusiast Scale (alpha=.50)

- I love the options at my finger-tips today, watching videos on my phone, texting, streaming films. (M=5.4)
- I can hardly wait to see what technology comes next. (M=5.4)
- I think I'm getting less patient and am glad I have a smartphone or other digital options to fill the time. (M=5.2)

Com Traditionalist Scale (alpha=.73)

- I'm more a traditionalist, preferring to read physical copies of books, magazines, and newspapers rather than digital versions. (M=5.1)
- I like the variety of entertainment available today but sometimes feel it's too much. (M=5.3)
- I think that the new technologies have begun to dominate our lives, occupying too much of our time. (M=5.2)
- I'd still rather talk to people over the phone than text. (M=5.1)

Unlike the fitful and weak relationships found in the 2015 Users Survey, the two scales in 2021 were related to virtually all the media behaviors (see Table 8.7). The traditionalist item included a couple with reservations about technology but that doesn't seem to cancel out an enthusiasm for using them.

The importance of these roles may vary by social categories. We found that the audience role is only related to not being White, and the consumer role is only related to higher education, higher income, and being African American. The creator, sender role is positively related to level of education and not being White, or being African American. Age is not related to any of the roles [Table available online].

Since the focus of this book is viewing film and TV genres, we checked to see whether the strength of these roles told us anything about the popularity of the different film and TV genres. Analyses show that the audience role is related to the most popular film genres, but not slasher films, chick flicks, mockumentaries, film noir, or science fiction films. Interestingly, the sender or creator role is related to all the film and TV genres. The consumer role is related to all film genres but the westerns, animated films, foreign films, romantic comedies, and superhero films, and to all TV genres except news magazine and science fiction programs [Table available online].

TABLE 8.7 Correlations between Media Use and Orientations toward Technology in the Pandemic Context (2021 Users Survey)

Media Use	Tech Enthusiast Scale	Com Traditionalist Scale
Watch TV	.29★★★	.28★★★
Listen to the radio	.21★★	.38★★★
Listen to podcasts	.24★★★	.23★★★
Read a magazine	.20★★	.39★★★
Read a book	.22★★	.31★★★
Read a newspaper	.31★★★	.32★★★
Go out to see films in a theater	.20★★	.37★★★
Watch a film on a tablet/ computer/cell phone	.33★★★	.38★★★
Watch a TV programs tablet/ computer/cell phone	.30★★★	.31★★★
Stream a movie on home TV	.26★★★	.21★★
Stream a TV program on home TV	.24★★★	.21★★
Check my email	.23★★	.38★★★
Go on Facebook	.30★★★	.38★★★
Post photos on Facebook	.29★★★	.47★★★
Post videos on Facebook	.26★★★	.49★★★
Browse YouTube for videos to watch	.32★★★	.23★★★
Post videos on YouTube	.25★★★	.46★★★
Browse TikTok for videos to watch	.27★★★	.41★★★
Post videos on TikTok	.22★★	.42★★★
Play video games on some device	.26★★★	.22★★
Watch videos on a smartphone	.30★★★	.28★★★
Text family of friends rather than call them on the phone	.25★★★	.18★★

Note: Surfing the Internet for pleasure, not work was not related to either measure and was omitted from the table. n=195. ★★p<.01; ★★★p<.001

Audience Processes of the Moving Image in the Pandemic Context

We see that the pandemic kept people indoors and stimulated use of some media, and this could have also changed how audiences process the moving image. As we saw in the previous section, people's roles as processors, creators, and consumers are strongly related to how often they use the mass media. The reduced mobility appears to have enhanced people's appreciation for services utilizing online and other technologies as well as accessing options for viewing the moving image. Here we probe further into these viewing decisions by looking at the extent to which people seek out novelty, maximize their interest, look for variety, and engage in binge watching.

When you're cooped up inside and have reduced mobility, audiences may tire of the "same old thing" and seek novel experiences in choosing different films and television programs. The 2021 Users Survey gave us an opportunity to measure novelty seeking with a set of items that speak directly to the current viewing environment. The 5-item scale was adapted from Lee and Crompton (1992). The items formed a robust novelty seeking scale.

Novelty Seeking (alpha=.82, *n*=207) (Scale adapted from "Change from Routine" Dimension, Lee & Crompton, 1992; 1 = strongly disagree and 7 = strongly agree).

- I like to watch films and TV shows that allow me to explore new things. (*M*=5.3)
- I want to experience new and different things when watching films and TV shows. (*M*=5.5)
- I want to encounter customs and cultures different from those in my own environment when watching films and TV shows. (*M*=5.3)
- My ideal film or TV watching experience involves looking at things I have not seen before. (*M*=5.3)
- I want there to be a sense of discovery involved in my watching of films and TV shows. (*M*=5.5)

We would expect those seeking novelty to have broader genre sampling repertoires for both film and television genres. As Table 8.8 shows, that's precisely the case. Those who seek novelty have broader film and TV genre repertoires. They also avoid fewer genres altogether, as the negative correlations suggest.

TABLE 8.8 Relationships between Film and TV Genre Repertoires and Novelty Seeking (2021 Users Survey)

Film and TV Genre Repertoires	*Novelty Seeking*
Cumulative Measures of Film Genre Repertoire	
Frequent Film Repertoire (no. of film genres watched very often or all the time)	.49★★★
Often Film Repertoire (no. of film genres watched often, very often, or all the time)	.40★★★
Film Sampling Repertoire (no. of film genres watched once in a while, often, very often, or all the time)	.28★★★
Never Film Repertoire (no. of film genres never watched)	-.23★★★
Cumulative Measures of TV Genre Repertoire	
Frequent TV Repertoire (no. of TV genres watched very often or all the time)	.47★★★
Often TV Repertoire (no. of TV genres watched often, very often, or all the time)	.39★★★
TV Sampling Repertoire (no. of TV genres watched once in a while, often, very often, or all the time)	.22★★
Never TV Repertoire (no. of TV genres never watched)	-.15★

Note: ★*p*<.05; ★★*p*<.01; ★★★*p*<.001

We know that people's viewing choices have changed dramatically from the days when audiences had single rather than multiplex theaters and access to no more than three channels on their home televisions. The standing joke from years ago was that people were couch potatoes who watched whatever was on TV because they were too lazy to get up and change channels. In fact, the networks counted on this inertia and programmed schedules in hopes of passing on audiences. The diffusion of the remote changed that picture, and then the explosion of options at home through cable, satellite and streaming, and growth of 24-screen multiplexes created the era of abundance for viewing the moving image (e.g., Mittell, 2010). The film and TV genre repertoires in the earlier section illustrate one facet of the viewing experience. But abundance also allows audiences to deliberately seek variety, to maximize their interests—perhaps with repeat viewing, or to engage in "binge watching." These viewing processes were tapped in the 2021 Users Survey using the following items (all measured on a 1 = strongly disagree to 7 = strongly agree response scale):

Variety Seeking (correlation between the two items=.34★★★)

- I really like a lot of variety in my life, especially in the types of films I watch in theaters or on TV. (M=5.3)
- I often flip through the channels available to find something new, some type of film or program I've not seen before. (M=5.1)

Interest Maximization (correlation between the two items=.17★)

- I know what I like the most and search through my options to find them. (M=5.4)
- When I try something new, I often find it a waste of time and abandon viewing to watch something familiar, that I know I'll enjoy. (M=5.0)

Binge Watching

- I did more binge watching of TV programs (during the pandemic). (M=5.3)

Interest is a tricky variable, and we see that in how items tapping interest maximization, variety seeking (to find something interesting) and binge watching (lots of the same programs one after the other or in a condensed time frame) relate to each other. They fit into the same scale (alpha=.60), but don't exactly measure the "same" thing, so we examined relationships involving the five-item score as well as the separate measures of all three concepts—variety seeking, interest maximization, and binge watching. As Table 8.9 shows, the three processes are strongly related to frequent viewing of the moving image, with a couple of exceptions.

TABLE 8.9 Correlations between Watching the Moving Image and Three Processes—Variety Seeking, Interest Maximization and Binge Watching (2021 Users Survey)

Frequency of Viewing the Moving Image During the Pandemic	Composite 5-item score	Variety Seeking	Interest Maximization	Binge Watching
Watch television	.35★★★	.40★★★	.20★★	.29★★★
Go out to see a film in a theater	.28★★★	.23★★★	.28★★★	
Watch a film on a tablet/computer/ cell phone	.42★★★	.44★★★	.26★★★	.17★
Stream a movie on home TV	.25★★★	.22★★	.16★	.25★★★
Stream a TV program on home TV	.29★★★	.26★★★	.20★★	.20★★
Browse YouTube for videos to watch	.15★	.22★★		
Browse TikTok for videos to watch	.29★★★	.28★★★	.24★★★	.13#
Watch videos on a smartphone	.36★★★	.32★★★	.29★★★	.25★★★

Note: #.05<*p*<.10; ★*p*<.05; ★★*p*<.01; ★★★*p*<.001

But what film and TV genres are chosen by those seeking variety or trying to maximize their interests one way or another? When we use the 2021 Users Survey to look at relationships between how often one sees each genre and the five scores measuring variety seeking, interest maximization, and binge watching, we learn that all the correlations are statistically significant, with one exception: Those who watch film noir are not seeking variety. So people seek variety in their own subset of film and television genres, and, similarly, maximize their interests the same way. Apparently, one can binge watch and maximize one's viewing of film noir, even though it's not chosen for variety seeking.

Who is it that is more likely to seek novelty, variety, or engage in interest maximization or binge watching? There are no differences noted for age or gender, but education is positively related to four of the five scores and the correlation with novelty seeking approaches statistical significance. Binge watching is only associated with education, while White ethnicity is negatively related and Black ethnicity positively related to novelty seeking, variety seeking and interest maximization (see Table 8.10).

In Chapter 7, the concept of genre hybridity was discussed at a macro level. We also measured our viewers' affinity for the phenomenon of hybridity with three items in the 2021 Users Survey, which allows us to examine relationships at the individual level. The items were:

TABLE 8.10 Correlations between Novelty Seeking, Variety Seeking, Interest Maximization, and Binge Watching and Social Categories *(2021 Users Survey)*

	Education	*Household Income*	*White Ethnicity*	*Black Ethnicity*
Novelty seeking	.13#	.13#	-.19★	.18★
Interest maximization 5-item score	.17★	.14#	-.18★	.18★
Interest maximization 2-item score	.18★		-.20★★	.14★
Variety seeking	.15★	.15★	-.16★★	.18★
Binge watching	.15★			

Note: There were no statistically-significant relationships involving age or gender. Total *n*=207; *n*=195 with missing data; #.05<*p*<.10; ★*p*<.05; ★★*p*<.01

Hybridity (alpha=.65)

- I like it when a traditional film or TV program challenges me with different conventions, making me think a bit more. (*M*=5.4)
- I really enjoy mashups of genres in film or TV. (*M*=5.3)
- I think it's great when film or TV content has a reference back to other content that I know. (*M*=5.3)

Who are the folks expressing the greatest interest in such viewing? We did not uncover any relationships with age or gender. The strength of one hybridity item is positively related to education level. We also find that the hybridity score is positively correlated with how often respondents watch each film and television genre, suggesting hybridity is a film "fan-favorite" expectation. Hybridity is also related to being a tech enthusiast, a com traditionalist, and all three roles described earlier (processor-viewer role, sender-creator role, and the consumer role), as well as the viewing processes: Novelty seeking (*r*=.64, *p*<.001), variety seeking (*r*=.54, *p*<.001), the 5-item interest maximization scale (*r*=.51, *p*=.002), the 2-item interest maximization score (*r*=.52, *p*<.001), and binge watching of TV programs (*r*=.31, *p*<.001). Hybridity is also positively related to both the film genre and the TV genre repertoires.

Those with a strong affinity for hybridity are more frequent media users in general—watching TV, listening to the radio, listening to podcasts, reading all three print media, going out to see films in a theater or watch films or TV programs on a tablet, computer or cell phone, streaming movies or TV programs on home TV, and watching videos on a smartphone.

But we specifically asked whether they engaged in use of the various media *more often* during the pandemic, and we find a similar strong pattern of relationships with hybridity: Watching TV, listening to the radio, listening to podcasts, reading magazines, books, and newspapers, going out to see films in a theater or watching films or TV programs on a tablet, computer or cell phone, streaming TV programs on home TV, and browsing YouTube and TikTok for videos to watch.

In general, it looks like these factors represent a mixed bag–film fans like the notion of hybridity, and they generally are heavier media users and engaged in even more use during the pandemic.

A Concluding Note

The present chapter set out to profile viewing during the pandemic, including the migration of viewing from theaters to emerging streaming technologies. Education, the most influential social locator here, is positively related to film going and several dimensions of social media use. In particular, education is also related to the producer role (e.g., posting photos on Facebook as well as videos on YouTube, TikTok, and Facebook). Age is inversely related to browsing TikTok for videos to watch. Our survey data are consistent with national data (e.g., Pew, 2020) suggesting that most increased their consumption of video at home during the pandemic, as 40–50% of respondents reported increasing their use of legacy media (e.g., reading books, magazines, or newspapers, and listening to the radio or podcasts).

But these audiences also did less Internet surfing for pleasure while checking their email more often—perhaps as a function of working at home. Older respondents were less likely to go outside to see films in theaters. Focusing on genre preferences, subscription to both cable and satellite stimulate greater viewing of most television genres and more than half of film genres. Subscribers of cable television, satellite subscribers, and larger numbers of streaming services have larger film genre repertoires, compared to nonsubscribers.

The 2021 Users Survey focused on several concepts related to viewing behaviors and communication roles as members of the audience (processors of images), as creators of images and messages, and the consumer role. Our data suggest that the audience role is only related to Nonwhite ethnicity, and the consumer role is only related to higher education, higher income, and being African American. The creator, sender role is positively related to level of education and not being White, or being African American. Whereas prototypical scales from the 2015 Users survey revealed a weak set of relationships, the 2021 scales were related to virtually all of the media behaviors.

Study data also reveal that the audience role is related to the most popular film genres, and the sender or creator role is related to all of the film and TV genres. Those seeking novelty enjoy broader genre sampling repertoires for both film and television genres. Moreover, those who are more likely to see each genre are also more likely to engage in binge watching, interest maximization, and variety seeking.

Again, education emerges as the most explanatory of the social locators. Importantly, hybridity appreciation is also positively related to education level and also related to being a technology enthusiast and communication traditionalist, as well as the film and TV genre repertoires. Generally, film fans like the notion of hybridity, and they're heavier media users, particularly during the pandemic.

9

FINAL THOUGHTS

This book has focused on audience perceptions of film and television genres, but what's the significance of the hours of time spent by audiences watching the moving image that are crafted by creative people? We have little data on the "effects" of the moving image, and this has long been the major focus of our research into mass media other than film (e.g., Eadie, 2022). Film itself has long been considered a creative art, and the literature addressing it—focused on artistic and humanistic dimensions of the moving image—reflects that fact (e.g., Mittell, 2004). But it's useful to remember that Hollywood's chief professional honorary organization is known as the "Academy of Motion Picture Arts *and Sciences*" (emphasis added).

Broadening the latter rubric to include the social sciences, this volume makes the case for the utility of empirical scholarly data in film studies. After examining the literature on the concept of genre and introducing the four surveys in Chapter 1, we lay out the features and structure of 31 film and 11 TV genres. Drawing from the work of film scholars and observers, we then compare those artistic genre conceptions with audience perceptions in Chapter 2, finding high agreement among audiences and scholars of the moving image. In Chapter 3, we see a profile of viewers and identify patterns of viewing for popular genres, with comedy, action, drama, adventure, and animated films emerging as the most popular categories.

In Chapter 4, we focus on the creator role as audiences shift from being "merely" members of the audience to creator and entrepreneurial roles, using technology to create moving images, especially for social media. Half of respondents in the 2021 Users Survey post photos or videos on Facebook daily or more often, and half post several times a week or more often on YouTube and TikTok. And it's the gratification of feeling a sense of achievement,

DOI: 10.4324/9781003264828-9

connecting to other people, and feeling productive that drive this activity. Moreover, study data reveal a split between the general population and young creators in the topics featured. The broader group favor social issues, pets and animals, and beautiful images of nature, while the younger creators focus on things that feature them, their lifestyles, and their own image. Stories that make people smile or laugh are popular with both groups.

In Chapter 5, we develop and test concepts that capture film and television genre repertoires (the number of genres viewed most regularly), finding that larger genre repertoires are found for those seeking novelty or to maximize their interests. In Chapter 6, we look at how viewers' genre preferences are related to the size of screens—in the theater, at home on TV, and on mobile vehicles such as laptops and cell phones.

Chapter 7 builds content theory, finding for example, that the uses and gratifications that audiences seek are related to numerous film and television genres. Examining macro data, we learn that audience agreement on expectations is highest for the musical, followed by the western and horror film. TV sitcoms have the most consensus for TV genres. This chapter also examines the notion of hybridity, how many genres share similar features. External influences such as reviews (Ma & Atkin, in press), the general buzz and influence from friends drive the frequency viewers go out to see particular films. In a theoretical discussion, Chapter 7 looks at genre-bending, genre hybridity, and trope appropriation. In Chapter 8, we look at how viewers respond to the COVID-19 pandemic in a streaming environment, finding that use of streaming services, as well as cable and satellite subscription, are related with larger film and TV genre repertoires, as is novelty seeking. We also find that watching television, streaming and browsing for videos are related to binge watching, variety seeking, and interest maximization.

Many of the findings described here uncover consensus and agreements, putting audiences on common ground. Although one could question whether or not Americans have shared a "common culture," most would agree that any consensus has been fractured in politics and culture. As institutions that once seemed to promote unity have lost much influence, popular culture has long been regarded as neutral ground, especially that found in visual media–film and television. When Lucy appeared pregnant on television in 1952, the entire country paid attention. Final episodes of major series drew large audiences to the small screen, to find out who shot JR (*Dallas*, 1978-91), or how the Korean War ended for a series of doctors (*M*A*S*H*, 1972-83). In more recent years, only national spectacles such as the Super Bowl or World Series have managed to capture the attention of broader audiences. But even these are fitful meeting grounds for the larger populace, much less sports fans.

Several theories speak to how mass media, which includes film and television genres, affect audiences. Cultivation theory as initially portrayed, said that media pull people together and act as a homogenizing force, as did Meyrowitz's

(1985) thesis that television erases differences between people and generations. In fact, it was the thesis that all such "content" essentially conveyed the same message that was at the basis of research arguing that time spent watching TV impacted our perceptions of crime and, in some cases, promoted violent or aggressive behavior. Countering this line of thought, Robinson's (1976) videomalaise construct and the literature criticizing the media for alienation and stimulating conflict argues the reverse, that media act as a disintegrating force for society. Putnam (2000) saw these mass media diversions destroying social capital through the end of the 20th century.

This conception of social displacement—as "we amuse ourselves to death" (Postman, 1985)—was recently eclipsed by a social influence model (Nowak et al., 2010) reflecting a revolution in social capital wrought by digital media. The society and media system that existed when videomalaise views were prevalent have thus been transformed by emerging digital media. And the results covered in this book provide a case that the "media of abundance"—with their proliferation of platforms, film and television genres—divide rather than pull people together. Audiences no longer need to convene on a few choices for what to watch (both film and TV genres as well as news reports). The media and popular culture of an earlier era once allowed Americans to share the same "moving images" (and reading material too); this likely helped create a common culture. But today more and more Americans are not even watching the same moving images, at the theater or at home on television. So even this institution may now contribute to the divisions in our country.

Does the proliferation of different media options contribute to social alienation, as people feel disconnected from others in American society? Karl Marx's theory of alienation saw workers being made to feel foreign to the products of their own labor (Marx & Elster, 1986). But it's through cultural alienation that the media can be seen as affecting people—who now seek out the "moving images" that are comfortable and support "their" subcultures rather than the broader culture. Though our surveys were not devised to address issues of media effects, we see examples of differences in our data as well as consensus on perceptions. While Democrats in the 2021 Users Survey are more likely to agree that TV portrays the world pretty much as it really is ($r=.20$, $p=.004$), being a Republican is not related to that perception, one way or another.

The results indicating the existence of a "common ground" for audiences of the moving image is quite strong. For example, a consensus was found in what people expect for the bulk of the film and television genres studied. Those who have the largest film and TV genre repertoires in the 2015 Users Survey also are more likely to see themselves as a happy person (correlations with the TV and film "often" genre repertoires, respectively, $r=.17$, $p<.001$, and $r=.11$, $p<.05$), so sampling more genres at a static level is positively related to feeling good about oneself. And another hint is found in the relationship between repertoires and perceptions of life. Those with larger TV and film "often" genre repertoires also are more likely to think TV portrays the world pretty much as it really is (correlations of TV and film genre repertoires, respectively, $r=.21$, $p<.001$, and $r=.30$, $p<.001$). Similar positive relationships are found in the 2021 Users Survey. Thus, those who think of themselves as a happy person have larger *often TV genre repertoires* ($r= .22$, $p<.001$) and *often film genre repertoires* ($r=.24$, $p<.001$). Those relationships are even stronger with perceptions that TV portrays the world pretty much as it really is, with larger *often TV genre repertoires* correlated at $r=.47$ ($p<.001$) and with *often film genre repertoires* at $r=.50$ ($p<.001$). We offer these observations to underscore the need for more empirical research in film studies.

The debate over hegemony and cultural imperialism of the 1970s and 1980s seems almost quaint today, as moving images from variegated sources move around the world between cultures with growing rapidity. Modernization has brought technology even to remote places, and the dominance of American culture has declined as the tail wags the dog (e.g., Lau & Atkin, 2012; Tunstall, 2008). Hollywood films need the huge Chinese market, as it now tailors casts and content for the broadest appeal. If there's a dominant "culture" today, it's consumerism, which national cultures can reinforce with their own cultural forms, e.g., K-pop, seen by Korea as "soft power."

In the United States itself, questions persist about what binds people together during times of great political and cultural division. A couple decades ago, some suggested that the norms and values characterizing most Americans have become less common and that "popular culture" is somehow expected to provide the glue that binds citizens together (e.g., McLuhan, 1965; Meyrowitz, 1985). Thus, the moving images that we collectively view—across our various screens—generate a common experience (e.g., Gitlin, 1979). But with the growth of different options and unlimited variety (e.g., "a la carte" streaming), that may no longer be the case, as Americans segregate themselves into cultural bubbles that reinforce tastes, norms, and values. Thus, is the growing variety further dividing us?

National integration refers to the creation of territorial nationality that overshadows or eliminates subordinate loyalties. This is the most common use of the term "national integration" (e.g., Deutsch, 1953). Van Dyke (1977, p. 367) notes that "all countries of the world are in some degree heterogeneous...Virtually all states are polyglot in the sense that they are multilingual, multiracial, multi-religious, or multinational." Or as Jeffres et al. (2011, p. 102) note, "American society is increasingly pluralistic and its media have come to represent that pluralism not only in terms of ethnic diversity but also through a more complex pattern of stories and images that embody little certainty and much relativism. Some would describe the current climate as a 'postmodern' environment where fragmentation rules and no set of values dominates society, at least not to the extent it once did in earlier decades and centuries."

Media fragmentation may break down our shared set of cultural values, pushing people to construct communities based on beliefs and values rather than geography (Bucy et al., 2007). The resulting disaggregation of the audience (Turow, 1997) could balkanize the larger culture into "small groups of like-minded individuals who do not interact with other groups or with society as a whole and choose to receive only the news and information that reinforces their beliefs and values" (Pavlik & McIntosh, 2004, p. 24).

The historical cultivation theory of George Gerbner and his associates assumed a homogeneous media message for cultural effects on audiences. Unfortunately, there is little theory on the impact of a fragmented media on national cultures. Sunstein (2017) explains how the Internet creates "echo chambers and 'cybercascades' that, in the broader political realm, exploit 'confirmation bias,' and promotes 'polarization entrepreneurs.'" These fragmentation dynamics in the broader body politic, then, echo the broader centripetal dynamics reflected in the narrowing genre taste publics found for film genres here. Taken together, these narrowcast alternatives undermine the pillars of the common culture upon which our shared experiences and languages are based, which Sunstein sees as the "lifeblood" of democracy.

Chaffee and Metzger (2001) asked if the changes wrought by new communication technology were ushering in an era that could mark the end of mass communication. That is, was mass communication a "fleeting idea, a purely, 20th-century phenomenon"? (p. 366). Alas, mass communication theories may now be eroding—alongside the mass audience generally—as converging media now deliver voice, video and data to audiences via narrowcast digital channels.

In theoretical terms, then, the rather inconsistent audience understandings uncovered in some research may reflect the moderating impact of fragmented "daily me" media constellations (e.g., Bucy et al., 2007). These shifting conceptions continue to question the mass audience exposure assumptions underpinning classic theories ranging from hegemony to cultivation and agenda setting (e.g., Atkin et al., 2015). Jeffres et al. (2001), for instance, observed the weakening of media influences on public opinion undermining conventional "mainstreaming" effects, casting that as a "scatter-streaming" dynamic. Similarly, emerging media may be "levelling" the narrative playing field for program distribution. This "scatter-streaming" of genre types and forms can help explain some of the conceptual disagreement among audiences and creators.

These processes also emulate those for public opinion theories like agenda setting, established in the late 20th century, based on the bedrock assumption that content influence processes flow from traditional, mass media to the public (e.g., Atkin et al., 2015). Here too, traditional top-down conceptions of political influence have been joined by "reverse agenda setting" conceptions, whereby legacy media are increasingly the recipients of agendas from grassroots stakeholders and the general public, via social media.

This book provides empirical answers to questions about audience perceptions and exposure to television and film genres, but we need studies designed to answer questions about the influence genres have on audiences. We hope this text stimulates movement in this area. Within film studies, some scholars have called for more empirical work (e.g., The Society for Cognitive Studies of the Moving Image), but thus far such publications are rather rare and non-programmatic. This leaves the considerable and valuable scholarship on film genres "without empirical tests of prevalence or of spectator response" (Egizii et al., 2018). The studies reported in this volume have begun to provide such tests.

The various studies profiled here document how the rapidly changing digital media environment is forcing a reconceptualizion of traditional notions of visual media content structures and their influence processes. For instance, Bryan Stetler mentioned that he no longer opens his CNN newscast with a temporal greeting (e.g., "Good morning"), because it is now offered 24-7 via podcast streaming. Future studies should continue to reimagine the ways in which such changes alter these symbolic interactions between audiences and creators, big or small.

With nearly three-quarters of film box office coming from the offshore international market, research will also need to document how these increasingly globalized consumption patterns continue to influence digital production and consumption patterns as well. Director Bong Joon-ho famously remarked that "Once you overcome the one-inch-tall barrier of subtitles, you will be introduced to so many more amazing films" (Freyman, 2022, para 1). Later work should consider the influence of these variegated screen sizes, outlined in Chapter 6, as the consumption of moving images continues to be transformed by such platforms as streaming, mobile film/television (and gamification), etc.

As digital media continue to reshape this playing field, later research could also profitably expand the present empirical profiles—alongside critical, qualitative, and other methods—amidst different media and national contexts. Such inquiry would benefit from more rigorous methods such as structural equation modeling to evaluate theoretical models for complex processes underpinning exposure and effects dynamics surrounding popular media use. Ideally, scholars could also include matching content analyses—to supplement survey, experimental, and/or qualitative approaches—to gain a deeper understanding of the moving image consumption and influence processes explored here.

[See the website at https://film-tv-genre-expectations.research.uconn.edu for additional material, tables, and instruments pertaining to the surveys reported in this text.]

REFERENCES

Abelman, R., & Atkin, D. J. (2011). *The televiewing audience: The art and science of watching TV* (2nd ed.). Peter Lang.

Adams, W. J. (1993). TV program scheduling strategies and their relationship to new program renewal rates and rating changes. *Journal of Broadcasting & Electronic Media, 37*(4), 465–474.

Adgate, B. (2021, April 13). The impact COVID-19 had on the entertainment industry in 2020. *Forbes.* https://www.forbes.com/sites/bradadgate/2021/04/13/the-impact-covid-19-had-on-the-entertainment-industry-in-2020/?sh=7019c038250f

Al Ghamdi, E., Yunus, F., Da'ar, O., El-Metwally, A., Khalifa, M., Aldossari, B., & Househ, M. (2016). The effect of screen size on mobile phone user comprehension of health information and application structure: An experimental approach. *Journal of Medical Systems, 40*(1), 1–8.

Allen, R. C. (2002). From exhibition to reception: Reflections on the audience in film history. In G. A. Waller (Ed.), *Moviegoing in America* (pp. 300–307). Blackwell Publishers.

Allocca, K. (2018). *Videocracy: How YouTube is changing the world...with double rainbows, singing foxes, and other trends we can't stop watching.* Bloomsbury.

Altman, R. (1984). A semantic/syntactic approach to film genre. *Cinema Journal, 23*(3), 6–18.

Altman, R. (2004). *Film/genre.* British Film Institute.

Anderson, C. (1988). Biographical film. In W. D. Gehring (Ed.), *Handbook of American film genres* (pp. 331–352). Greenwood Press.

Anderson, C. (2004, October 1). The long tail. *Wired.* https://www.wired.com/2004/10/tail/

Anderson, C. (2008). *The long tail: Why the future of business is selling less of more.* Hyperion.

Armstrong, S. J., & Hird, A. (2009). Cognitive style and entrepreneurial drive of new and mature business owner-managers. *Journal of Business & Psychology, 24*(4), 419–430.

Atkin, D. J., Hunt, D. S., & Lin, C. A. (2015). Diffusion theory in the new media environment: Toward an integrated technology adoption model. *Mass Communication and Society, 18*(5), 623–650.

Atkin, D., & Litman, B. (1986). Network TV programming: Economics, audiences, and the ratings game, 1971-1986. *Journal of Communication, 36*(3), 32–50.

Atkinson, S. (2016). *Beyond the screen: Emerging cinema and engaging audiences.* Bloomsbury.

Aubrey, J. S., Olson, L., Fine, M., Hauser, T., Rhea, D., Kaylor, B., & Yang, A. (2012). Investigating personality and viewing-motivation correlates of reality television exposure. *Communication Quarterly, 60*(1), 80–102.

Austin, B. A., & Gordon, T. F. (1987). Movie genres: Toward a conceptualized model and standardized definitions. In B. A. Austin (Ed.), *Current research in film: Audiences, economics, and law* (Vol. 3, pp. 12–33). Ablex.

Barker, D. (1991). The emergence of television's repertoire of representation, 1920-1935. *Journal of Broadcasting and Electronic Media, 35*(3), 305–318.

Barnes, B., & Sperling, N. (2022, March 26). Streaming took over Hollywood. Will it take best picture, too? *The New York Times.*

Barnouw, E. (1993). *Documentary: A history of the non-fiction film* (2nd revised ed.). Oxford University Press.

Baruh, L. (2009). Publicized intimacies on reality television: An analysis of voyeuristic content and its contribution to the appeal of reality programming. *Journal of Broadcasting & Electronic Media, 53*(2), 190–210.

Bauder, D. (2021, January 1). From TV to digital sites, viewership taking big hit. *Hartford Courant*, B4.

Belton, J. (1992). *Widescreen cinema.* Harvard University Press.

Belton, J. (1996). New technologies. In G. Nowell-Smith (Ed.), *The Oxford history of world cinema* (pp. 483–490). Oxford University Press.

Belton, J. (2002). Spectator and screen. In G. A. Waller (Ed.), *Moviegoing in America* (pp. 238–246). Blackwell Publishers.

Berg, C. R. (2012). Immigrants, aliens, and extraterrestrials: Science fiction's alien "other" as (among other things) new Latino imagery. In B. K. Grant (Ed.), *Film genre reader IV* (pp. 402–432). University of Texas Press.

Berger, A. A. (1992). *Popular culture genres: Theories and texts.* SAGE Publications.

Berlyne, D. E. (1951). Attention to change. *British Journal of Psychology, 42*, 269–278.

Berlyne, D. E. (1960). *Conflict, arousal, and curiosity.* McGraw-Hill.

Bevins, R. A. (2001). Novelty seeking and reward: Implications for the study of high-risk behaviors. *Current Directions in Psychological Science, 10*(6), 189–193.

Biocca, F. (1991). *Mental models of television: Toward a theory of the semantic processing of television.* Paper presented to the Information Systems Division at the annual conference of the International Communication Association, Chicago.

Bizumic, B., & Duckitt, J. (2018). Investigating right wing authoritarianism with a Very Short Authoritarianism scale. *Journal of Social and Political Psychology, 6*(1), 129–150.

Black, R. W. (2006). Language, culture, and identity in online fanfiction. *E-Learning, 3*(2), 170–184.

Black, R. W. (2007). Fanfiction writing and the construction of space. *E-Learning, 4*(4), 384–397.

Borde, R., & Chaumeton, E. (1996). Towards a definition of *film noir.* In A. Silver & J. Ursini (Eds.), *Film noir reader* (pp. 17–25). Limelight Editions.

Bornstein, R. F., Kale, A. R., & Cornell, K. R. (1990). Boredom as a limiting condition on the mere exposure effect. *Journal of Personality and Social Psychology, 58*(5), 791–800.

Bottomore, S. (1999). The panicking audience?: Early cinema and the "train effect." *Historical Journal of Film, Radio, and Television, 19*(2), 177–216.

Bourget, J.-L. (2012). Social implications in the Hollywood genres. In B. K. Grant (Ed.), *Film genre reader IV* (pp. 69–77). University of Texas Press.

Bowser, E. (1990). *The transformation of cinema, 1907–1915.* University of California Press.

Bracken, C. C., Lombard, M., Neuendorf, K. A., Denny, J., & Quillin, M. (2004, August). *Do 3-D movies really reach out and grab you? The case of Spy Kids 3-D.* Proceedings of the Seventh Annual International Meeting of the Presence Workshop, Valencia, Spain, pp. 283–286.

Bracken, C. C., Neuendorf, K. A., & Jeffres, L. W. (2003, July). *Source credibility, presence, and screen size.* Paper presented to the Visual Communication Division of the Association for Education in Journalism and Mass Communication, Kansas City, MO.

Braudy, L. (1976). *The world in a frame: What we see in films.* Anchor/Press/Doubleday.

Brooks, T. (2007). A short history of network television. In T. Brooks & E. Marsh (Eds.), *The complete directory to prime-time network and cable TV shows, 1946-present* (9th ed., pp. x–xxi). Ballantine Books.

Brown, J. A. (2017). *The modern superhero in film and television: Popular genre and American culture.* Routledge.

Brown, J. D., Campbell, K., & Fischer, L. (1986). American adolescents and music videos: Why do they watch? *Gazette, 37,* 19–32.

Brownrigg, M. (2003). *Film music and film genre* [Doctoral dissertation]. University of Stirling.

Bucy, E. P., Gantz, W., & Wang, Z. (2007). Media technology and the 24-hour news cycle. In C. A. Lin & D. J. Atkin (Eds.), *Communication technology and social change* (pp. 143–163). Lawrence Erlbaum.

Burgoyne, R. (2008). *The Hollywood historical film.* Blackwell Publishing.

Bursztnsky, J., & Alessandrini, S. (2022, April 20). *Netflix closes down 35% wiping more than $50 billion off market cap.* https://www.cnbc.com/2022/04/20/netflix-plunges-trading-subscriber-loss.html

Buscombe, E. (1977). The idea of genre in the American cinema. In B. K. Grant (Ed.), *Film genre: Theory and criticism* (pp. 24–38). Scarecrow Press.

Cabral, J. (2021, September 23). *Complete searchable list of Netflix genres with links.* https://www.finder.com/netflix/genre-list

Cahill-Solis, T. L., & Witryol, S. L. (1994). Children's exploratory play preferences for four levels of novelty in toy constructions. *Genetic, Social and General Psychology Monographs, 120*(4), 393–419.

Camp, C. J., Dietrich, M. S., & Olson, K. R. (1985). Curiosity and uncertainty in young, middle aged, and older adults. *Educational Gerontology, 11*(6), 401–412.

Casey, B., Casey, N., Calvert, B., French, L., & Lewis, J. (Eds.). (2008). *Television studies: The key concepts* (2nd ed.). Routledge.

Cawelti, J. G. (1974). Savagery, civilization and the western hero. In J. Nachbar (Ed.), *Focus on the western* (pp. 57–63). Prentice-Hall, Inc.

Chaffee, S. H., & Metzger, M. J. (2001). The end of mass communication? *Mass Communication and Society, 4*(4), 365–379.

Clover, C. J. (1987). Her body, himself: Gender in the slasher film. *Representations, 20,* 187–228.

Collins, J. M. (1988). The musical. In W. D. Gehring (Ed.), *Handbook of American film genres* (pp. 269–284). Greenwood Press.

Coyle, J. (2021, November 11). Who's going back to the movies? So far, not everyone. *AP News.* https://apnews.com/article/coronavirus-pandemic-entertainment-life-style-business-arts-and-entertainment-a4e505df1bcfff8717662721521f282a

Creeber, G. (2006). The joy of text?: Television and textual analysis. *Critical Studies in Television: The International Journal of Television Studies, 1*(1), 81–88.

Creeber, G. (Ed.). (2015). *The television genre book* (3rd ed.). Palgrave.

Cromie, S. (2000). Assessing entrepreneurial inclinations: Some approaches and empirical evidence. *European Journal of Work and Organizational Psychology, 9*(1), 7–30.

Cunningham, N. R., & Eastin, M. S. (2017). Second screen and sports: A structural investigation into team identification and efficacy. *Communication & Sport, 5*(3), 288–310.

Dam, L., Roy, D., Atkin, D. J., & Rogers, D. (2018). Applying an integrative technology adoption paradigm to health app adoption and use. *Journal of Broadcasting & Electronic Media, 62*(4), 654–672.

Davis, N. Z. (2002). *Slaves on screen: Film and historical vision.* Harvard University Press.

Derry, C. (1985). Television soap opera: "Incest, bigamy, and fatal disease." In S. M. Kaminsky & J. H. Mahan (Eds.), *American television genres* (pp. 85–110). Nelson-Hall.

Deutsch, K. W. (1953). *Nationalism and social communication.* John Wiley & Sons.

Dirks, T. (2020). *Main film genres.* Filmsite.org. https://www.filmsite.org/genres.html

Dominick, J. R., & Pearce, M. C. (1976). Trends in network prime-time programming, 1953-74. *Journal of Communication, 26*(1), 70–80.

Donohew, L., & Tipton, L. (1973). A conceptual model of information seeking, avoiding, and processing. In P. Clarke (Ed.), *New models for mass communication research* (pp. 243–268). SAGE.

Douglas, D. (1989). *Horrors!* The Overlook Press.

Dovey, J. (2015). Reality TV: Introduction. In G. Creeber (Ed.), *The television genre book* (3rd ed., pp. 159–160). Palgrave.

Duckitt, J., Bizumic, B., Krauss, S. W., & Heled, E. (2010). A tripartite approach to right-wing authoritarianism: The authoritarianism-conservatism-traditionalism model. *Political Psychology, 31*(5), 685–715.

Duckworth, K. L., Bargh, J. A., Garcia, M., & Chaiken, S. (2002). The automatic evaluation of novel stimuli. *Psychological Science, 13*(6), 513–519.

Duncan, M. C., & Brummett, B. (1989). Types and sources of spectating pleasure in televised sports. *Sociology of Sport Journal, 6*(3), 195–211.

Durgnat, R. (1977). Epic, epic, epic, epic, epic. In B. K. Grant (Ed.), *Film genre: Theory and criticism* (pp. 108–117). Scarecrow Press.

Eadie, W. F. (2022). *When communication became a discipline.* Lexington.

Earle, T. C., & Cvetkovich, G. (1997). Culture, cosmopolitanism, and risk management. *Risk Analysis, 17*(1), 55–65.

Ebert, R. (2011, July 27). *Where the deer and the bug-eyed monsters play.* https://www.rogerebert.com/reviews/cowboys-and-aliens-2011

Ebert, R. (2020). *Roger Ebert's journal.* https://www.rogerebert.com/rogers-journal

Eberwein, R. (2010). *The Hollywood war film*. Wiley-Blackwell.

Egizii, M. L., Neuendorf, K. A., Denny, J., Skalski, P. D., & Campbell, R. (2018). Which way did he go? Film lateral movement and spectator interpretation. *Visual Communication, 17*(2), 221–243.

Eisenberger, R., Sucharski, I. L., Yalowitz, S., Kent, R. J., Loomis, R. J., Jones, J. R., Paylor, S., Aselage, J., Mueller, M. S., & McLaughlin, J. P. (2010). The motive for sensory pleasure: Enjoyment of nature and its representation in painting, music, and literature. *Journal of Personality, 78*(2), 599–638.

Ekelund, J., Lichtermann, D., Järvelin, M.-R., & Peltonen, L. (1999). Association between novelty seeking and the type 4 dopamine receptor gene in a large Finnish cohort sample. *American Journal of Psychiatry, 156*(9), 1453–1455.

Elert, G. (Ed.). (2009). *The physics factbook*. https://hypertextbook.com/facts/index-authors.shtml

Emmanouloudis, A. A. (2015). *You are not alone. The emergence of fan communities around user-generated content: A comparative analysis* [Master's thesis]. University of Amsterdam.

Ferguson, D. A., & Melkote, S. R. (1997). Leisure time and channel repertoire in a multichannel environment. *Communication Research Reports, 14*(2), 189–194.

Ferris, A. L., Smith, S. W., Greenberg, B. S., & Smith, S. L. (2007). The content of reality dating shows and viewer perceptions of dating. *Journal of Communication, 57*(3), 490–510.

Ferriss, S., & Young, M. (Eds.). (2008). *Chick flicks: Contemporary women at the movies*. Routledge.

Feuer, J. (1992). Genre study and television. In R. C. Allen (Ed.), *Channels of discourse, reassembled: Television and contemporary criticism* (pp. 138–159). Routledge.

Feuer, J. (1993). *The Hollywood musical* (2nd ed.). Indiana University Press.

Feuer, J. (2015). Situation comedy, part 2. In G. Creeber (Ed.), *The television genre book* (3rd ed., pp. 100–101). Palgrave.

Fischer, S., Lienhart, R., & Effelsberg, W. (1995). *Automatic recognition of film genres*. University of Mannheim.

Fiske, J. (1992). The cultural economy of fandom. In L. A. Lewis (Ed.), *The adoring audience: Fan culture and popular media* (pp. 30–49). Routledge.

Foxman, M., Leith, A. P., Beyea, D., Klebig, B., Chen, V. H. H., & Ratan, R. (2020, November 2–4). Virtual reality genres: Comparing preferences in immersive experiences and games. *CHI PLAY'20 EA*. Canada.

Freyman, N. (2022, March 13). Editor's Note. *Morning Brew*. https://www.morning-brew.com/daily/issues/latest

Gallagher, M. (2006). *Action figures: Men, action films, and contemporary adventure narratives*. Palgrave MacMillan.

Galpin, S. A. (2016). Harry Potter and the hidden heritage films: Genre hybridity and the power of the past in the Harry Potter film cycle. *Journal of British Cinema and Television, 13*(3), 430–449.

Gans, H. J. (1999). *Popular culture and high culture: An analysis and evaluation of taste* (revised and updated edition). Basic Books.

Garcia, L. F., Aluja, A., Garcia, O., & Cuevas, L. (2005). Is openness to experience an independent personality dimension? Convergent and discriminant validity of the openness domain and its NEO-PI-R facets. *Journal of Individual Differences, 26*(3), 132–138.

Geduld, H. M., & Gottesman, R. (1973). *An illustrated glossary of film terms*. Holt, Rinehart and Winston.

Gehring, W. D. (1983). *Screwball comedy: Defining a film genre*. Ball State University Press.

Gehring, W. D. (1986). *Screwball comedy: A genre of madcap romance*. Greenwood Press.

Gehring, W. D. (1988a). Black humor. In W. D. Gehring (Ed.), *Handbook of American film genres* (pp. 167–188). Greenwood Press.

Gehring, W. D. (Ed.). (1988b). *Handbook of American film genres*. Greenwood Press.

Gehring, W. D. (1999). *Parody as genre: "Never give a saga an even break."* Greenwood Press.

Gehring, W. D. (2002). *Romantic vs. screwball comedy: Charting the difference*. Scarecrow Press.

Gehring, W. D. (2016). *Genre-busting dark comedies of the 1970s: Twelve American films*. McFarland & Company, Inc.

Gehring, W. D. (2019). *Hitchcock and humor: Modes of comedy in twelve defining films*. McFarland & Company, Inc.

Geiwitz, P. J. (1966). Structure of boredom. *Journal of Personality and Social Psychology*, *3*(5), 592–600.

Giannetti, L. (2011). *Understanding movies* (12th ed.). Allyn & Bacon.

Giannetti, L. D., & Eyman, S. (2010). *Flashback: A brief history of film* (6th ed.). Pearson Education/Allyn & Bacon.

Gil de Zúñiga, H., Garcia-Perdomo, V., & McGregor, S. C. (2015). What is second screening? Exploring motivations of second screen use and its effect on online political participation. *Journal of Communication*, *65*(5), 793–815.

Gitlin, T. (1979). Prime time ideology: The hegemonic process in television entertainment. *Social Problems*, *26*(3), 251–266.

Gitlin, T. (2000). *Inside prime time*. University of California Press.

Glass, A. L., & Waterman, D. (1988). Predictions of movie entertainment value and the representativeness heuristic. *Applied Cognitive Psychology*, *2*(3), 173–179.

Gocłowska, M. A., Ritter, S. M., Elliot, A. J., & Baas, M. (2019). Novelty seeking is linked to openness and extraversion, and can lead to greater creative performance. *Journal of Personality*, *87*(2), 252–266.

Gorbman, C. (1987). *Unheard melodies: Narrative film music*. BFI Publishing.

Gordon, C. L., & Luo, S. (2011). The Personal Expansion Questionnaire: Measuring one's tendency to expand through novelty and augmentation. *Personality and Individual Differences*, *51*(2), 89–94.

Grant, A. E. (1994). The promise fulfilled? An empirical analysis of program diversity on television. *Journal of Media Economics*, *7*(1), 51–64.

Grant, A., & Meadows, J. (2020). *Communication technology update and fundamentals*. Routledge.

Grant, B. K. (Ed) (1977). *Film genre: Theory and criticism*. Scarecrow Press.

Grant, B. K. (Ed.). (1984). *Planks of reason: Essays on the horror film*. Scarecrow Press.

Grant, B. K. (Ed). (1986). *Film genre reader*. University of Texas Press.

Grant, B. K. (Ed.). (2003). *Film genre reader III*. University of Texas Press.

Grant, B. K. (2007). *Film genre: From iconography to ideology*. Wallflower Press.

Grant, B. K. (Ed.). (2012a). *Film genre reader IV.* University of Texas Press.

Grant, B. K. (2012b). *The Hollywood film musical*. Wiley-Blackwell.

Grindon, L. (2011). *The Hollywood romantic comedy: Conventions, history, controversies*. Wiley-Blackwell.

Groombridge, N. (2002). Crime control or crime culture TV? *Surveillance & Society, 1*(1), 30–46.

Gunning, T. (1990). The cinema of attractions: Early film, its spectator and the avant-garde. In T. Elsaesser & A. Barker (Eds.), *Early cinema: Space, frame, narrative* (pp. 56–62). BFI Publishing.

Haberlin, K. A., & Atkin, D. J. (2022, January). Mobile gaming and Internet addiction: When is playing no longer just fun and games? *Computers in Human Behavior, 126.*

Haghighat, R. (2007). The development of the Brief Social Desirability Scale (BSDS). *Europe's Journal of Psychology, 3*(4).

Hall, A. (2005). Audience personality and the selection of media and media genres. *Media Psychology, 7*(4), 377–398.

Hall, S. (1980). Encoding/decoding. In Centre for Contemporary Cultural Studies (Ed.), *Culture, media, language: Working papers in cultural studies, 1972-1979* (pp. 128–138). Hutchinson.

Hardy, P. (1984). *The encyclopedia of science fiction movies.* Woodbury Press.

Hardy, P. (Ed.). (1995). *The Overlook film encyclopedia: Horror* (2nd ed.). The Overlook Press.

Hartley, J. (2015). Situation comedy, part 1. In G. Creeber (Ed.), *The television genre book* (3rd ed., pp. 96–98). Palgrave.

Henningham, J. P. (1985). Relations between television news gratifications and content preferences. *Gazette, 35,* 197–208.

Hillier, J. (Ed.). (1986). *Cahiers du Cinéma, The 1950s: Neo-realism, Hollywood, New Wave.* Harvard Film Studies.

Hoberman, J. (1994). On how the western was lost. In R. T. Jameson (Ed.), *They went thataway: Redefining film genres a National Society of Film Critics video guide* (pp. 51–56). Mercury House.

Höijer, B. (2000). Audiences' expectations and interpretations of different television genres: A socio-cognitive approach. In I. Hagen & J. Wasko (Eds.), *Consuming audiences? Production and reception in media research* (pp. 189–207). Hampton Press, Inc.

Horton, A., & Rapf, J. E. (Eds.). (2012). *A companion to film comedy.* Wiley-Blackwell.

Horton, D., & Wohl, R. R. (1956). Mass communication and para-social interaction. *Psychiatry, 19*(3), 215–229.

Hunt, D. S., Lin, C. A., & Atkin, D. J. (2014, November). Photo-messaging: Adopter attributes, technology factors and use motives. *Computers in Human Behavior, 40,* 171–179.

Ijsselsteijn, W. (2003). Presence in the past: What can we learn from media history? In G. Riva, F. Davide, & W. A. Ijsselsteijn (Eds.), *Being there: Concepts, effects and measurement of user presence in synthetic environments* (pp. 18–40). IOS Press.

IMDb. (2020). *Popular TV show and movie genres.* https://www.imdb.com/feature/genre/

Independent Cinema Office. (2022). *Understanding audiences.* https://www.independentcinemaoffice.org.uk/advice-support/how-to-start-a-cinema/understanding-audiences/

Jameson, R. T. (Ed) (1994). *They went thataway: Redefining film genres a National Society of Film Critics video guide.* Mercury House.

Jamison, A. (2013). *Fic: Why fanfiction is taking over the world.* Smart Pop.

Jaramillo, D. L. (2002). The family racket: AOL Time Warner, HBO, *The Sopranos,* and the construction of a quality brand. *Journal of Communication Inquiry, 26*(1), 59–75.

Jeffres, L. W. (1974, August). *Functions of media behaviors*. Paper presented to the Theory and Methodology Division of the Association for Education in Journalism, San Diego, CA.

Jeffres, L. W. (1978). Cable TV and interest maximization. *Journalism Quarterly, 55*(1), 149–154.

Jeffres, L. W. (1994). *Mass media processes*. Waveland Press.

Jeffres, L., & Atkin, D. (1996). Predicting use of technologies for communication and consumer needs. *Journal of Broadcasting & Electronic Media, 40*(3), 318–330.

Jeffres, L. W., Atkin, D., Bracken, C. C., & Neuendorf, K. (2004). Cosmopoliteness in the Internet age. *Journal of Computer-Mediated Communication, 10*(1), Article 2.

Jeffres, L. W., Atkin, D. J., Lee, J.-W., & Neuendorf, K. (2011). Media influences on public perceptions of ethnic groups, generations and individuals. *Howard Journal of Communications, 22*(1), 101–121.

Jeffres, L. W., Atkin, D. J., & Neuendorf, K. A. (2001). Expanding the range of dependent measures in mainstreaming and cultivation analysis. *Communication Research Reports, 18*(4), 408–417.

Jeffres, L. W., Atkin, D. J., Neuendorf, K. A., & Lin, C. A. (2004). The influence of expanding media menus on audience content selection. *Telematics and Informatics, 21*(4), 317–334.

Jeffres, L. W., Bracken, C. C., Atkin, D., & Neuendorf, K. (2010). Moving from theorizing to application: Predicting audience enjoyment of TV formats. *American Journal of Media Psychology, 3*(3/4), 156–179.

Jeffres, L. W., Bracken, C. C., Neuendorf, K., Kopfman, J., & Atkin, D. J. (2014). Cosmopoliteness, cultivation and media use. *Journal of Communication and Media Research, 6*(1), 1–24.

Jeffres, L. W., & Dobos, J. (1989, November). *Entrepreneurship and communication*. Paper presented at the annual conference of the Midwest Association for Public Opinion Research, Chicago, IL.

Jeffres, L. W., Kumar, A., Neuendorf, K. A., Atkin, D. J., McCall, K., Carlisle, P. W., Fisher, M., & Franz, J. (2014). Influences on United States communication professionals' decisions to become entrepreneurs. *Journal of Communication and Media Research, 6*(2), 93–120.

Jeffres, L., Neuendorf, K., & Atkin, D. (2000, June). *Media use and public leisure activities: competition or symbiosis?* Paper presented to the Popular Communication Division at the annual conference of the International Communication Association, Acapulco, Mexico.

Jeffres, L., Neuendorf, K., & Giles, D. (1990, November). *Film genre: Matching audience expectations with critical assessments*. Paper presented at the annual meeting of the Midwest Association for Public Opinion Research, Chicago, IL.

Jenkins, H. (1992). *What made pistachio nuts? Early sound comedy and the vaudeville aesthetic*. Columbia University Press.

Jenkins, H., Ford, S., & Green, J. (2013). *Spreadable media: Creating value and meaning in a networked culture*. New York University Press.

Jenner, M. (2015). The detective series. In G. Creeber (Ed.), *The television genre book* (3rd ed., pp. 20–22). Palgrave.

Jennings, W. (1988). Fantasy. In W. D. Gehring (Ed.), *Handbook of American film genres* (pp. 249–265). Greenwood Press.

Johnson, S. (2005). *Everything bad is good for you: How today's popular culture is actually making us smarter*. Penguin Books.

Jonason, P. K., & Webster, G. D. (2010). The dirty dozen: A concise measure of the dark triad. *Psychological Assessment, 22*(2), 420–432.

Joy, S. (2004). Innovation motivation: The need to be different. *Creativity Research Journal, 16*(2/3), 313–330.

Kaminsky, S. M. (1985). *American film genres* (2nd ed.). Nelson-Hall.

Kaminsky, S. M., & Mahan, J. H. (1985). *American television genres*. Nelson-Hall.

Kane, K. (1988). The World War II combat film. In W. D. Gehring (Ed.), *Handbook of American film genres* (pp. 85–102). Greenwood Press.

Karrer, F. (2021). *The average U.S. household subscribes to four streaming services*. https://mountain.com/blog/the-average-u-s-household-subscribes-to-four-streaming-services-2/#:~:text=The%20survey%20also%20found%20that,watch%20ad%2Dsupported%20services).

Katz, E. (2015). Where are opinion leaders leading us? *International Journal of Communication, 9*, 1023–1028.

Katz, E., Blumler, J. G., & Gurevitch, M. (1974). Utilization of mass communication by the individual. In J. G. Blumler & E. Katz (Eds.), *The uses of mass communications: Current perspectives on gratification research* (pp. 19–32). SAGE.

Katz, E., Gurevitch, M., & Haas, H. (1973). On the use of the mass media for important things. *American Sociological Review, 38*(2), 164–181.

Kawin, B. F. (2012). Children of the light. In B. K. Grant (Ed.), *Film genre reader IV* (pp. 360–381). University of Texas Press.

Kendall, E. (1990). *The runaway bride: Hollywood romantic comedy of the 1930s*. Anchor Books.

Kerr, W. (1975). *The silent clowns*. Alfred A. Knopf.

Kim, J., Seo, M., Yu, H. S., & Neuendorf, K. (2014). Cultural differences in preference for entertainment messages that induce mixed responses of joy and sorrow. *Human Communication Research, 40*(4), 530–552.

Knobloch-Westerwick, S., Westerwick, A., & Sude, D. J. (2020). Media choice and selective exposure. In M. B. Oliver, A. A. Raney, & J. Bryant (Eds.), *Media effects: Advances in theory and research* (4th ed.; pp. 146–162). Routledge.

Koszarski, R. (1990). *An evening's entertainment: The age of the silent feature picture, 1915–1928*. Simon & Schuster Macmillan.

Krasinski, M. (n.d.). *The Long Tail Effect theory in practice explained*. https://miloszkrasinski.com/the-long-tail-effect-theory-in-practise-explained/

Krishnan, A., & Atkin, D. (2014, November). Individual differences in social networking site users: The interplay between antecedents and consequential effect on level of activity. *Computers in Human Behavior, 40*, 111–118.

Kunst, A. (2022, March 2). Share of Americans who watched dramas on TV in 2021, by age. *Statista* https://www.statista.com/statistics/229099/tv-viewers-who-typically-watch-dramas-usa/#:~:text=This%20statistic%20presents%20the%20share%20of%20Americans%20who,watched%20dramas%20on%20TV%20in%202021%2C%20by%20age

Lau, T.-Y., & Atkin, D. (2012). Competition and the decline in Western television program popularity in Indonesia during the 1990s. *Asian Journal of Communication, 22*(3), 320–333.

Leach, J. (1977). The screwball comedy. In B. K. Grant (Ed.), *Film genre: Theory and criticism* (pp. 75–89). Scarecrow Press.

Lee, T.-H., & Crompton, J. (1992). Measuring novelty seeking in tourism. *Annals of Tourism Research, 19*(4), 732–751.

Lieberman, E. A., Neuendorf, K. A., Denny, J., Skalski, P. D., & Wang, J. (2009). The language of laughter: A quantitative/qualitative fusion examining television narrative and humor. *Journal of Broadcasting & Electronic Media, 53*(4), 497–514.

Lightfoot, C. (1997). *The culture of adolescent risk-taking.* Guilford Press.

Lin, C. A. (1996). Looking back: The contribution of Blumler and Katz's uses of mass communication to communication research. *Journal of Broadcasting & Electronic Media, 40*(4), 574–581.

Lin, C. A. (2009). Effects of the Internet. In J. Bryant & M. B. Oliver (Eds.), *Media effects: Advances in theory and research* (3rd ed., pp. 567–591). Routledge.

Lin, C. A., & Atkin, D. J. (2002). *Communication technology and society: Audience adoption and uses.* Hampton Press.

Lin, C. A., & Atkin, D. J. (2007). *Communication technology and social change: Theory and implications.* Lawrence Erlbaum.

Litman, B. R. (1978). Is network ownership in the public interest? *Journal of Communication, 28*(2), 51–59.

Litman, B. R. (1979). The television networks, competition and program diversity. *Journal of Broadcasting, 23*(4), 393–409.

Litman, B., Hasegawa, K., Shrikhande, S., & Barbatsis, G. (1994). Measuring diversity in U.S. television programming. *Studies in Broadcasting, 30*, 131–153.

Litman, J. A., & Spielberger, C. D. (2003). Measuring epistemic curiosity and its diversive and specific components. *Journal of Personality Assessment, 80*(1), 75–86.

Livingstone, S. M. (1988). Why people watch soap opera: An analysis of the explanations of British viewers. *European Journal of Communication, 3*(1), 55–80.

Lombard, M., & Ditton, T. (1997). At the heart of it all: The concept of presence. *Journal of Computer-Mediated Communication, 3*(2).

Lombard, M., Reich, R. D., Grabe, M. E., Bracken, C. C., & Ditton, T. B. (2000). Presence and television: The role of screen size. *Human Communication Research, 26*(1), 75–98.

L'Pree Corsbie-Massay, C. (2021). *20th century media and the American psyche.* Routledge.

Ma, B., Greer, T., Knox, D., & Narayanan, S. (2021). A computational lens into how music characterizes genre in film. *PLoS One, 16*(4), e0249957.

Ma, J., & Atkin, D. J. (in press). Cognition under simultaneous exposure to competing heuristic cues in online movie reviews. *Journal of Communication and Media Studies.*

Mallet, P., & Vignoli, E. (2007). Intensity seeking and novelty seeking: Their relationship to adolescent risk behavior and occupational interests. *Personality and Individual Differences, 43*(8), 2011–2021.

Martin, R. A., & Ford, T. E. (2018). *The psychology of humor: An integrative approach* (2nd ed.). Academic Press.

Marx, K., & Elster, J. (1986). *Karl Marx: A reader.* Press Syndicate of the University of Cambridge.

Mast, G. (1979). *The comic mind: Comedy and the movies* (2nd ed.). University of Chicago Press.

Maynard, R. A. (1974). *The American west on film: Myth and reality.* Hayden Book Company, Inc.

McArthur, C. (1977). The iconography of the gangster film. In B. K. Grant (Ed.), *Film genre: Theory and criticism* (pp. 118–123). Scarecrow Press.

McCarthy, A. (2015). Studying soap opera. In G. Creeber (Ed.), *The television genre book* (3rd ed., pp. 73–75). Palgrave.

McClintock, P. (2019, November 27). Will "The Irishman" Netflix debut ding Thanksgiving box office? *The Hollywood Reporter.*

McConnell, F. D. (1977). Leopards and history: The problem of film genre. In B. K. Grant (Ed.), *Film genre: Theory and criticism* (pp. 7–15). Scarecrow Press.

McCrae, R. R. (1996). Social consequences of experiential openness. *Psychological Bulletin, 120*(3), 323–337.

McCrae, R. R., & Costa, P. T. (2003). *Personality in adulthood: A five-factor theory perspective* (2nd ed). Guilford.

McLuhan, M. (1965). *Understanding media: The extensions of man.* McGraw Hill.

McReynolds, P. (1956). A restricted conceptualization of human anxiety and motivation. *Psychological Reports, 2*, 293–312.

Menegaldo, G. (2004). *Flashbacks in film noir.* https://journals.openedition.org/sillagescritiques/1561

Meyrowitz, J. (1985). *No sense of place: The impact of electronic media on social behavior.* Oxford.

Mikulas, W. L., & Vodanovich, S. J. (1993). The essence of boredom. *The Psychological Record, 43*(1), 3–12.

Miller, L. (2022, January 31). How the ending of Netflix's new show perfectly skewers "The Woman in the Window." *Slate.* https://slate.com/culture/2022/01/woman-in-the-house-netflix-ending.html

Miller, M. M. (1972). Task orientation and salience as determinants of source utility. *Journalism Quarterly, 49*(4), 669–673.

Mills, B. (2015). Contemporary sitcom: "Comedy verité." In G. Creeber (Ed.), *The television genre book* (3rd ed., pp. 106–107). Palgrave.

Minnebo, J. (1999). Relaxing tension: Motives for viewing and the role of emotions in reality TV. *Communicatie, 28*, 45–58.

Mitchell, E. (2012). Apes and essences: Some sources of significance in the American gangster film. In B. K. Grant (Ed.), *Film genre reader IV* (pp. 255–264). University of Texas Press.

Mittell, J. (2004). *Genre and television: From cop shows to cartoons in American culture.* Routledge.

Mittell, J. (2010). *Television and American culture.* Oxford University Press.

Mittell, J. (2015). Children's television as genre. In G. Creeber (Ed.), *The television genre book* (3rd ed., pp. 112–113). Palgrave.

Mordden, E. (1988). *The Hollywood studios: House style in the Golden Age of the movies.* Simon & Schuster Inc.

Moulla, F. (2002). *Cosmopoliteness and diffusion of information about a critical event in an Internet environment* [Master's thesis]. Cleveland State University.

Munson, B. (2021, March 29). U.S. streaming video subscribers will total 385M by end of 2021: analyst. *Fierce Video.* https://www.fiercevideo.com/video/u-s-streaming-video-subscribers-will-total-385m-by-end-2021-analyst

Musser, C. (1991). *Before the nickelodeon: Edwin S. Porter and the Edison Manufacturing Company.* University of California Press.

Nachbar, J. (Ed.). (1974). *Focus on the western.* Prentice-Hall, Inc.

Nachbar, J. (1988). Film noir. In W. D. Gehring (Ed.), *Handbook of American film genres* (pp. 65–84). Greenwood Press.

NATO. (2020). *Advancing the moviegoing experience.* https://www.natoonline.org/data/us-movie-screens/

NBC News. (2014, June 11). *World's biggest TV is a custom-made, $1.6 million 370-inch monster.* https://www.nbcnews.com/tech/gift-guide/worlds-biggest-tv-custom-made-1-6-million-370-inch-n128771

Neale, S. (2012). Questions of genre. In B. K. Grant (Ed.), *Film genre reader IV* (pp. 178–202). University of Texas Press.

Neale, S., & Krutnik, F. (1990). *Popular film and television comedy.* Routledge.

Neenan, M. (2018, April 8). What you should know about influencer marketing on YouTube. *Digital marketing.* https://blogs.brighton.ac.uk/mn202/2018/04/08/whatyoushouldknowaboutinfluencermarketingonyoutube/

Neuendorf, K. A. (2019). Content analysis and thematic analysis. In P. Brough (Ed.), *Advanced research methods for applied psychology: Design, analysis and reporting* (pp. 211–223). Routledge.

Neuendorf, K. A. (2020). Media and humor. In J. Van den Bulck, D. Ewoldsen, M.-L. Mares, & E. Scharrer (Eds.), *The international encyclopedia of media psychology.* John Wiley & Sons, Inc.

Neuendorf, K. A., Atkin, D. J., & Jeffres, L. W. (2001). Reconceptualizing channel repertoire in the urban cable environment. *Journal of Broadcasting and Electronic Media, 45*(3), 464–482.

Neuendorf, K. A., & Baumgartner, M. (2022). *Emotional tone and narrative anticipation: Film scoring and spectator response.* Unpublished manuscript in progress.

Neuendorf, K. A., Egizii, M., Rudd, J., & Campbell, R. (2012, November). *A voice from past and present: The impact of first-person documentary narrative on perceptions about children of incarcerated mothers.* Presentation to the National Communication Association, Orlando, FL.

Neuendorf, K. A., & Fennell, T. (1988). A social facilitation view of the generation of humor and mirth reactions: The effects of a "laugh track." *Central States Speech Journal, 39*(1), 37–48.

Neuendorf, K. A., Jeffres, L. W., & Atkin, D. (2000). The television of abundance arrives: Cable choices and interest maximization. *Telematics and Informatics, 17*(3), 169–197.

Neuendorf, K. A., & Lieberman, E. A. (2010). Film: The original immersive medium. In C. C. Bracken & P. D. Skalski (Eds.), *Immersed in media: Telepresence in everyday life* (pp. 9–38). Routledge.

Neuendorf, K. A., Lieberman, E. A., Ying, L., & Lindmark, P. (2009, August). *Too wide to please? A comparison of audience responses to widescreen vs. pan and scan presentation.* Paper presented to the Visual Communication Division of the Association for Education in Journalism and Mass Communication, Boston, MA.

Neuendorf, K. A., Rudd, J. E., Palisin, P., & Pask, E. B. (2015). Humorous communication, verbal aggressiveness, and father-son relational satisfaction. *Humor: International Journal of Humor Research, 28*(3), 397–425.

Neuendorf, K. A., Skalski, P. D., Denny, J., Egizii, M., & Campbell, R. (2012, October). *The role of post-production formal features in the prediction of presence.* Paper presented to the International Society for Presence Research "Presence Live!" conference, Philadelphia, PA.

Neuendorf, K. A., Skalski, P. D., Jeffres, L. W., & Atkin, D. (2014). Senses of humor, media use, and opinions about the treatment of marginalized groups. *International Journal of Intercultural Relations, 42*, 65–76.

Neuendorf, K. A., & Sparks, G. G. (1988). Predicting emotional responses to horror films from cue-specific affect. *Communication Quarterly, 36*(1), 16–27.

Newcomb, H. (Ed.). (2007). *Television: The critical view* (7th ed.). Oxford.

Nichols, B. (1992). *Representing reality: Issues and concepts in documentary.* Indiana University Press.

Nowak, K. L., Hamilton, M. A., Atkin, D. J., & Rauh, C. (2010). Effect of media access and use on the political involvement, communication, and attitudes of college students. *American Journal of Media Psychology, 3*(1/2), 5–31.

NPR (National Public Radio) (2019, October 23). *'Parasite' is a genre-bending look at capitalism.* https://www.npr.org/2019/10/22/772309445/parasite-is-a-genre-bending-look-at-capitalism

Ocasio, A. (2012, February 2). *Reality TV by the numbers.* http://screenrant.com/reality-tv-statistics-infographic-aco-149257

O'Neil-Hart, C., & Blumenstein, H. (2016, July). *Why YouTube stars are more influential than traditional celebrities.* https://www.thinkwithgoogle.com/marketing-strategies/video/youtube-stars-influence/

Palmgreen, P., & Rayburn, J. D. II (1982). Gratifications sought and media exposure: An expectancy value model. *Communication Research, 9*(4), 561–580.

Palmgreen, P., & Rayburn, J. D. II (1985). An expectancy-value approach to media gratifications. In K. E. Rosengren, L. A. Wenner & P. Palmgreen (Eds.), *Media gratifications research: Current perspectives* (pp. 11–37). SAGE.

Papacharissi, Z., & Mendelson, A. L. (2007). An exploratory study of reality appeal: Uses and gratifications of reality TV shows. *Journal of Broadcasting & Electronic Media, 51*(2), 355–370.

Papazian, T. (1998). *Medium rare: The evolution, workings, and impact of commercial television.* Media Dynamics.

Parsons, T. (1951). *The social system.* The Free Press.

Pautz, M. (2002). The decline in average weekly cinema attendance, 1930-2000. *Issues in Political Economy, 11*, 54–65.

Pavlik, J., & McIntosh, S. (2004). *Converging media: An introduction to mass communication.* Allyn & Bacon.

Pearson, P. H. (1970). Relationships between global and specified measures of novelty seeking. *Journal of Consulting and Clinical Psychology, 34*(2), 199–204.

Perez, S. (2019, January 15). *Nielsen: 16M U.S. homes now get TV over-the-air, a 48% increase over past 8 years.* https://techcrunch.com/2019/01/15/nielsen-16m-u-s-homes-now-get-tv-over-the-air-a-48-increase-over-past-8-years/

Perrin, A., & Atske, S. (2021, April 2). *7% of Americans don't use the internet. Who are they?* https://www.pewresearch.org/fact-tank/2021/04/02/7-of-americans-dont-use-the-internet-who-are-they/

Pew. (2020, August 7). *U.S. adults regularly turn to a variety of activities to help cope with coronavirus outbreak.* Pew Research Center. https://www.pewresearch.org/religion/2020/08/07/u-s-adults-regularly-turn-to-a-variety-of-activities-to-help-cope-with-coronavirus-outbreak/

Picard, R. G. (Ed.). (2000). *Measuring media content, quality, and diversity: Approaches and issues in content research.* Turku School of Economics and Business Administration.

Postman, N. (1985). *Amusing ourselves to death: Public discourse in the age of show business.* Viking.

Potter, W. J. (2016). *Introduction to media literacy.* SAGE.

Prawer, S. S. (1980). *Caligari's children: The film as tale of terror.* Da Capo.

Putnam, R. D. (2000). *Bowling alone: The collapse and revival of American community.* Simon and Schuster.

Pye, D. (2012). The western (genre and movies). In B. K. Grant (Ed.), *Film genre reader IV* (pp. 239–254). University of Texas Press.

Qiao, X., & Zhu, Y. (2011). A review of theory and research based on uses and gratifications in HCI. In S. Lin & X. Huang (Eds.), *Advances in Computer Science, Environment, Ecoinformatics, and Education, CSEE 2011. Communications in Computer and Information Science* (Vol. 216; pp. 232–236). Springer.

Rader, K., Neuendorf, K. A., & Skalski, P. D. (2016). International film and audiovisual translation: Intercultural experience as moderator in audience recall and enjoyment. *Journal of Intercultural Communication*, (42), article 6.

Raeburn, J. (1988). The gangster film. In W. D. Gehring (Ed.), *Handbook of American film genres* (pp. 47–64). Greenwood Press.

Rammstedt, B., & John, O. P. (2007). Measuring personality in one minute or less: A 10-item short version of the Big Five Inventory in English and German. *Journal of Research in Personality, 41*(1), 203–212.

Reio, T. G. Jr., & Choi, N. (2004). Novelty seeking in adulthood: Increases accompany decline. *The Journal of Genetic Psychology, 165*(2), 119–133.

Richard, J. (2004). *Henri Langlois: Phantom of the Cinematheque* [film]. Kino Lorber.

Rieser, K. (2001). Masculinity and monstrosity: Characterization and identification in the slasher film. *Men & Masculinities, 3*(4), 370–392.

Rigby, J. M., Brumby, D. P., Cox, A. L., & Gould, S. J. J. (2016). *Watching movies on Netflix: Investigating the effect of screen size on viewer immersion.* Proceedings of the 18th International Conference on Human-Computer Interaction with Mobile Devices and Services Adjunct (pp. 714–721).

Ritzer, I., & Schulze, P. W. (2016). *Genre hybridisation: Global cinematic flow.* Schuren.

Robinson, J. P., & Zill, N. (1997). Matters of culture. *American Demographics, 19*(9), 24–27.

Robinson, M. J. (1976). Public affairs television and the growth of political malaise: The case of "The Selling of the Pentagon". *American Political Science Review, 70*(2), 409–432.

Rodríguez-Fidalgo, M. I., & Paíno-Ambrosio, A. (2020). Use of virtual reality and 360° video as narrative resources in the documentary genre: Towards a new immersive social documentary? *Catalan Journal of Communication & Cultural Studies, 12*(2), 239–253.

Rose, B. (2003). TV genres re-viewed. *Journal of Popular Film & Television, 31*(1), 2–4.

Rotten Tomatoes. (2020). *Movies by genre.* https://editorial.rottentomatoes.com/hub-subpage/movies-by-genre-4/

Rubin, A. M. (2009). Uses-and-gratifications perspective on media effects. In J. Bryant & M. B. Oliver (Eds.), *Media effects: Advances in theory and research* (3rd ed., pp. 165–184). Routledge.

Rubin, R. (2022, March 14). *Global entertainment industry revenue rebounds from pandemic, thanks to streaming boom.* https://variety.com/2022/film/news/entertainment-industry-revenues-streaming-box-office-recovery-1235203582/?fbclid=IwAR1uPpT-5THLT06aiIKqqiYwktKV-JX-r2FJTXcde4Zlp7vzF1bySp2VZFQA

Rubin, R. B., & McHugh, M. P. (1987). Development of parasocial interaction relationships. *Journal of Broadcasting & Electronic Media, 31*(3), 279–292.

Rushdie, S. (2001, June 9). Reality TV: A dearth of talent and the death of morality. *The Guardian* (p. 1).

Ryan, T., & Xenos, S. (2011). Who uses Facebook? An investigation into the relationship between the Big Five, shyness, narcissism, loneliness, and Facebook usage. *Computers in Human Behavior, 27*(5), 1658–1664.

Sanders, J. (2009). *The film genre book.* Auteur/Columbia University Press.

Sayre, N. (1977). Winning the weepstakes: The problems of American sports movies. In B. K. Grant (Ed.), *Film genre: Theory and criticism* (pp. 182–194). Scarecrow Press.

Scharrer, E., & Blackburn, G. (2018). Is reality TV a *Bad Girls Club*? Television use, docusoap reality television viewing, and the cultivation of the approval of aggression. *Journalism & Mass Communication Quarterly, 95*(1), 235–257.

Schatz, T. (1981). *Hollywood genres.* Temple University Press.

Schatz, T. (1988a). *The genius of the system: Hollywood filmmaking in the studio era.* University of Minnesota Press.

Schatz, T. (1988b). The western. In W. D. Gehring (Ed.), *Handbook of American film genres* (pp. 25–46). Greenwood Press.

Scheurer, T. E. (1977). The aesthetics of form and convention in the movie musical. In B. K. Grant (Ed.), *Film genre: Theory and criticism* (pp. 145–160). Scarecrow Press.

Scheurer, T. E. (2008). *Music and mythmaking in film: Genre and the role of the composer.* McFarland.

Schrader, P. (2012). Notes on film noir. In B. K. Grant (Ed.), *Film genre reader IV* (pp. 265–278). University of Texas Press.

Schumpeter, J. A. (1971). *Can capitalism survive?* Harper & Row.

Seel, P. B. (2012). *Digital universe: The global telecommunication revolution.* Wiley-Blackwell.

Shattuc, J. (2015). The celebrity talk show. In G. Creeber (Ed.), *The television genre book* (3rd ed., pp. 194–195). Palgrave.

Sheehan, K. B., & Pittman, M. (2016). *Amazon's Mechanical Turk for academics: The HIT handbook for social science research.* Melvin & Leigh, Publishers.

Shimamura, A. P. (Ed.). (2013). *Psychocinematics: Exploring cognition at the movies.* Oxford University Press.

Shon, J.-H., Kim, Y.-G., & Yim, S.-J. (2014). Classifying movies based on audience perceptions: MTI framework and box office performance. *Journal of Media Economics, 27*(2), 79–106.

Siegel, S., & Siegel, B. (1994). *American film comedy.* Prentice Hall.

Signorielli, N. (1986). Selective television viewing: A limited possibility. *Journal of Communication, 36*(3), 64–75.

Skalski, P. D., Neuendorf, K. A., Lieberman, E. A., & Denny, J. (2008, May). *The parallel development of film and video game technologies: History and implications.* Paper presented to the International Communication Association, Montreal, Canada.

Skalski, P., & Whitbred, R. (2010). Image versus sound: A comparison of formal feature effects on presence and video game enjoyment. *PsychNology Journal, 8*(1), 67–84.

Slater, M. (2018). Immersion and the illusion of presence in virtual reality. *British Journal of Psychology, 109*(3), 431–433.

Sobchack, T. (1977). Genre film: A classical experience. In B. K. Grant (Ed.), *Film genre: Theory and criticism* (pp. 39–52). Scarecrow Press.

Sobchack, T. (1988). The adventure film. In W. D. Gehring (Ed.), *Handbook of American film genres* (pp. 9–24). Greenwood Press.

Sobchack, V. (1988). Science fiction. In W. D. Gehring (Ed.), *Handbook of American film genres* (pp. 229–248). Greenwood Press.

Spiegel, S. (2017). The big genre mystery: The mystery genre. In B. Beil, H. Schwaab, & D. Wentz (Eds.), *Lost in media* (pp. 29–46). Medien' Welten.

Staiger, J. (1997). Hybrid or inbred: The purity hypothesis and Hollywood genre history. *Film Criticism*, *22*(1), 5–20.

Staiger, J. (2012). Hybrid or inbred: The purity hypothesis and Hollywood genre history. In B. K. Grant (Ed.), *Film genre reader IV* (pp. 203–217). University of Texas Press.

Steinberg, L. (2003, September). *Risk-taking in adolescence: What changes and why?* Paper presented at the meeting of the New York Academy of Sciences on Adolescent Brain Development.

Stoner, S. B., & Spencer, W. B. (1986). Age and sex differences on the State-Trait Personality Inventory. *Psychological Reports*, *59*(3), 1315–1319.

Sunstein, C. R. (2017). *#Republic: Divided democracy in the age of social media*. Princeton University Press.

Sussman, R. (1989). Curiosity and exploration in children: Where affect and cognition meet. In K. Field, B. J. Cohler, & G. Wool (Eds.), *Learning and education: Psychoanalytic perspectives* (pp. 245–266). International Universities Press.

Tarratt, M. (2012). Monsters from the id. In B. K. Grant (Ed.), *Film genre reader IV* (pp. 382–401). University of Texas Press.

Tefertiller, A., & Sheehan, K. (2019). TV in the streaming age: Motivations, behaviors, and satisfaction of post-network television. *Journal of Broadcasting & Electronic Media*, *63*(4), 595–616.

Time Magazine (2007, January 1). Magazine cover.

Tudor, A. (1977). Genre. In B. K. Grant (Ed.), *Film genre: Theory and criticism* (pp. 16–23). Scarecrow Press.

Tudor, A. (2012). Genre. In B. K. Grant (Ed.), *Film genre reader IV* (pp. 3–11). University of Texas Press.

Tunstall, J. (2008). *The media were American: U.S. mass media in decline*. Oxford University Press.

Turow, J. (1997). *Breaking up America: Advertisers and the new media world*. University of Chicago Press.

Van Dyke, V. (1977) The individual, the state, and ethnic communities in political theory. *World Politics*, *29*(3), 343–369.

Vidal, B. (2012). *Heritage film: Nation, genre, and representation*. Wallflower.

Vodanovich, S. J. (2003). Psychometric measures of boredom: A review of the literature. *The Journal of Psychology*, *137*(6), 569–595.

Waggoner, E. B. (2012). *Television and fanfiction online: Finding identity, meaning, and community* [Master's thesis]. Gonzaga University.

Waisbord, S. (2004). McTV: Understanding the global popularity of television formats. *Television & New Media*, *5*(4), 359–383.

Wakshlag, J., & Adams, W. J. (1985). Trends in program variety and the prime time access rule. *Journal of Broadcasting & Electronic Media*, *29*(1), 23–34.

Wallace, R. (2018). *Mockumentary comedy: Performing authenticity*. Palgrave Macmillan.

Waller, G. A. (Ed.). (2002). *Moviegoing in America*. Blackwell Publishers.

Watson, A. (2020, August 25). *Streaming in the U.S. – statistics & facts.* Statista.com. https://www.statista.com/topics/1594/streaming/

Weimann-Saks, D., Ariel, Y., & Elishar-Malka, V. (2020). Social second screen: WhatsApp and watching the World Cup. *Communication & Sport, 8*(1), 123–141.

Wentworth, N., & Witryol, S. L. (2003). Curiosity, exploration, and novelty-seeking. In M. H. Bornstein, L. Davidson, C. L. M. Keyes, & K. A. Moore (Eds.), *Well-being: Positive development across the life course* (pp. 281–294). Erlbaum.

White, D. L. (1977). The poetics of horror: More than meets the eye. In B. K. Grant (Ed.), *Film genre: Theory and criticism* (pp. 124–144). Scarecrow Press.

White, M. (1985). Television genres: Intertextuality. *Journal of Film and Video, 37*(3), 41–47.

WHO. (2021a, 30 March). *Weekly epidemiological update on COVID-19.* https://www.who.int/publications/m/item/weekly-epidemiological-update-on-covid-19---31-march-2021

WHO. (2021b). *WHO Coronavirus (COVID-19) Dashboard.* https://covid19.who.int/

Wicks, R. H. (1989). Segmenting broadcast news audiences in the new media environment. *Journalism Quarterly, 66*(2), 383–390.

Williams, E. R. (2018). *The screenwriters' taxonomy: A roadmap to collaborative storytelling.* Routledge.

Wills, T. A., Vaccaro, D., & McNamara, G. (1994). Novelty seeking, risk taking, and related constructs as predictors of adolescent substance use: An application of Cloninger's theory. *Journal of Substance Abuse, 6*(1), 1–20.

Wojcik, S., & Hughes, A. (2019, April 24). *Sizing up Twitter users.* Pew Research Center. https://www.pewresearch.org/internet/2019/04/24/sizing-up-twitter-users/

Wood, B. (2004). A world in retreat: The reconfiguration of hybridity in 20th-century New Zealand television. *Media, Culture & Society, 26*(1), 45–62.

Wood, G. C. (1988). Horror film. In W. D. Gehring (Ed.), *Handbook of American film genres* (pp. 211–228). Greenwood Press.

INDEX

For Product Safety Concerns and Information please contact our EU
representative GPSR@taylorandfrancis.com
Taylor & Francis Verlag GmbH, Kaufingerstraße 24, 80331 München, Germany

www.ingramcontent.com/pod-product-compliance
Lightning Source LLC
Chambersburg PA
CBHW050351270326
41926CB00016B/3700

* 9 7 8 1 0 3 2 2 0 1 3 1 3 *